Library Automation

Library Automation

Core Concepts and Practical Systems Analysis

Third Edition

Dania Bilal

Foreword by Marshall Breeding

 LIBRARIES UNLIMITED

AN IMPRINT OF ABC-CLIO, LLC
Santa Barbara, California • Denver, Colorado • Oxford, England

Library of Congress Cataloging-in-Publication Data

Bilal, Dania, 1956–
    Library automation : core concepts and practical systems analysis/ Dania Bilal ; foreword by Marshall Breeding. — Third edition.
        pages cm
    Reshaped and expanded edition of: Automating media centers and small libraries. Second edition. 2002.
    Includes bibliographical references and index.
    ISBN 978-1-59158-922-8 (pbk.) — ISBN 978-1-59158-923-5 (ebook)
1. Libraries—Automation.   2. Integrated library systems (Computer systems)   3. Open source software—Library applications.   I. Bilal, Dania, 1956– Automating media centers and small libraries.   II. Title.
    Z678.9.B54   2014
    025.00285—dc23   2013044228

ISBN: 978-1-59158-922-8
EISBN: 978-1-59158-923-5

18 17 16 15 14   1 2 3 4 5

This book is also available on the World Wide Web as an eBook.
Visit www.abc-clio.com for details.

Libraries Unlimited
An Imprint of ABC-CLIO, LLC

ABC-CLIO, LLC
130 Cremona Drive, P.O. Box 1911
Santa Barbara, California 93116-1911

This book is printed on acid-free paper ∞
Manufactured in the United States of America

*In memory of my beloved inspirational father,
Moustafa B. Bilal, my greatest mentor,
brother, and friend.*

Contents

Illustrations

Foreword

Given my intense interest in the field of library technology, I was delighted to have the chance to read the manuscript for Dania Bilal's latest book, *Library Automation: Core Concepts and Practical Systems Analysis, Third Edition*.

I have been aware of Dr. Bilal's work as a specialist in our shared field of interest for many years. In 1998 and 1999 Bilal and her colleagues at the University of Tennessee, for example, produced the *Library Journal* Automation Marketplace feature that summarizes the major activities, product developments, and trends in the industry. Since 2002 I have taken the reins of the Automation Marketplace article, representing at least as a symbolic link between her work in the field of library automation and mine, even though we have not had the opportunity to collaborate directly.

It has also been interesting to observe the transformation of this book over the years. When the initial edition of *Automating Media Centers and Small Libraries: A Microcomputer-Based Approach* was initially published by Libraries Unlimited in 1998, libraries were just beginning to feel the impact of the web and their work primarily centered on print collections. Integrated library systems that operated on personal computers represented the state of the art in the practice of library automation at that time, especially for smaller libraries. The first edition of this book was an important text for both graduate students in programs of library and information science or for systems librarians needing to master the realm of library automation. The second edition released in 2002 brought the material up to date for that time.

This book, though retaining some of the structure of the earlier two editions, takes a fairly large step of departure from previous editions. One cannot overstate the changes in libraries and in technology that have taken place in the decade since its last edition. For most libraries, involvement with print continues, though electronic and digital materials increasingly dominate. The tools that libraries need to manage and deliver access to these collections of diverse media have changed dramatically, some through gradual evolution, others in more revolutionary ways. The web has become ubiquitous as the means for accessing content and operating software applications. Social networks add a new dimension in the way that we interact with our personal and professional communities. Search engines make information of all sorts available in an instant. How individuals use the web in daily life likewise shapes their expectations for library services. Technology today is all about cloud computing, service-oriented architectures, and computer applications delivered as services operated through web browsers, eclipsing the earlier age of client/server computing.

In response to these foundational shifts, Bilal has reshaped and conceptualized the underlying concepts of the book in addition to updating the specific products and technologies addressed. The previous orientation toward smaller libraries has been expanded to a broader perspective, covering concepts and trends in automation systems that apply to libraries of all types. Bilal frames portions of the book around a conceptual framework called the Library Automation Life Cycle that describes a reference model for the stages a library can follow as it evaluates, selects, and implements its technology environment. The author taps her experience in systems analysis and human–computer interaction in developing the material presented.

Libraries today require technology infrastructure to help with all aspects of their operations. Readers will encounter information not only on the traditional modules of the integrated library system, but will also learn about some of the more recent tools that help with the management of electronic resources and digital assets and the new generation of discovery tools that enable patrons to search and gain access to all aspects of the library's collection. This book provides a wealth of context, perspective, and advice to guide the process of identifying the library automation products available that best align with a library's strategic requirements, not just in terms of functionality, but in overall design and orientation to its size and complexity. While presented in terms of the products and genres of software that prevail today, these principles should remain viable as new options take the stage over time.

I trust that readers will share my impressions this book by Dr. Dania Bilal as a practical and informative tool for gaining a better understanding of this interesting realm of library automation.

Marshall Breeding
Independent Consultant
Founder of *Library Technology Guides*
Editor, *Smart Libraries Newsletter*
Columnist for *Computers in Libraries*

Acknowledgments

I wish to extend my greatest gratitude to my beloved mother, Yusra A. Bilal, who has always been proud of my efforts and achievements and has provided continuous support and encouragement throughout the writing of this book. I offer my sincere appreciation to my sisters, brothers, nieces, and nephews: to my beloved aunt Rajaa and her family, and to my cousins and friends for their sustained support and enthusiasm throughout the writing process. I give my special thank you to my colleagues in the United States and colleagues overseas, especially Drs. Imad Bachir and Fawz Abdallah, professors at the Lebanese University, College of Communication and Information Management in Beirut, Lebanon, for supporting my efforts and encouraging me to complete this book.

I offer my sincere thanks and warmest regards to Marshall Breeding for writing the Forward and for sharing his knowledge and invaluable expertise throughout the research and authoring of this book. I give many thanks to Barbara Ittner, Editor at ABC-CLIO for her patience, guidance, and encouragement throughout the writing of this book. I extend my appreciation to Susan Earl, library director at Brentwood Municipal Center in Brentwood, Tennessee and Maria Sochor, librarian at the Brentwood Municipal Center, for granting me permission to include the Request for Proposal document they had developed to procure an integrated library system for the center as an Appendix in this book. I give my gratitude to the reviewers who have shared their views and expertise and provided valuable comments and suggestions for improving the book. I give a special thank you to David Ratledge, associate professor and head of digital initiatives at The University of Tennessee Libraries at Hodges Library in Knoxville, Tennessee for taking the time to talk with me about the changing nature of the library's network management. I extent an equal special thank you to Scot Samuel Smith, school librarian at Robertsville Middle School in Oak Ridge, Tennessee for explaining the shift in roles and responsibilities of managing the school library's network. I thank all my graduate teaching assistants (Eve Bevill, Reid Boehm, and Sarah Webb) for assisting me through the research for this book and helping with graphics, proofreading, and formatting. Finally, I thank all my graduate students who had taken my class, Information Systems: Design and Implementation, and provided feedback on the chapters I have assigned as readings.

Introduction

Today, users' expectations are much higher than those of previous generations. While the quality of integrated library system (ILS) interfaces have improved over the past years, today's users expect interfaces to be more tangible and modeled after Google's interface, especially in relation to simplicity in design, search functionality, "universal" information retrieval, relevancy ranking of search results, and personalization, among other features. The rise of Web 2.0 has shifted users' roles from consumers of information to contributors and generators of content. From the web to mobile smart technologies, users' expectations have gravitated toward information access and retrieval "on the move," anytime, anywhere. Changes in user expectations, continued advances in computing technologies (e.g., cloud computing, Application Programming Interface, Service-Oriented Architecture), and increase in digital content have provoked automation companies and open-source firms to design innovative ILS solutions. Libraries have adopted federated search tools to enhance the user's information discovery experience in the ILS. However, due to the limitations of these tools, many libraries have implemented front-end *discovery* interfaces with their existing ILSs. These interfaces are based on Web 2.0 technologies and support a single search box for searching across all types of materials and allow for filtering information by format (e.g., books, audios, videos, maps, images, and journal titles). Retrieved information is ranked by relevancy; topics relevant to a user's search are displayed in clusters, and user engagement is supported through tagging, reviews, and social media. These interfaces have rendered the traditional online catalogs interfaces obsolete. However, a full integration of collection formats including journal articles from a library's subscription online databases into retrieved search results was lacking in these interfaces. The need to provide users with "universal" information retrieval that includes journal articles relevant to a given search similar to what Google retrieves, has led to a new shift in information discovery—the next-generation discovery interfaces or *discovery services*. While not all libraries have adopted discovery services, most have implemented discovery interfaces. Today, mobile apps with discovery interfaces are made available by proprietary ILS vendors or developed by libraries using open-source ILS software.

The past few years have witnessed an increase in libraries' digital collections, including eBooks. As most ILSs are built around print collections, libraries, especially large academic ones with a high volume in digital materials, have begun to consider migration to library services platforms (LSPs). These proprietary next-generation ILSs are based on the open system platform concept and take advantage of the latest advances in computing technologies (e.g., cloud computing), employ discovery services, integrate and streamline the management of all types of collections (print, digital, and electronic) and operations, among other things. In fact, LSPs are reshaping the library automation landscape.

The rapidly evolving technologies, ubiquitous use of smartphones and other mobile devices, increase in users' expectations combined with the changing nature of library collections and operations have led to the writing of this book. While one may argue that most libraries in the United States are already automated, there are many libraries in rural areas that negotiate user information needs and fulfill them using the traditional card catalog. In addition, libraries with existing traditional ILSs will not be able to support the expectations of today's users in the near future. Thus, rethinking these old ILSs and migrating to new ones will eventually happen.

Unlike the book published by Bilal in 2002, *Automating Media Centers and Small Libraries*: *A Microcomputer-Based Approach,* this book is not geared toward specific types of libraries; rather, it is general in focus and covers major recent developments in automation at the small and large library fronts. In addition, it describes ILS software and products, proprietary and open source, for all types of libraries. Moreover, this book is conceptualized in the context of the system development life cycle (SDLC), which has been modified to create the library automation life cycle (LALC), as the conceptual framework used to describe the five iterative phases and procedures for carrying out a library automation project in any library environment. This framework is built on relevant theoretical conceptions derived from areas of study in the field of system analysis and development, library and information science, and human–computer interaction to inform practice.

THE ILS AS AN INFORMATION SYSTEM

As defined in this book, an information system consists of a set of inter-related components or entities and subcomponents that are designed to interact together to perform specific tasks, functions, and operations and achieve a purpose. An information system is used to access and retrieve information from resources stored in the system based on user information need. Libraries, regardless of type, use different information systems to support access to and retrieval of information. These systems include ILS, online databases, and digital repositories. Web search engines are also information systems. In the library and information science arena, these systems are known as information retrieval systems. As an information retrieval (IR) system, an ILS has software designed specifically to manage library operations including but not limited to circulation, cataloging, public access, acquisitions, serials, digital content management, and media management. Of these, circulation, cataloging, and public access are the basic modules. The other modules can be acquired as add-ons to the basic ILS. As to the public access module, traditionally known as the online public access catalog (OPAC), it is being overlaid with a discovery interface or discovery service. The latter is the next-generation discovery interface used by many libraries to enhance the user's information discovery experience. That is, retrieval of all types of materials, including journal articles (citations and/or full-text) from a library's subscription to online databases (in the case of discovery service). By doing so, a user can perform a search using a single search box to retrieve all types of relevant materials in search results similar to what Google does.

Software and hardware work together to support the operation of the ILS. Different types of ILSs exist for different types of libraries—academic, public, special, and school. The latest development in automation management systems is the LSP, a term coined by Marshall Breeding. Most LSPs are proprietary ILSs targeted for academic and large libraries. An open-source LSP is Kuali OLE that has been designed and developed by a team of academic and research institutions in the United States.

Many options exist for embarking on a new library automation project or for migrating from a legacy system to a new ILS. For example, a library may adopt an open-source ILS and contract out a firm that services the selected ILS, thus freeing most of the chores that library staff perform, including, but not limited to, installation, implementation, and technical support. Another option is for a group of libraries to join efforts to build their own ILS using open-source technologies. This option requires financial resources and the availability of staff with technical expertise. Small libraries with limited financial resources, however, may join a consortium of libraries of similar size to share the ILS used by these libraries.

LIBRARY AUTOMATION LIFE CYCLE (LALC)

The classical System Development Lifecycle described by Valacich, George, and Hoffer (2011) consists of four main phases: (1) systems planning and selection; (2) systems analysis; (3) system design; (4) system implementation and operation. Each phase includes a set of processes and tasks to complete based on the defined project. These phases have been modified to fit the library automation environment, resulting in the LALC, which encompasses five instead of four phases: (1) system identification and planning; (2) gathering user requirements; (3) structuring user requirements/selecting a system; (4) implementing the system; (5) evaluating the system through usability.

GOALS OF THE BOOK

This book is written for graduate students and educators in Library and Information Science (LIS) programs, practitioners, and researchers in the library automation arena. Graduate students will learn about the complexity and challenges of library automation in today's rapidly evolving technologies and changes in today's users' expectations. They will learn about the entire life cycle of the library automation project (LALC) from initiation to usability assessment. They will become aware of advances in computing technologies that are impacting on the nature of library automation. Using the LALC as a backbone, LIS educators who teach courses in systems analysis and design and those that teach courses in library automation will find that this book provides a consolidated approach for teaching a basic course that covers both areas of study. Practitioners in various types of libraries who are automating their collection for the first time or are migrating from an existing ILS to another will gain firsthand knowledge about the whole process of library automation and basic understanding of the computing and information communication technologies that are driving forces in library automation. They will develop understanding of the varied automation options available for their library environments. Researchers can benefit from learning about today's rapid developments in library automation and the directions it has taken, as well as the theories, models, and processes used as foundations for understanding users and for designing user-centered interfaces. The usability methods described in this book are useful to all these constituencies, from students to researchers, as they can be employed to evaluate an institution's website, a library website, and an ILS discovery interface or discovery service in various settings.

ORGANIZATION OF THE BOOK

This book is organized into 10 chapters. Chapter 1 provides a definition of ILS that is conceptualized within the context of an information system. It provides a brief description of the characteristics of an information system that are shared with an ILS. These include core components such as software and hardware: modules that exist based on the scope of the ILS, its boundary, purpose, input and output, constraints, and interfaces. In addition, this chapter describes the types of ILS software (i.e., proprietary and open source), modularity, modules, and functions. The chapter discusses differences between a discovery interface and a traditional online catalog interface, and between a discovery interface and discovery service. It describes the basic and add-on modules for an ILS (cataloging, circulation, acquisitions, serials, interlibrary loan, authority control, media management, electronic resource management, and textbook management). It describes the changing nature of the ILS, noting the next-generation library management solutions called LSPs and their influence on reshaping the future of library automation. It points to leading proprietary LSP products such as Ex Libris' Alma, OCLC WorldShare Management Services, Innovative Interfaces' Sierra, Serials Solutions' Intota, and VTLS Open Skies, as well as the open-source Kuali OLE. The chapter concludes with a summary, a list of references, and a list of relevant websites.

Chapter 2 illustrates the LALC (Figure 2.1) and describes phase 1 of this cycle: System Identification and Planning. It covers the basic knowledge needed and sources to consult in acquiring this knowledge. In addition, it describes different types of ILSs and models, planning the automation project, and assessing the feasibility of the project. The latter includes technical, budgetary, operational, schedule, political, and legal feasibility. It has a section on the role of the project manager in assessing potential risks and finding ways to circumvent them. This role also extends to preparing staff for change, assigning tasks and responsibilities, and communicating the project's progress to stakeholders. Moreover, this chapter delineates tangible and intangible benefits of the ILS and provides two work sheets (Tables 2.1 and 2.2) to use in estimating projected tangible onetime and tangible ongoing costs of the project. The chapter concludes with a summary, list of references, and a list of relevant websites.

Chapter 3 covers phase 2 of LALC, Gathering User Requirements. It describes general characteristics of gathering user requirements, from simple to complex, depending on the type of the library. It discusses methods for gathering these requirements using quantitative and qualitative approaches. It includes interviews, observation, diaries, or journal logs, web analysis, analysis of work documents and procedures, and unit analysis as approaches to consider in gathering information from staff and users. In addition, this chapter discusses the outcomes of the data-gathering techniques and illustrates them in Table 3.1. The chapter concludes with a summary, a list of references, and a list of relevant websites.

Chapter 4 describes phase 3 of LALC, Structuring User Requirements/ Selecting a System. Because ILS software (proprietary and open source) are well established in the automation marketplace, phase 3 of the original SDLC (systems design) is not employed in the context of the system development process; rather, the system selection process is used for structuring the requirements of an ILS. In this context, the chapter describes sources for identifying ILS software, prioritizing the software based on the library's needs, goals of the automation project, and financial resources. It discusses the importance of developing a request for proposal (RFP) for proprietary and open-source software and delineates the advantages and disadvantages of the RFP. In addition, it provides detailed guidelines for preparing the RFP document along with a list of criteria for evaluating vendor responses to the RFP and makes the case for negotiating a contract for the chosen ILS. The chapter has a reference to a full RFP document that is provided in the Appendix of the book. This part of the chapter concludes with a summary and is followed with a section on selected ILS products.

The section on ILS products described in this chapter is divided into two categories: ILS for small libraries and ILS for large libraries. For school libraries, five proprietary ILSs are described: Destiny Library Manager (Follett), Alexandria (COMpanion Corporation), Atriuum (Book Systems), LibraryWorld (LibraryWorld), and Library.Solution (The Library Corporation). Selected proprietary ILSs for special small libraries include EOS.Web (EOS International), Inmagic (Sydney Plus International), Sydney Plus (Sydney Plus International), and Cuadra Star (Cuadra Associates). The selected proprietary ILSs for small public libraries are Apollo (Biblionix), Agent VERSO (Auto-Graphics), Atriuum (version for public libraries) (Book Systems), and Library.Solution (version for public libraries) (The Library Corporation).

In the open-source small library arena, the ILS products included are Koha and OPALS as two well-established software. Evergreen is described as the most well-established open-source ILS suitable for small public libraries in consortia and for individual large public libraries. In addition, two social media ILS, Social OPAC (SOPAC) and LibraryThing, are described. Moreover, this chapter has a section on software for large libraries that covers both proprietary and open-source ILS products. It begins with a description of LSPs such as Alma (Ex Libris Group), WorldShare Management Services (OCLC), Sierra Services Platform (Innovative Interfaces Inc.), and Intota (Serials Solutions). It also includes a section on ILS for large public libraries that describes Symphony (SirsiDynix), Polaris (Polaris), and Carl.X (The Library Corporation). This section is followed with a description of selected ILS software suitable for large academic libraries that covers Aleph (Ex Libris Group), Millennium (Innovative Interfaces), and Symphony.

Moreover, this chapter provides a description of open-source ILS suitable for large public and academic libraries. It covers Evergreen and Kuali OLE. In addition, this chapter lists other open-source ILSs and provides their URL addresses. The chapter concludes with a list of references and a list of websites.

Chapter 5 covers the first part of phase 4 of the LALC, System Implementation. It introduces the collection preparation process, which covers collection weeding, weeding circulation records, collection inventory, shelflist analysis, and retrospective conversion (Recon). It describes weeding the library's collection, cleaning up and exporting circulation and patron records, inventorying the collection, and options for preparing retrospective conversion of records (Recon). It covers specifications for Recon and three Recon options: outsourcing, in-house, and hybrid. For each option, the process is detailed and guidelines are provided for choosing a Recon outsourcing vendor and also the advantages and disadvantages of using each option. Moreover, it includes reputable sources for subscribing to fee-based MARC 21 services such as Book Where from WebClarity Software Inc., ITS.MARC from The Library Corporation, eZcat from Book Systems, as well as sources for creating MARC records in-house using Mitinet MARC Magician software. A list of selected Recon companies and contact information is given in Table 5.1. Furthermore, this chapter covers advantages and disadvantages of fee-based Web MARC services and MARC records available free of charge on the web. It is followed with a description of the hybrid Recon process and a cost analysis for outsourcing Recon. A Recon scenario is provided along with a calculated cost of Recon options that is illustrated in Tables 5.2 and 5.3. The Program Evaluation Review Technique (PERT) formula is used to estimate the expected time for completing a Recon project along with an example of applying the formula.

In addition, Chapter 5 contains a major section on bibliographic standards including MARC 21, MARCXML, Functional Requirements for Bibliographic

Records (FRBR), Anglo-American Cataloging Rules Second Revised Edition (AACR2R), and Resource Description and Access (RDA). The most frequently used MARC 21 tags are illustrated in Table 5.4. RDA refs and data elements are described in Table 5.5. This section is followed by a description of International Standard Bibliographic Description (ISBD), linked data and schema (schema. org) that use uniform resource identifiers (URIs) to identify entities or concepts, and Resource Description Framework (RDF) to describe links between data. The last part of this chapter describes barcoding the collection using traditional barcodes (smart and dumb) and radio frequency identification (RFID) tags for print and digital media. It is followed with a brief section describing QR codes and the purpose for using them in libraries. This chapter concludes with a summary, list of references, and a list of relevant websites.

Chapter 6 describes the second part of phase 4 of LALC, System Implementation. It covers ILS software installation, testing, facility, training, and ILS data tracking. It describes options for on-site installation of the ILS (direct, parallel, single location, and phase), options for testing the on-site hosted ILS (incremental testing, integrated, and full testing), as well as testing the installation of open-source ILS. In addition, this chapter covers a section on configuring the ILS including data import for circulation, cataloging, and other add-on modules acquired by the library. The acquisition of a new ILS may require purchase of new pieces of hardware and preparation of the library facility. This chapter describes hardware such as computers for public access, staff workstations, and printers, as well as furniture. Moreover, it briefly covers ILS documentation and provides a section on ILS maintenance. The latter includes environmental care for hardware, data backup, network and computer security, and antitheft security gates. A list of selected companies of security systems and accessories is provided in Table 6.1. In addition, this chapter describes the importance of maintaining the integrity of the database after the records have been imported into the ILS. It follows with a section on staff and patron training in using the ILS. Finally, this chapter provides a section on evaluating use of the ILS through transaction data extracted from the circulation and other modules, data analytics (as applicable), and other web log transactions. This chapter concludes with a summary, a list of references, and a list of relevant websites.

Chapter 7, "Software, Hardware, and Network Architecture," covers the varied architectures employed in libraries. It describes software architecture in relation to deployment models available for libraries to host the ILS, which include on-site hosting, cloud software hosting, software-as-a-service (SaaS), multitenant and single-tenant hosting, as well as traditional remote hosting. The advantages and disadvantages of each hosting solution are provided. Similarly, hardware architecture covers the options for hosting computers, servers, and devices to access the ILS. It describes the on-site hosting model and its advantages and disadvantages. In addition, it discusses the two main cloud hardware hosting models, platform-as-a-service (PaaS) and infrastructure-as-a-service (IaaS). In addition, there is a section that explains cloud computing and its advantages and disadvantages. This is followed by a section with guidelines on negotiating a contract with a cloud service provider and essential questions to ask of the provider under consideration.

The section on network architecture describes the changing nature of managing and maintaining the library's network. It provides real-world examples describing the shift in responsibilities for managing the library's network from the building level to the parent institution's IT unit. It provides a basic description of various telecommunications available for connecting to the Internet and especially broadband. The latter is explained and includes the digital subscriber line (DSL), coaxial cable, fiber-optic cable, and wireless access. In addition, it explains the network protocol, Internet Protocol version 6 (IPv6), network topologies especially modern Ethernet, as well as the current network standards and categories used in modern Ethernet networks. Moreover, this chapter has three tables describing the categories of twisted-pair cables (Table 7.1), Ethernet type, name, and data rates by cable category (Table 7.2), and a list of selected companies for finding network products and media (Table 7.3). It concludes with a summary and a list of references.

Chapter 8, "System (ILS) Migration," defines migration from one ILS to another, describes reasons for migration, and lists the tasks to undertake for completing data migration in-house. It provides detailed guidelines for data extraction from the library's current ILS and running tests on sample MARC 21, circulation, and other records, as applicable. In addition, this chapter describes the process of data migration through outsourcing, includes criteria for choosing a data migration company or firm, and has a list of questions to ask of the outsourcing company in relation to circulation and bibliographic data. Moreover, this chapter includes tips for successful migration from one ILS to another. The chapter concludes with a summary, a list of references, and websites.

Chapter 9, "Evaluating System Use Through Usability," is the final phase of LALC. It discusses usability assessment methods for evaluating one or more components of the organization's website, library's website, discovery interface, or discovery service. Usability focuses on the effectiveness of interface design elements and how users interact with the interface to achieve certain goals. This chapter provides both the theoretical and practical perspectives from the human–computer interaction and information behavior fields of study. It covers three essential dimensions for understanding user interaction with an interface, including user characteristics (children, adults, older adults, and users with special needs), system attributes (memorability, learnability, errors, and satisfaction), and task attributes (closed and open-ended; assigned or imposed and self-selected). It describes two main methods for involving expert reviewers in such an evaluation. One method considers system inspection based on Jakob Nielsen's Ten Heuristics, Ben Shneiderman's and Catherine Plaisant's Nine Golden Rules, and Donald Norman's Principles. From the Information Behavior (IB) point of view, it describes selected IB models relevant to understanding users' information-seeking process. Another method is the cognitive walkthrough where expert reviewers evaluate an interface from users' point of view by predicting what the user would do and whether the user would be able to achieve a specific goal. It describes both the preparatory and analysis phases and provides examples of questions to ask during the evaluation process, as well as developing success and failure stories a user may experience during the interaction with an interface. In addition, this chapter describes the methods used for involving actual users in the evaluation process. These include observations, interviews, surveys, focus groups, contextual inquiry, task analysis, and experimental testing. Moreover, it describes how to get started on a usability assessment project, questions to ask, and sources to consult. The chapter concludes with a summary, list of references, and list of relevant websites.

Chapter 10, "Library Automation 'On the Move,' " discusses the dynamic nature of library automation in the rapidly changing computing and information technology environment. It describes cloud computing and software hosting models deployed in libraries such as SaaS and cloud hardware hosting using PaaS and IaaS as continued trends. Increase in use of application programming interface (API) based on service-oriented architecture (SOA), especially by proprietary ILS and LSP companies, have become very attractive to libraries seeking to implement modern automation solutions. The nature of library collections is changing rapidly due to increase in digital assets, e-resources, and eBooks. Large libraries with high volume in these formats have begun to rethink their existing ILSs in favor of LSPs. Continued migration from one ILS to another at both the proprietary and open-source fronts are expected to persist in the future. The rise of ILSs that are socially driven (e.g., SOPAC) and those that are built by consortia (e.g., OPALS) provide automation solutions for small libraries to establish web presence and serve their user communities. This chapter concludes with a list of references and a list of relevant websites.

The book contains an Appendix with a sample request for proposal (RFP) developed by the Brentwood Library Center for Fine Arts in Brentwood, TN, a glossary of terms, and an index.

Chapter 1

Integrated Library System (ILS) Defined

An integrated library system (ILS) is a computer-based information system consisting of a set of interrelated components or entities and subcomponents that are designed to interact together to perform specific tasks, functions, and operations and achieve a purpose. Valacich, George, and Hoffer (2011) identify the general nine characteristics of an information system: (1) components, (2) interrelated components, (3) boundary, (4) purpose, (5) environment, (6) interfaces, (7) input, (8) output, and (9) constraints. The ILS is an information system that shares many of these characteristics. The ILS is also an information retrieval system (IRS). This chapter describes the characteristics that ILS shares with a typical information system. It covers the following:

- ILS as an information system

- Types of ILS software

- ILS modularity, modules, and functions

  ○ Discovery interface versus online catalog interface

  ○ Discovery service versus discovery interface

- Cataloging module

- Circulation module

- Acquisitions module

- Serials module

- Interlibrary loan (ILL) module

- Authority control module

- Media management module

- Electronic resources management (ERM) module

- Digital asset management module

- Textbook management module (for schools)

ILS CHARACTERISTICS AS AN INFORMATION SYSTEM

The two core components that support the operation of the ILS are the software and hardware. ILS application software is designed to support the operation of the library's functions, processes, and tasks. The software may have different components or modules, including, but not limited to, circulation, cataloging, and public access, which is traditionally known as online catalog and online public access catalog (OPAC). This OPAC module comes with the traditional ILS. The new generation of online catalog user interface is referred to as a discovery interface. The next generation of a discovery interface is the discovery service. The discovery interface or discovery service is an add-on module to the traditional online catalog user interface. Other add-on modules are acquisitions, serials, media booking, ILL, ERM, digital asset management, and textbook management.

Each of these modules may have *subcomponents* or *submodules*. For example, the circulation module's subcomponents may consist of check-in, checkout, holds, account management, and reports management. In this case, the function of one component or subcomponent is tied up with the function or subfunction of another component. When a task in a subcomponent interacts with one or more subcomponents within the overall components, these components or subcomponents become *interrelated* or *interconnected* or *integrated*.

The second primary component of an ILS is the hardware on which the ILS application or system software operates. The hardware includes computer stations, servers, devices, printers, and peripherals. Data are stored and updated on the servers used over the network. Servers can be hosted by a cloud service provider for a fee or housed on the premises. In the former case, the ILS software is stored on a service provider's web server and is accessed remotely by the library's personnel and users over the web. Hardware may also be hosted in the cloud using the infrastructure-as-a-service (IaaS) solution. Cloud hosting has been gaining popularity in all types of libraries in the past few years. Additional information about cloud computing and cloud solutions is provided in Chapter 7.

The scope of the ILS is defined by its *boundary*, which consists of the internal entities (modules and submodules, or components and subcomponents).

The *boundary* separates the ILS from its environment or the world outside of it. The ILS interacts with its environment, taking inputs from patrons, for example, processing them, and returning outputs to the patron.

The interrelationship between the ILS components exists to achieve a *purpose*—to support and manage the library operations and services using the application software and hardware on which it operates. This purpose should be achieved by streamlining the operations, simplifying tasks, eliminating routine tasks, increasing productivity, and meeting staff needs as well as user needs and expectations.

Another characteristic of an ILS as an information system is the *environment*—everything external to it and interacting with it. Examples are library patrons, staff members, librarians, students, teachers, administrators, stakeholders, and book vendors.

Dominant ILS *interfaces* (e.g., search, retrieval) are based on the Graphical User Interface (GUI). GUI is "a computer program that enables a person to communicate with a computer through the use of symbols, visual metaphors, and pointing devices" (http://www.britannica.com/EBchecked/topic/242033/graphical-user-interface-GUI). GUI is also known as "a point-and-click interface" because it allows a user to use a mouse to click on an object and drag it into position rather than recall commands from memory to perform a specific function. GUI "takes advantages of features in display design such as text boxes, check boxes, option buttons, lists and drop-down list boxes, sliders and spin buttons, image maps, and tab control dialog boxes" (Kendall and Kendall 2011, 446). Windows Microsoft Office suite is an example of applications with GUI-based interfaces. In contrast, a character-based interface (also known as text-based) "is one where users navigate through a page or through a system using text links and text commands" (http://www.smartcomputing.com/editorial/dictionary/detail.asp?guid=&searchtype=&DicID=16688&RefType=Encyclopedia). An example of such interface is MS DOS. Today, web-based interfaces are the most dominant in the library automation marketplace.

ILS *constraints* are the limits to what the ILS can accomplish. For example, some of the software constraints in the traditional public access catalog are the lack of modern features, including, but not limited to, relevance ranking of search results, spell checking, and a single search box for searching across varied types of materials and formats. Hardware may also have constraints. This includes the speed of computer stations, storage capacity of web servers, and the amount of traffic over the network. In addition, a library's *external* environment such as a statewide budget cut may impose constraints on enhancing the ILS hardware to speed up applications.

Types of ILS Software

Today, there are two dominant types of ILS software in libraries: proprietary and open source. Traditionally, proprietary ILS software is supplied by a commercial vendor or company. The latter is responsible for maintaining, updating, providing technical support, and training. In this case, the software is stored on one of library's servers and is managed by the library. This type of software is also called *turnkey* or *off-the-shelf* because once installed, set up, and data are imported into the system, it should be ready for use. Typically, ILS companies restrict access to the software source code. However, a number of companies have moved toward the *open system* concept to allow libraries to customize their ILSs, harvest data, and share metadata, among other things, through application programming interface (API). The latter is a set of codes and specifications for software programs to follow in order to communicate with one another. API acts as an "intermediary" or interface between the software programs. In a library setting, staff may use the ILS software program to communicate with the respective automation company's ILS program through API in order to modify certain features and use process data. Despite this progress, proprietary ILS software has not totally moved toward the open system platform.

Open source ILS software provides access to the program source code (the actual computer program the developer has created) for modification and free distribution. To qualify as open source, the software must meet certain criteria: the program must include the source code; modification and customization of the source code must be allowed; the modified source code can be redistributed; the license must not require the exclusion of other software or must not interfere with the operation of other software; and the software must be reviewed and approved by the Open Source Initiative (for additional information, visit http://opensource.org/osd.html). Examples of widely used open-source ILS are Koha (http://www.koha.org) supported by Liblime (http://www.liblimekoha.org), ByWater Solutions (http://bywatersolutions .com), and Equinox; and Evergreen (http://open-ils.org) supported by Equinox Software (http://www.esilibrary.com/esi). Koha software supports academic and small libraries, whereas Evergreen targets public libraries.

Another example of open-source software is Kuali OLE, an open platform library management system that is built by state consortia, academic, research, and college libraries. Kuali is funded by the Andrew W. Mellon Foundation for creating community source software to manage and provide access to local print, digital collections, and licensed databases and services (http://kuali .org/OLE).

Prior to open-source software availability, a number of libraries developed their own ILS software in-house (totally from scratch). This type of software requires designing the ILS from ground up, a very costly and time-consuming process as it entails the creation of the source code, design of the database and internal data structures, design of interfaces, building retrieval algorithm, prototyping and testing the software, among other things. Technical staff, including, but not limited to, software designers and computer programmers, must be involved in the process. This is not an approach to justify today. With the availability of open-source ILSs, there is no need to start from scratch.

A few years ago, libraries created a "hybrid" ILS that combined software components developed in-house using open-source technologies with components provided by a proprietary ILS vendor. DaVinci, the Queens' Borough Public Library's ILS (in New York) is an example of a hybrid system that was developed in-house using the open-source Drupal content management system and other open-source elements, such as Apache Solr Search platform (for full text searching, facet searching, and clustering of results, etc.), a MySQL database, and Fedora Commons (for managing digital content). DaVinci was built on an architecture that includes customized components of VTLS Virtua. DaVinci was released in 2011 (Breeding 2011). The hybrid model of ILS development is no longer a common practice.

Libraries selecting an ILS for the first time, such as those located in rural areas where broadband technologies have recently become available, or those that are migrating from traditional "legacy" ILSs to modernized ones, have software and hosting options from which to choose. Selecting an option should be based on the nature of the library, its collection, personnel resources and their knowledge, financial resources, and environment (a single library versus a library in a consortia), among other things. For information about the selection process, see Chapter 4.

ILS Modularity, Modules, and Functions

A modular ILS consists of components or modules that are designed using specific application software to perform specific functions. Components or modules can be decomposed based on the tasks they are designed to perform. Each of the circulation, cataloging, and public access modules can be decomposed to create individual subcomponents or subfunctions. Decomposition of the circulation module, for example, will result in several subfunctions, including—but not limited to—check-in, checkout, fines, inventory, holds, account management, and management reports. Modularity and decomposition are important for understanding the individual ILS components and the tasks that each module is designed to perform.

Every library with an ILS has a traditional public access or online catalog module. Patrons use the online catalog to find items (books, names of journals, specific media, etc.) held by the library. Generally speaking, this module is equivalent to the traditional card catalog libraries used in the past to provide access to its collection. Today, libraries are using a *discovery interface* or *discovery service* to complement the "traditional" online catalog. The differences between the traditional online catalog and these discovery tools are discussed in the next section.

Discovery Interface versus Online Catalog Interface

A *discovery interface* is independent of the traditional ILS and can be supplied by the same ILS vendor or a third-party vendor. A *discovery interface* consists of "a layer of software that sits on top of any existing database or integrated library system (ILS) . . . ingesting records in many formats, including MARC and XML, and providing a best-of-breed, web-based search interface for users" (Jacobsen 2011). The *discovery interface* is actually the next-generation online catalog (Breeding 2010). In 2011, this interface was considered as one of the "hottest new trends in the library Online Public Access Catalogue (OPAC) sphere" (Jacobsen 2011). Unlike the traditional ILS online catalog, a *discovery interface* retrieves multiple library resources including print, digital, and journal articles from a library's subscription databases. "With this approach, information is brought out of silos, and users need only use a single interface to access disparate resources" (Jacobsen 2011). As a next-generation online catalog, this interface is based on Web 2.0 features, meaning that it provides a spell-check, relevance ranking of retrieved search results, recommender services/features (e.g., More Like This, Similar Sites), and faceted searching or guided navigation (allows users to refine or navigate search results using multiple facets of a subject term and create their own custom navigation) (Lemieux 2009). In addition, the *discovery interface* allows patrons to generate their own content for materials including reviews, summaries, and tags. User tagging of items can be used by technical services staff to create folksonomies (subject categories or headings organized on the basis of tagged content created by patrons) to augment keywords and subject headings, and subsequently, enhance the user's discovery experience. Another feature supported by Web 2.0 technologies is Really Simple Syndication (RSS); a subscription to the RSS feed keeps the user abreast of items relating to search results that are added to the discovery interface.

Like the traditional public access or online catalog, a *discovery interface* supports many features, including, but not limited to, searching by author, title, phrase, and keywords combined with Boolean operators (AND, OR, NOT). A user can limit a search to a specific time period, publication date, and type of materials, among others. Search results can be saved, e-mailed, exported, and formatted according to a specific bibliographic style available to users. Examples of discovery interface products suited for small libraries are Follett's Destiny Quest, the Library Corporation's Library.Solution for Schools LS2 PAC, and Mandarin Library Automation M3 Web OPAC. Examples of discovery interfaces for larger libraries include Ex Libris's Primo (http:// www.exlibrisgroup.com/category/PrimoOverview), Innovative Interfaces Inc.'s Encore, Online Computer Library Center's (OCLC's) WorldCat Local, and SirsiDynix Social Library. Additional discovery products are provided by Breeding (2013) in the Digital Shift Automated Marketplace 2013 (http:// www.thedigitalshift.com/2013/04/ils/automation-marketplace-2013-the-rush-to-innovate/). Note that Breeding reported on these and other discovery products based on ILS company sales to libraries in 2012.

Every library can benefit from adding a *discovery interface* to its current ILS (Jacobsen 2011) especially as most of these interfaces are interoperable with third-party ILSs. The nature of the library's ILS (for schools, public libraries, academic libraries, etc.) will determine whether a third-party interface is interoperable with the existing ILS. Finding reviews about discovery interfaces offered by companies is recommended.

Discovery Service versus Discovery Interface

A *discovery service* is a cloud-based *next-generation discovery interface* that goes beyond federated searching to enrich the user's information discovery experience. This service is based on the *open platform* framework and harvests data from aggregated scholarly e-resources including eBooks, journal articles, newspaper articles, and digital repositories. A discovery service integrates with a library's collections to provide access to a library's print and digital contents in a single interface. A user can search for materials using one single search box and the service retrieves materials in all formats including journal articles (citations and/or full text) that are ranked by relevancy and based on the library's subscription to online databases and services. Leading discovery services include Serials Solutions' Summon (http://www.serialssolutions .com/en/services/summon), OCLC WorldCat Local (http://www.oclc.org/ worldcatlocal/default.htm), Primo Central Index (http://www.exlibrisgroup .com/category/PrimoCentral), and EBSCO Discovery Service. Discovery services are implemented in academic and large-sized libraries. Currently, most ILS companies that target small libraries are utilizing discovery interfaces rather than discovery services.

Discovery services enjoy these main benefits:

- Design of the interface is based on one single search box to facilitate searching across different types of materials.

- Journal articles are retrieved in search results along with other types of materials in various formats (print and digital) similar to what Google retrieves for a user's search.

- Retrieved search results to a user's search are ranked by relevancy.

- Access to both local content and remotely hosted content saves the user time in finding information (Freeman 2011).

However, discovery services have limitations. These include the following:

- A search often yields results that are inconsistent with those retrieved from a library's traditional online catalog interface.

- The amount of information retrieved may be overwhelming to users.

- Users may not be able to distinguish between various types of materials retrieved.

• Research and academic libraries are the target audience for discovery services. However, small libraries that are a part of library consortia may save on the cost of these services while providing faster services to users.

Cataloging Module

Cataloging library materials and storing the metadata for cataloged items are accomplished in the cataloging module. One can create MARC records using the Machine-Readable Cataloging for the 21st Century (MARC 21) protocol; import such records from services such as the OCLC WorldCat or other MARC databases provided by book or automation vendors; or copy and input such records from the Library of Congress Z39.50 Gateway. Other ways for finding MARC records are through access to specific libraries' web-based online catalog or discovery interface or service. The cataloging module has many additional features, including—but not limited to—searching, editing, saving, deleting, indexing, and exporting records. Editing or cleaning up MARC records can be achieved by purchasing software such as MARC Magician by Mitinet Library Services (http://www.mitinet.com/Products/MARCMagician.aspx) that is designed for this purpose. MARC records can also be exported onto an external medium such as a flash or hard drive and sent to an automation vendor to clean up. Cleaning up each MARC record individually in-house can also be achieved although it is very time consuming.

When a MARC record is saved in the cataloging database and indexed (keywords are assigned from various fields), a user will be able to find it through the online catalog or discovery interface or service. An item or holdings statement is attached to the MARC record during the cataloging process to make it available for circulation.

The latest development in the area of cataloging has been the Resource Description and Access (RDA). RDA "is the new standard for resource description and access designed for the digital world. Built on the foundations established by AACR2R, RDA provides a comprehensive set of guidelines and instructions on resource description and access covering all types of content and media"(http://www.rdatoolkit.org/background). The Library of Congress has implemented RDA on March 13, 2013 (http://www.rdatoolkit.org). One of the main benefits of RDA lies in the conceptual models of functional requirements for bibliographic data (FRBR) and functional requirements for authority data (FRAD) that will be applied to cataloging resources. FRBR "is a conceptual model that defines four different entities in an attempt to alter the ways in which catalogers catalog items so that they can be more uniform, more trimmed down, and more accessible by users. FRBR is not a data format like MARC 21 or a rule set like AACR2, or a mark-up language like Extensible Markup Language (XML); rather, it is a set of structured ideas about what bibliographic records must contain to meet user needs." For more information, visit LISwiki website: http://liswiki.org/wiki/FRBR#What_is_FRBR.3F. XML is being used to code data in MARC 21 records.

Circulation Module

This module covers tasks and processes for managing the circulation function. This includes but is not limited to item check-in, checkout, inventory, fines, overdue notices, holds, account management, and reports management. Circulation deals with both patron records and item records created during the cataloging process. Patron records include patron information such as the name, identification number, address, phone number, and so forth. This module also contains circulation policies, calendar of due dates and holidays, tables that hold current circulation transactions, tables with item records, and patron privileges, among other things.

Acquisitions Module

Materials ordering and management is covered in this module. This includes ordering, receiving, invoicing, claiming, fund allocation and encumbrance, vendor performance tracking, and reporting, among other functions. Materials may be onetime orders, standing orders, on approval, or subscriptions. Orders can be transmitted electronically to a vendor using the Electronic Data Interchange (EDI) manager that is based on the EDI protocol. When materials are received in the library, they are checked against the orders to ensure accuracy. Encumbered funds are released to the vendor and funds are adjusted. In an ILS with an acquisitions module, status and availability of ordered materials are reflected. When an item is placed on order, it is reflected in the discovery interface or service. When the item is received and a MARC record is generated for it or imported in the cataloging module, the user will be able to identify its availability if the circulation module is integrated with cataloging. In small libraries such as those in public schools, the acquisitions module is centralized at the district or county level where the ordering and processing of materials are performed.

Serials Module

Ordering and processing annuals, periodicals, newspapers, and like materials are accomplished in this module. Additional functions include cancellation of subscriptions, claiming late issues of journals or magazines, routing of journals (passing issues to interested users), allocating and encumbering funds, tracking vendor performance, binding, and management reports. This module allows for searching and browsing serials records using different options (e.g., title, ISSN, publisher), editing, deleting, and merging serials records.

In an ILS with an integrated serials module, the status and availability of a magazine or journal, for example, will appear in the discovery interface (on order, claimed, at the bindery). As the status of the magazine or journal changes from claimed to received, the serial record for that item is updated and reflected in the discovery interface. Academic, public, and special libraries use this module to perform the described functions, among other things. In school libraries, this module, if it exists, will be at the district level, like the acquisitions module.

Interlibrary Loan Module

Borrowing and lending materials are achieved in this module. When an item is not owned by a library, a registered patron can place and track a request for the item electronically via the library website. ILL is a form of resource sharing among libraries; it is based on the International Organization for Standardization (ISO) ILL Protocol, which is an international standard that allows "libraries to exchange interlibrary loan requests and responses electronically, even when using different systems" (Kelsall 2008). The standard provides a unified structure for all ILL requests, thus facilitating the tracking and management of requests. The ISO ILL 10160 is Information and Documentation, Open Systems Interconnection, and Interlibrary Loan Application Service Definition; and the ISO ILL 10161 is Information and Documentation, Open Systems Interconnection, and Interlibrary Loan Application Protocol Specification. For additional information about the ISO ILL, visit the Auto-Graphics website: http://www4 .auto-graphics.com/standards/isoillprotocol.htm.

Borrowing and lending is based on a reciprocal agreement among participating libraries. Not all types of materials can be requested through ILL. For example, a library may not allow the borrowing of textbooks or reference materials that is not circulated. In many situations, ILL is managed through software independent from the existing ILS. However, the existing ILS should have features to support resource sharing in a consortia environment.

While many large libraries use the OCLC for ILL services, small libraries with an ILS that is shared in a consortia environment may connect to a statewide network for borrowing and lending materials. OCLC's ILL system is ISO ILL compliant. Libraries that wish to use the OCLC ISO ILL will need to have an ISO ILL compliant system to interact with OCLC ILL (http://www .oclc.org/isoill/default.htm). OCLC's service is fee-based and may be costly to small libraries operating on limited budgets.

Authority Control Module

The creation and management of headings (author names, titles, series, and subjects) of MARC 21 bibliographic records created in the Cataloging module are performed in this module. It links authority-controlled headings with their respective authority records through use of a list of standardized headings. Variant forms of a heading (e.g., author name) existing in bibliographic records are brought together under one authority-controlled heading and cross references (See and See Also) associated with the heading are generated for use in the online catalog or discovery interface. Authority control allows for maintaining consistency in the heading formats of bibliographic records, leading users to the headings used in catalog in one single place. This module is an add-on to the ILS and can be purchased from the ILS vendor or a third-party vendor.

Media Management Module

Reserving multimedia materials and booking equipment are provided through this module, which is also an add-on to an ILS. Through this module, one can schedule, book, search, and track these resources. Videos, audio CDs, DVDs, Blu-ray Disks, and the like materials are the types of media managed in this module; also included are study rooms, conference rooms, and labs. This module also allows for a better management of multimedia resources, such as use by type and the generation of various kinds of management reports.

Electronic Resource Management Module

Management of electronic resources (e.g., eBooks, eJournals) is performed in this module. Tasks supported are license methods, access, distribution channels, record creation, usage statistics, and report management, among other things. Increased use of eBooks in libraries in the past few years makes this module an essential add-on to the ILS or as a separate stand-alone module. The integration of eBooks in the ILS will provide a seamless approach for the management and patron's access to eBooks. This integration is a trend that ILS companies are pursuing. For example, The eResource Central solution offered by SirsiDynix allows the integration of eBooks from a number of eBooks service providers with whom the company has agreements. Among these providers are OverDrive and Oxford University Press (http://www.thedigitalshift .com/2013/04/ils/automation-marketplace-2013-the-rush-to-innovate/). Other companies are expected to offer similar integration of eBooks into their electronic resource management modules in the near future.

Digital Asset Module

The purpose of this module is to organize, manage, and maintain digital collections such as special collections, repositories, images, digitized texts, and other materials in digital format. Large academic libraries and other libraries with large digital collections are the target audience for this module.

Library patrons can use this module to search for and retrieve all types of digital assets using one single search in the ILS discovery interface.

Textbook Management Module

This add-on module is mainly geared for schools. It allows for effective management of textbooks, viewing a district-wide inventory of textbooks and other curriculum materials, transferring textbooks between schools, and replacing them, among other things. Managing textbooks through this module may result in improving accountability as it reduces cost associated with the replacement of textbooks, among other things. Many automation companies with ILSs designed for schools and other small libraries offer this module.

THE CHANGING NATURE OF THE ILS

The past few years have witnessed shifts from the traditional ILS to cloud-based, library services platforms that are founded on the open platform framework. Ex Libris Group, for example, released Alma, a new unified resource management system that handles print, electronic, and digital resources and "supports the entire suite of library operations-selection, acquisition, meta-data management, digitization, and fulfillment-for the full spectrum of library materials, regardless of format and location" (http://www.exlibrisgroup.com/category/AlmaOverview). In 2012, Ex Libris Group reported 17 contracts for 71 libraries that will use Alma. Similarly, OCLC has implemented its WorldShare Management Services (WSMS), a system that offers unified functions including acquisitions, circulation, inventory, and patron management, cataloging with digital collection management, along with WorldCat Local, its discovery service (http://www.oclc.org/webscale). OCLC had 163 total contracts for WMS in 2012. Innovative Interfaces had 117 contracts benefiting 303 libraries that will use its Sierra Services Platform. Another library services platform is Serials Solutions' Intota, which was announced in January 2012 and expected for release in late 2014 (http://www.thedigitalshift .com/2013/04/ils/automation-marketplace-2013-the-rush-to-innovate). Intota is designed around library workflows, unlike legacy systems, and supports the entire resource life cycle, from selection to discovery of all types of materials. According to the company's website, Intota was conceived around the principles of interoperability, linked data, and software-as-a-service (SaaS) to lower the cost of library ownership and management of the software. Intota was developed with six partners that include academic, public, college, and private libraries (http://www.serialssolutions.com/en/news/detail/serials-solutions-announces-intota-development-partners).

On the small library front, OCLC announced on February 14, 2012, its new Website for Small Libraries project that will allow small libraries with collections of 20,000 items or less to have a presence on the web. Libraries can provide basic access to their collections, circulate materials in and out, manage user accounts, and promote services and events. Users create their accounts, search library materials, and place holds on items. This service is not a full-featured library management service, but it provides basic automated functionalities. Based on OCLC, the implementation of this project is scheduled in 2014. However, as of September 2013, OCLC has not released any information about the status of this project. Libraries wishing to learn more about this project should visit the WorldCat website: http://beta.worldcat.org/lib. Libraries can import and export their collection and patron data during the trial period and continue to do so throughout the duration of their memberships (http://www.librarytechnology.org/ltg-displaytext.pl?RC=16561).

These open platform products are evolving rapidly and may compete with legacy ILSs (e.g., SirsiDynix Symphony) and open-source systems (e.g., Koha and Evergreen). While these unified resource management solutions are available for large libraries, similar products for smaller libraries are very few. One of these products is Apollo by Biblionix, a multitenant ILS that has been successful for small public libraries nationwide (Breeding 2013).

SUMMARY

This chapter described the components of an ILS within the framework and nine characteristics of an information system. It described various ILS modules and functionalities and provided a comparison between the ILS traditional online catalog and a discovery interface, and between a discovery service and discovery interface.

A discovery interface is a software layer installed over an existing ILS. The interface supports Web 2.0 features and federated searching. A discovery service is a next-generation discovery interface that is cloud-based and offered in next generation ILSs called Library Services Platforms (LSPs). The discovery service provides a unified search box for searching all types of content from a library's print and digital materials. A discovery service goes beyond federated searching and retrieves information from across all types of materials including books, eBooks, eJournals, journal articles based on a library's subscription to online databases and other services, and newspapers, among other resources, and ranks results by relevancy, similar to what Google and other leading web search engines retrieve to a user's query. While traditional ILSs focus on existing collections, the next-generation ILSs focus on content management of all types of resources and are founded on the open platform framework. Currently, discovery services are more common in academic and public libraries than in school or other smaller libraries.

At the forefront of open-source ILSs for large libraries is Kuali Ole, a Library Services Platform designed and developed by and for college and university libraries. While Kuali Ole is being implemented, Koha and Evergreen are well established in the automation marketplace.

Use of LSPs in libraries is on the rise. Leading companies offering LSPs include OCLC's WMS, Ex Libris Group's Alma, Innovative Interfaces Inc.'s Sierra Services Platform, as well as Serials Solutions' Intota, and VTLS Open Skies, which is under development.

REFERENCES

Auto-Graphics, Inc. "ISO ILL Protocol (10160/10161)." 2006–2012. http://www4.auto-graphics.com/company-standards-support.asp. Accessed February 4, 2013.

Breeding, Marshall. "Discovery Interfaces Add New Facet to the Marketplace." *Automation Marketplace 2012: New Models, Core Systems.* 2010. http://www.libraryjournal.com/article/CA6723662.html. Accessed December 5, 2012.

Breeding, Marshall. "Perceptions 2012: An International Survey of Library Automation." 2013. http://www.librarytechnology.org/perceptions2012.pl. Accessed March 2, 2013.

Breeding, Marshall. "Queens Library Develops daVinci to Deliver its New Integrated Web Site." 2011. http://www.librarytechnology.org/ltg-displaytext.pl?RC=16144. Accessed on March 13, 2013.

Britannica.com. "Graphical User Interface (GUI)." http://www.britannica.com/EBchecked/topic/242033/graphical-user-interface-GUI. Accessed January 3, 2013.

Freeman, Daniel A. "Jason Vaughan Discusses Web Scale Discovery Systems." 2011. http://www.alatechsource.org/blog/2011/02/jason-vaughan-discusses-web-scale-discovery-systems.html. Accessed January 17, 2013.

Jacobsen, Jonathan. "Discovery Interfaces: A New OPAC for Libraries." 2011. http://www.andornot.com/blog/post/Discovery-Interfaces-A-New-OPAC-For-Libraries.aspx. Accessed February 7, 2013.

Kelsall, Paula. "The ISO ILL Protocol: A "State of the Standard" Report." NISO Resource Sharing Forum. 2008. http://www.niso.org/news/events/2008/resshar08/agenda/5_resshar08_kelsall.pdf. Accessed January 4, 2013.

Kendall, Kenneth E., and Julie E. Kendall. *Systems Analysis and Design.* 8th ed. Upper Saddle River: NJ: Prentice Hall, 2011.

Lemieux, Stephanie. "Designing for Faceted Search," *KM World.* 2009. http://www.uie.com/articles/faceted_search. Accessed January 20, 2013.

LIS Wiki. "FRBR." 2012. http://liswiki.org.wiki/FRBR#What_is_FRBR.3F. Accessed February 7, 2013.

OCLC. "ISO ILL: The International Standard for Interlibrary Loan." 2012. http://www.oclc.org/isoill/default.htm. Accessed February 4, 2013.

RDA Toolkit: Resource Description & Access. "RDA Background." 2010. http://www.rdatoolkit.org/background. Accessed January 7, 2013.

Valacich, Joseph S., Joey F. George, and Jeffrey A. Hoffer. *Essentials of Systems Analysis and Design.* 5th ed. Upper Saddle River, NJ: Prentice Hall, 2011.

WEBSITES

ByWater Solutions. http://bywatersolutions.com/.

The Digital Shift. http://www.thedigitalshift.com.

Evergreen. http://open-ils.org.

Equinox Software. http://www.esilibrary.com/esi.

Ex Libris (Alma). http://www.exlibrisgroup.com/category/AlmaOverview.

Ex Libris (Primo). http://www.exlibrisgroup.com/category/PrimoCentral.

Koha. http://www.koha.org.

Kuali OLE. http://kuali.org/OLE.

Liblime Koha. http://www.liblimekoha.org.

OCLC. Website for Small Libraries. http://www.librarytechnology.org/ltg-displaytext.pl?RC=16561.

OCLC WorldCat Local. http://www.oclc.org/worldcatlocal/default.htm.

OCLC WorldShare Management Services. http://www.oclc.org/webscale. Open Source Initiative. http://opensource.org/osd.html.

Serials Solutions. http://www.serialssolutions.com/en/news/detail/serials-solutions-announces-intota-development-partners.

Chapter 2

Library Automation Life Cycle (LALC) Phase I

SYSTEM IDENTIFICATION AND PLANNING

Embarking on a full-scale or partial library automation project involves several processes. While one may assume that all libraries in the United States already have an integrated library system (ILS) in place, there are still many libraries in rural areas (e.g., Appalachia and East Tennessee) that have just started preparing for automation, or have outdated ILSs and cannot upgrade or migrate to a new ILS due to financial reasons. Breeding (2012) echoed on this reality in his article on the status of automation in small libraries in the United States, saying "many small public libraries in rural areas and small towns either rely on outdated systems or have no automation at all . . . as I track the automation trends in libraries, I have been concerned for a long time about how many public libraries in the U.S. lag behind in automation . . ." Therefore, planning for library automation is necessary regardless of its magnitude. This chapter describes the planning process within the framework of the Library Automation life cycle (LALC), a method applied in many organizations to guide these processes. This chapter covers the following main topics:

- System identification and planning
- Acquiring basic knowledge

- Project planning
- Project feasibility
  - Technical feasibility
  - Budgetary feasibility
  - Operational feasibility
  - Schedule feasibility
  - Political feasibility
  - Legal feasibility
- Assessing potential risks
- Role of the project manager

Today, libraries are in a strong position when it comes to selecting an ILS due to the varied types of software and hosting models available. The primary types of ILSs are proprietary and open source. A library may choose a proprietary ILS to host on-site or use the ILS vendor to host the software in the cloud. In the latter case, the library will save on the cost of hiring technical personnel to troubleshoot software problems. However, the library will pay an annual subscription for the cloud-based hosting service.

The latest development in proprietary offerings is library services platforms (LSPs) that allow for sharing resources—from cataloging to acquisitions to policies—making sharable data available to them. Breeding (2013) reports on the implementation activity of these platforms by Ex Libris (Alma), Innovative Interfaces Inc. (Sierra Services Platform), and Online Computer Library Center (OCLC) WorldShare Management Services. Serials Solutions' Intota platform is under development and is expected for release by the end of 2014.

Open-source software (OSS) is a software application where the *source code* is available free of charge to use, copy, modify, and distribute. OSS must comply with 10 specific criteria outlined by the Open Source Initiative (http:// opensource.org/osd.html). Use of an OSS ILS requires technical expertise with source code modification to customize features and functionalities based on a library's needs. OSS ILS can be hosted on-site or in the cloud through an ILS service provider. Koha and Evergreen are examples of OSS ILSs. Another OSS ILS is Open Integrated Library System (OPALS), a web-based system that was built through the joints efforts of schools, colleges, private, and special libraries. Currently, MediaFlex supports OPALS (http://www.mediaflex.net/ showcase.jsp?record_id=52).

Regardless of the library environment you are in, it is important that you acquire an adequate level of knowledge about the automation process, ILS software model or architecture, and evolving technologies that are impacting on the nature of automated library systems. Webber and Peters (2010) note that the availability of varied ILS software models will require decisions on an ILS that best fits the needs of library users and in the meantime is the most cost effective. Thus, learning about the various phases of the automation project and the tasks to undertake in each phase should provide a good foundation for carrying out a successful automation project.

LIBRARY AUTOMATION LIFE CYCLE

The classical SDLC described by Valacich, George, and Hoffer (2011) is a conceptual model that defines four phases and tasks to complete at each phase of the project development process. It is used by systems designers, managers, and developers to guide systems-related projects. It consists of four main iterative phases: (1) systems planning and selection; (2) systems analysis; (3) systems design; and (4) systems implementation and operation. The SDLC has been modified to fit the library automation environment. This has resulted in the Library Automation Life Cycle (LALC), which encompasses five iterative phases: (1) system identification and planning; (2) gathering user requirements; (3) structuring user requirements/selecting a system; (4) implementing the system; and (5) evaluating the system through usability (Figure 2.1).

Figure 2.1 Library Automation Life Cycle (LALC)

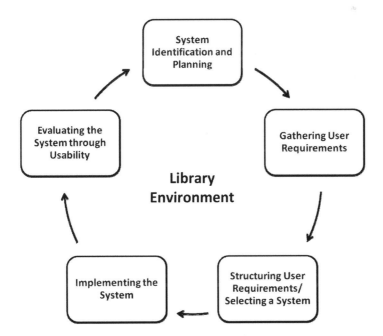

LALC PHASE 1: SYSTEM IDENTIFICATION AND PLANNING

A proposal for automating library functions for the first time, for migrating from an existing ILS to another, or for adding a *discovery interface* or other modules to the current ILS may begin as a result of a top–down administrative decision or as a bottom–up initiative at the unit or department level (e.g., user and access services). Automating a library or migrating form one ILS to another may be requested by the administration in order to join a consortium and share resources through use of a specific ILS.

The idea of undertaking a full-scale or partial automation project may also stem from the needs of the library staff. An administrator may lay out several projects for the library and appoint a project manager who will recruit staff to examine and rank these projects based on needs and funding available. The level of activities involved in the project will differ based on the existing library environment; that is, acquiring an ILS for the first time, adding a third-party discovery interface, or migrating from a proprietary ILS to an open-source one. The selection of the project as a priority should be aligned with the mission and goals of the library, including its strategic and recent technology plan, as well as the mission of its parent institution.

Most importantly is to empower yourself (if you are the project manager) and the project team with adequate knowledge of library automation including how to research, evaluate, select, and implement an ILS. Knowledge about the following is essential: available software and software models; changes in the automation industry since the existing ILS was purchased (if one is already in place); modules available as add-ons from third-party vendors; software and hardware terminology; and trends in technology (e.g., cloud computing and open system framework) that are driving library automation. In addition, you need to become familiar with the various operations of the library and users' expectations and the changing nature of their information behavior and needs.

Acquiring Basic Knowledge

Begin by researching the literature on library automation and focus on changes in the past three years. This is because advances in technologies are rapidly evolving and impacting on the automation marketplace. A key source to use is *Library Journal*, which features an annual article about the library automated marketplace in its April issue. Marshall Breeding, who writes extensively on library automation, authors the article. It is based on an annual survey of automation vendors or companies and covers software, vendor profiles, trends in the automation marketplace, and software sales to different types of libraries. Starting in 2012, this featured article has become part of *The Digital Shift* (http://www.thedigitalshift.com) of *Library Journal* (http://lj.libraryjournal.com/). In the issue dated April 2, 2013 (http://www.thedigitalshift.com/2013/04/ils/

automation-marketplace-2013-the-rush-to-innovate/), Breeding noted that the state of the automation industry continues to expand both at the national and international levels with the industry-wide shift to software-as-a-service (SaaS) and other hosting arrangements, increased investment in the academic library sector in discovery products, and subscriptions to electronic content products. In the 2012 issue of *The Digital Shift* (http://www.thedigitalshift .com/2012/03/ils/automation-marketplace-2012-agents-of-change), Breeding reflected on a decade of developments in the industry (from 2002 to 2012) and elaborated on key accomplishments in this arena. The main themes he covered include the state of the industry, sales for the last three years, emergence of new library service platforms, leaders in ILS sales for academic and public libraries, sales by product category covering vendors offering web-scale library management solutions (now called LSPs), discovery interfaces, federated search tools, mobile products, digital library management systems, electronic resource management, link resolver tools, resource sharing, radio frequency identification (RFID) support, and archives management products. In each issue, Breeding provides charts reporting ILS sales, a profile of selected ILS companies including those offering OSS, and trends in the industry.

Breeding's article includes automation companies that replied to his survey in 2011. *Computers in Libraries Buyer's Guide*, edited by Owen O'Donnell, and provides a comprehensive listing of automation companies and the software they support. The hard copy of the guide is published in the July/ August issue of every year. The online version of the guide is located at http:// bg.computersinlibraries.com. Besides automation software, this guide covers software and hardware used in libraries including online databases, books, periodicals, and supplies. There is an alphabetical list of ILS companies, the software they offer, types of libraries they serve, operating systems they support, and profiles. The keyword search feature allows one to find information by a company's name or the name of the software. The search menu also includes software, hardware, information for sale/lease (e.g., databases, books), supplies, and services sold (services provided by a company-retrospective conversion, cataloging services, IT training, etc.). The hardware section includes products such as networking devices, antitheft systems and devices, scanners, and barcode readers, among others.

Computers in libraries also publishes Pamela Cibbarelli's 2010 guide, *Helping You Buy ILS: Guide to ILS Vendors & Products*, available in a pdf format at (http://www.infotoday.com/cilmag/CILMag_ILSGuide.pdf). In this guide, Cibbarelli provides an alphabetical listing of ILS vendors that responded to her survey, describing each vendor's mission in brief, number of sites, marketplace it targets, address, phone number, URL, and e-mail.

Another guide is *American Libraries' Buyers Guide* (http://americanlibra iesbuyersguide.com/), which offers a comprehensive section on automation software, vendors, and services (http://americanlibrariesbuyersguide.com/ index.php?category=Automation&category_id=799). It includes companies under different categories such as integrated library systems, discovery services platform, cataloging, federated search, inventory management, to name a few. The address, phone number, and names of software and products provided by each company along with a link to the company's website are included. Like Cibbarelli's guide, this source does not include evaluation of ILS software or products.

Additional sources to consult are the *Library Technology Guides* (LTG) (http://www.librarytechnology.org) authored by Marshall Breeding. This site includes the most recent news about the library automation field, technology products, individual automation company news, library news in relation to automation, trends, synopsis of articles and links to the *Library Journal, Automated System Marketplace*, articles published in *Library Technology Reports*, trends in technology that impact libraries, a guide to discovery interfaces used in libraries (http://www.librarytechnology.org/discovery.pl), and *lib-web-cats* (a directory of library websites and online catalogs worldwide) (http://www.librarytechnology.org/libwebcats). By searching *lib-web-cats*, one can locate library online catalogs in a specific geographical area. Breeding's LTG is another good starting point for learning about the automation marketplace.

The American Library Association's (ALA's) bibliography, *Automating Libraries: A Selected Annotated Bibliography*, *ALA Fact Sheet Number 21* (http://www.ala.org/tools/libfactsheets/alalibraryfactsheet21), covers relevant articles from 2006 to 2012. ALA's *Library Technology Reports* offers featured reports on varied topics in the automation arena. In its October 2011 (vol. 47, issue 7), for example, there is a 54-page report by Andrew Nagy titled, *Analyzing The Next Generation Catalog* (http://www.alatechsource.org/taxonomy/term/106/analyzing-the-next-generation-catalog) that discusses these topics: defining the next-generation catalog; open source versus commercial solutions; deploying the next-generation service; understanding the impact; and case studies of selected universities that implemented next-generation catalogs.

Blogs are additional sources one can use to learn about and keep updated on recent developments in the ILS environment. *ALA Tech Source Blog* (http://www.alatechsource.org/blog), for example, has the "Tech Set" section covering interviews with book authors who publish books on the library automation arena. In a blog submitted on June 14, 2012, for example, there is a recorded audio interview with Marshall Breeding about his book, *Cloud Computing for Libraries*, published in 2011. The ALA blog page is an important source for learning about the latest developments in library automation and the technologies driving it. Another blog is Marshall Breeding's *Guide Posts Perspective and Commentary Blog Archive* (http://www.librarytechnology.org/blog.pl?Archive=2012–6&BlogID=1).

Google blogsearch (http://www.google.com/blogsearch) is an effective tool for finding blogs. For example, entering the term *ILS open source* in the blogsearch box retrieved relevant results on the first results page. Other blog search tools are found at, (http://websearch.about.com/lr/blog_search_engines/368771/1/). This site also has descriptions of the top Twitter search tools in real time. (http://websearch.about.com/od/enginesanddirectories/tp/twitter-search-engines.htm).

Attending national and state conferences where product showcases and vendor exhibits are available is highly recommended for becoming familiar with various products, using them on-site, and for connecting with specific library automation vendors. The ALA, American Association of School Librarians, and Special Library Association annual conferences are examples of these professional venues. Early in the planning process, view demos of products at these conferences to gain understanding of the various features that ILSs have to offer; visit vendors' websites, and explore these products further. Identify libraries that have recently implemented the products and discuss them with colleagues (via blogs, listservs, tweets, etc.). Forming a partnership with nearby libraries that have recently implemented ILSs to learn from their experiences will enrich your knowledge of library automation.

In retrospect, learning about library automation includes the following topics:

- Automation steps or processes

- Sources for different types of ILS software (proprietary and open source)

- Existing software models (in-house versus cloud hosting) and LSPs

- ILS software and hardware terminology

- ILS software technology components or back ends (operating systems–supported, web servers, programming languages, database query languages, etc.)

- ILS software technology components or front ends (traditional online catalog interfaces versus discovery interfaces versus discovery services)

- Technology advances impacting on library automation industry

Project Planning

Normally, a project manager is appointed, and teams with project leaders are formed to plan the project. In a small library setting, this situation may apply at the system level (a number of libraries working together to achieve a common goal in automation). The size of the teams depends on the number of staff members available in the various affiliated libraries. The project manager identifies the scope of the project, cost, and time it may take to complete the project. The manager establishes a project baseline plan (PBP) that includes the project name, description, feasibility assessments (see the next section), and management issues (Valacich, George, and Hoffer 2011). A library may develop its own baseline plan to document the work undertaken in completing the project.

The manager assigns tasks, roles, and responsibilities to team members and leaders; he or she identifies potential project risks, develops alternative plans to tackle the risks, and oversees the feasibility studies performed. The project manager does not work in isolation; instead, he or she collaborates with the teams on many tasks and communicates problems, issues, challenges, as well as progress on the project. Project management is essential throughout the project life cycle especially if the ILS is to be implemented by the in-house staff rather than by a vendor or firm that will assign a project manager to guide you through the whole process.

Selecting or migrating to a new ILS or library services platform will require justification for upper level administrators and a buy-in by stakeholders, especially in terms of tangible and intangible benefits to the library, patrons, staff, and stakeholders.

Tangible benefits are concrete and can be measured in monies and with certainty based on using existing data. In other words, these benefits are quantifiable. Examples of these benefits include, but are not limited to, time saved by streamlining library operations (e.g., cataloging, circulation, and acquisitions), reduction in the number of errors made, increase in accuracy, efficiency, and effectiveness in performing tasks, and also cost saving on migrating to a cloud-based software model. Note that these benefits should be researched and /or documented based on published literature, stories collected from other libraries, and consultation with ILS vendors and colleagues.

Intangible benefits are those that cannot be measured in monies and with certainty. These benefits tend to be abstract rather than concrete in nature. For example, the benefits patrons may gain by using a discovery service instead of the ILS traditional online catalog include the ability to retrieve locally hosted content in varied formats (print, digital, electronic, and journal articles of subscription databases); that is, using one unified search interface instead of four different interfaces (books, media, journal databases, and digital repository). Leckie, Givens, and Campbell (2008) argue that despite advancements in information technologies, the traditional web-based online catalogs that come with the ILS have not resolved the long-standing difficulties users have experienced with online catalogs. Therefore, adding a *discovery interface* or *discovery service* may help users overcome these difficulties by saving time in finding information, navigating search results, and judging relevancy of the results (Tam, Cox, and Bussey 2009; Luther and Kelly 2011). In the issue of *The Digital Shift* dated April 2, 2013, Breeding notes that libraries, especially in the academic arena, continue to invest in discovery products to enhance user access to the library's collection in varied formats (http://www.thedigitalshift.com/2013/04/ils/automation-marketplace-2013-the-rush-to-innovate/); other libraries may need to consider a discovery interface to enrich the user's experience and access to resources.

Project Feasibility

Part of the planning process is performing a preliminary cost-benefit analysis that includes both onetime cost and ongoing cost. The costs will vary based on the software type and model to be considered, in addition to the nature of library facilities, technology infrastructure, staffing, and budget. These factors can be unraveled through conducting various feasibility studies.

Technical Feasibility

Existing technical resources should be assessed in terms of hardware and the adequate level of knowledge and skills of technical personnel who may be involved in the project. The project manager should assess the adequacy of existing computer hardware. There may be a need for an upgrade of the hardware or the purchase of new computers to accommodate the proposed ILS software. This is especially true in case the library may consider local hosting of the hardware. The capacity of technical staff with computer and technology skills should also be identified to determine whether the technical expertise is available in support of the future operability of the ILS. Assessment of personnel resources, availability, skills, and willingness to participate in the project in various capacities is essential at this stage in the process to ensure smooth planning.

Budgetary Feasibility

The project manager should estimate both the *tangible* and *intangible cost* of the automation project. *Tangible cost* includes both onetime cost and ongoing cost. *Tangible onetime cost* (see Table 2.1) involves the software (to be purchased from a proprietary vendor, licensed as open source, or hosted in the cloud as SaaS, hardware and requirements for client stations and servers, cost of devices and peripherals such as collection inventory devices, self-checkout scanners, and cost of hardware as a service (HaaS) hosted in the cloud by an ILS vendor or company (if this option is under consideration). In addition, budgetary feasibility should include assessment of the existing network capacity for accommodating local and remote access to the ILS and the cost of increasing bandwidth of the

Table 2.1
Projected tangible onetime cost work sheet

Indicate the item, quantity needed, item description, and cost for each of the items shown in this worksheet. Add items as needed. Indicate N/A (not applicable) inside the cell that does not apply.

Item	Quantity	Description	Cost
Public access computers			
Staff workstations			
Server(s)*			
ILS basic software (on-site)*			

Table 2.1 (Continued)

Item	Quantity	Description	Cost
ILS add-on modules*			
Printers for public access			
Printers for staff			
Checkout device(s)— staff use			
Self-checkout device(s)			
Inventory device			
Anti-theft security system (EM, RF, or RFID)			
Network upgrade			
Network firewalls, virus protection software, and so on.			
Facilities renovation (chairs, tables, ramps, etc.)			
Collection—retrospective conversion (Recon) (outsourcing— including barcodes or tags)			
Collection—Recon (in-house alternative)			
Smart barcode generator software (or RFID tags)			
Staff training			
Feasibility studies			
Miscellaneous			
Total			

*If cloud hosting is being considered, the onetime cost should be removed from this work sheet and placed in the projected ongoing tangible cost work sheet. As applicable, some items should be removed based on the option being considered. Descriptions and cost of the items should be obtained for ILS vendors or companies that specialize in these products and services. The following chapters have lists of ILS companies, Recon vendors, and supplies to use for calculating the projected onetime tangible cost of the project.

network to speed up traffic and provide faster access to resources. In many environments, the IT personnel develop the architecture of the network, and assess the cost involved. Other onetime tangible cost is staff training (off- and on-site), attending conferences, renovating facilities, as needed (e.g., remodeling, carpeting, tables, chairs, ramps to support accessibility for people with disabilities), and collection services (e.g., retrospective conversion or Recon). The latter should include the cost of both in-house and outsourced Recon options. Note that onetime cost should also include the cost of the feasibility study.

Ongoing tangible cost covers supplies (e.g., printer paper, barcode printer paper, barcode labels or RFID tags, and annual software maintenance and vendor technical support). If OSS is considered, the ongoing cost of technical support is waived if the organization has qualified technical staff to do it. If the SaaS OSS model is under consideration, the annual cost of hosting should be included (Table 2.2).

Table 2.2
Projected tangible ongoing cost work sheet

Indicate the item, quantity needed, item description, and cost for each of the items shown in this **work sheet**. Add items as needed. Indicate N/A (not applicable) inside the cell that does not apply.

Item	Quantity	Description	Cost
Software maintenance (on-site hosting)			
Technical support (on-site hosting)			
Barcodes or RFID tags			
Paper for printers (staff)			
Paper for printers (users)			
Discovery interface add-on			
Cloud hosting service —software*			
Cloud hosting service—hardware (Paas or IaaS)*			
Miscellaneous			
Total			

*This cost is incurred if the library considers this option. As applicable, some items should be removed based on the option being considered (e.g., on-site hosting of software). The descriptions and cost of the items should be obtained for ILS vendors or companies that specialize in these products and services. The next chapters have lists of ILS companies, Recon vendors, networking companies, and supplies to use for calculating the projected onetime tangible cost of the project.

Intangible cost refers to items that cannot be measured in monies and with certainty. Loss of employees, time taken to hire new employees, decline in employee morale, resistance to change by users and employees, and decline in users' access to or privileges for certain services (e.g., recall of checked out materials before due date) are examples of this cost. Calculating tangible and intangible costs will provide a clear idea about the projected funds needed to support the project.

Operational Feasibility

One of the main purposes of initiating an automation project is to improve services and enhance the user experience and information discovery of locally and possibly remotely available materials. If an ILS is implemented but not heavily used as expected, the operation of the system will be limited, resulting in a waste of both financial and personnel resources. The ultimate goal of purchasing or developing an ILS lies in its acceptance, likeability, and regular use by patrons. Assessing and understanding user needs (including those of the staff)—and implementing an ILS that meets those needs—will most likely result in a smooth operation of the system. The operational feasibility of the proposed ILS may be based on an informal assessment of user and staff needs. The results of such assessment may be augmented with recent literature attesting to user reactions in interacting with ILSs in similar environments.

Schedule Feasibility

Schedule feasibility involves an analysis of the estimated amount of time it will take to complete the project successfully and within the set time frame or deadline using various resources and taking into account all possible internal and external constraints that could affect completing the project on time. Based on existing technical expertise, financial and human resources, input from administrators, stakeholders, and potential ILS vendors, the project manager should be able to assess whether the proposed ILS project timeline is reasonable. Failure to meet a mandatory deadline could have political, legal, and financial ramifications on the library and the ILS vendors (if the library chooses a proprietary ILS).

Political Feasibility

Political feasibility is an assessment of how the key stakeholders of the library within the parent institution perceive the need for the proposed ILS project and/or the value of it. For example, in a school library setting, school librarians, teachers, principals, superintendent, and district-level supervisors are key stakeholders. The ILS project cannot be carried out without the support of and input from these key personnel.

Legal Feasibility

Legal feasibility involves an analysis of risks or conflicts with existing legal requirements of the parent institution. Such risks may involve signing a contract for the ILS with a specific ILS vendor that requires consultation with a legal advisor or attorney. Data migration from one ILS to another could incur the risk of losing data or data corruption and copyright problems, and infringement of user privacy may also be at risk. Failure of the selected ILS vendor to deliver the converted data as promised or to deliver the ILS software on time, as well as changes in the ILS vendor's financial stability or company status (possible merger, buyout, or withdrawal from the automation marketplace) will have legal ramifications that could impact on the nature of the ILS project including its timeline.

Assessing Potential Risks

Every project has potential risks. The project manager should identify potential problems and outline ways of managing unexpected events. It has been estimated that 30 percent of all projects in organizations succeed; 20 percent fail; and 50 percent are behind the established timeline, over budget, or provide fewer features than originally promised or planned (Kendall and Kendall 2010). The project manager should plan for unexpected events including, but not limited to, staff resistance to change that may cause delay in the project, staff resignation or early retirement, budget cuts, absence of administrators and key personnel during the needs assessment phase, and staff delay in beginning work on the project due to delay in completing other projects. To minimize these risks, the project manager should assess the probability of occurrence of these and other events and calculate the value or cost of these unexpected events. The timeline for completing the project should be as flexible as possible to allow for project delay in case unexpected events take place. Another way of minimizing potential risks is to develop an alternative plan for carrying out the project, including phasing in the project overtime in the event of budget cuts. Note that the type of feasibility assessment to conduct depends on the library environment, size of the library, and the responsibilities and roles of librarians in the project, among other factors. In certain cases, it is not surprising to find that supervisors or top-level administrators make the ILS purchase decisions without consulting with school librarians. The outcome of the feasibility assessment studies is a report with a planning document summarizing the key elements of the proposed project, which is described in the next section.

Project Planning Document

The planning document, also known as the Baseline Project Plan (BPP) (Valacich, George, and Hoffer 2011), summarizes the results of the feasibility assessment studies on the first page or two pages of the feasibility assessment report. It provides the project scope, results of the feasibility studies, methods employed in assessment, justification for the project (all benefits), project requirements, cost estimate (tangible and intangible), resource requirements (both human and financial), recommendations, and level of success (Berrie 2008). If the results of the feasibility assessment studies show that the project is viable, a meeting with key personnel (upper level administrators) is scheduled to discuss the project plan in more detail, ensure common understanding of the project, its scope, benefits, cost, duration, and articulate clear ideas about the expectations and personnel issues.

ROLE OF THE PROJECT MANAGER

"The project manager's role in a nutshell is the overall responsibility for the successful planning, execution, monitoring, control and closure of a project" (Barry, n.d.). Barry (n.d.) identified these 10 top qualities of a project manager. These are:

- Capacity to inspire a shared vision
- Communication skills
- Integrity
- Enthusiasm
- Empathy
- Competence
- Ability to delegate tasks
- Levelheadedness under pressure
- Team building skills
- Problem-solving skills

A successful project depends, in most part, on the strong leadership skills of the project manager. The manager defines the overall project scope, time, cost, and quality. She sets the goals of the project, develops the project document plan, strategizes each phase of the LALC, selects the project teams and their leaders, assigns tasks, measures the quality of achieved tasks, and monitors task completion as scheduled. The manager should clearly define these tasks and develop criteria based on which completed tasks will be evaluated. She captures the tangible and intangible project cost in a budget sheet, conducts or monitors the various feasibility assessment studies, and manages the project financial resources. In addition, the project manager monitors the team leaders' progress on tasks, explores training opportunities to enhance inadequate skills, and coaches the teams as needed.

Staff may raise many of the "why" questions during planning and possibly other phases of the project: Why do we have to do this project? What is wrong with what we have been doing? How much time do we have to do these tasks? How will the new ILS be better than what we have now? How will the environment be different when the project is finished? (Dobson 2004; Kerzner 2009). Answering these questions effectively should provide staff with good understanding of the problems experienced with current practices and how solving these problems will improve the operations of the library and its environment.

Developing a collaboration tool (a website with a content management system, for example) is advisable to keep project documents and all communications with team members and other groups (administrators, potential users, vendors, and constituencies) in one place. In addition to assisting in accurate record keeping, this tool could be used for promoting the automation project and for keeping administrators, staff, and stakeholders up-to-date about its progress.

SUMMARY

The first phase in the LALC is the System Identification and Planning. At this phase of the LALC, and if you are a novice to library automation, you will need to acquire an adequate level of knowledge of the automation process by reading relevant literature on the topic. This should include sources to find ILSs suitable for your library's environment, reviews of varied ILS software, recent technology advances impacting on library automation, ILS trends, software and hardware terminology, and ILS software architecture. Main sources include the Automation Marketplace featured article on library automation. This article is authored by Marshall Breeding and appears in *The Digital Shift*, part of *Library Journal*, which appears annually in the April 2 issue. The articles reports on the status of the library automation industry, sales of ILSs, profiles of ILS companies, open-source ILS, and future trends. Another major source is *Computers in Libraries Buyer's Guide* published annually. However, this guide precludes reviews of the ILSs. Marshall Breeding's LTG website provides the latest news about automation including information about libraries migrating to new systems and vendors' new initiatives. Selected full-text articles on different "hot" topics in the automation arena are provided, as well as links to Breeding's published articles and reports. LTG contains articles and reports on important topics in automation. Learning from colleagues, attending professional conferences, and using subject-related blogs and other social media tools can be valuable during the planning process.

During the planning phase, the project manager assigned to the automation project (who could be you) will form teams and leaders to assist with the project. The manager has many responsibilities, including, but not limited to, setting project goals and the timeline, assigning roles and responsibilities to the teams and leaders, estimating the tangible (concrete) and intangible (abstract) benefits of the project, overseeing the feasibilities studies, assessing the preliminary costs of the project (onetime and ongoing), calculating a cost-benefit analysis, assessing potential risks, and providing solutions to overcome the risks. The manager prepares the planning document, measures performance on tasks, and produces a report describing the planning outcomes of the project.

REFERENCES

Barry, Timothy R. "Top Ten Qualities of a Project Manager." No date. http://www.projectsmart.co.uk/pdf/top-10-qualities-of-a-project-manager.pdf. Accessed on July 19, 2013.

Berrie, Michelle. "Initiating Phase—Feasibility Study Request and Report." 2008. http://www.pmhut.com/initiating-phase-feasibility-study-request-and-report. Accessed on August 25, 2011.

Breeding, Marshall. "Automation Marketplace 2013: The Rush to Innovate." *The Digital Shift*. April 2, 2013. http://www.thedigitalshift.com/2013/04/ils/automation-marketplace-2013-the-rush-to-innovate. Accessed on May 30, 2013.

Breeding, Marshall. "Lower the Threshold for Automation in Small Libraries." *Computers in Libraries*. April 2012. http://www.librarytechnology.org/ltg-displaytext.pl?RC=16732. Accessed on August 9, 2013.

Cibbarelli, Pamela. *Helping You Buy ILS: Guide to ILS Vendors & Products.* 2010. http://www.infotoday.com/cilmag/CILMag_ILSGuide.pdf. Accessed on July 31, 2013.

Dobson, Michael S. *The Triple Constraints in Project Management.* Vienna, VA: Management Concepts Inc., 2004.

Kendall, Kenneth E., and Julie E. Kendall. *Systems Analysis and Design.* 8th ed. Upper Saddle River, NJ: Pearson Prentice Hall, 2010.

Kerzner, Harold. *Project Management: A Systems Approach to Planning, Scheduling, and Controlling.* 10th ed. New York: Wiley & Sons, 2009.

Leckie, Gloria J., Lisa Givens, and Grant Campbell. "Technologies of Social Regulation: An Examination Library OPACs and Web Portals." *Information Technology in Librarianship: New Critical Approaches*, 2008.

Luther, Judy, and Maureen C. Kelly. "The Next Generation of Discovery." *Library Journal.* 2011. http://www.libraryjournal.com/lj/home/889250-264/the_next_generation_of_discovery.html.csp. Accessed on January 22, 2013.

Nagy, Andrew. "Analyzing the Next Generation Catalog." *LibraryTechnology Reports*, 47(7). 2011. See also, http://www.alatechsource.org/taxonomy/term/106/analyzing-the-next-generation-catalog. Accessed on July 22, 2013.

Tam, Winnie, Andrew M. Cox, and Andy Bussey. "Student User Preferences for Features of Next-Generation OPACs: A Case Study of University of Sheffield International Students." *Program: Electronic Library and Information Systems*, 43, no. 4 (2009): 349–74.

Valacich, Joseph S., Joey F. George, and Jeffrey A. Hoffer. *Essentials of Systems Analysis and Design*. Upper Saddle River, NJ: Prentice Hall, 2011.

Webber, Desiree, and Andrew Peters. *Integrated Library Systems*: *Planning, Selecting, and Implementing*. Santa Barbara, CA: ABC-CLIO, 2010.

WEBSITES

ALA Tech Source Blog. http://www.alatechsource.org/blog.

American Libraries Buyers Guide. http://americanlibrariesbuyersguide.com/.

Automating Libraries: A Selected Annotated Bibliography, ALA Fact Sheet Number 21. http://www.ala.org/tools/libfactsheets/alalibraryfactsheet21.

"Automation." *American Libraries' Buyers Guide*. http://americanlibrariesbuyers guide.com/index.php?category=Automation&categoryid=799.

Computers in Libraries Buyer's Guide. http://bg.computersinlibraries.com.

The Digital Shift. http://www.thedigitalshift.com. "Discovery Layer Interfaces." *Library Technology Guides*. http://www.librarytechnology.org/discovery.pl.

Google blogsearch. http://www.google.com/blogsearch.

Guide Posts Perspective and Commentary Blog Archive. http://www.librarytech nology.org/blog.pl?Archive=2012–6&BlogID=1.

Library Journal. http://lj.libraryjournal.com/.

Library Technology Guides. http://www.librarytechnology.org.

Lib-Web-Cats. http://www.librarytechnology.org/libwebcats.

Open Integrated Library System (OPALS). http://www.mediaflex.net/showcase .jsp?record_id=52.

Websearch.about.com. http://websearch.about.com/lr/blog_search_engines/ 368771/1.

Websearch.about.com. "Twitter search tools." http://websearch.about.com/od/ enginesanddirectories/tp/twitter-search-engines.htm.

Chapter 3

LALC Phase 2

GATHERING USER REQUIREMENTS

Gathering and understanding user requirements are essential steps that, if performed, analyzed, and interpreted accurately, can drive your decision making for purchasing an integrated library system (ILS), migrating to a new one, or adding a layer over an existing ILS such as a discovery interface. Requirements are the features and functionalities desired in the entire ILS or a specific module. By gathering user requirements early in the automation process, "you can gain understanding of such things as what users really want and need, how they currently work and would like to work, and their mental models or mental representations of their domain" (Courage and Baxter 2005, 4). These requirements are essential for selecting the ILS—the software and architecture—best satisfying the needs of the users, staff, administrators, and possibly stakeholders. The method(s) to employ will depend on the type of the library, timeline of the automation project, and personnel resources, among other things. While large libraries may use more than one method for gathering user requirements, small libraries may follow a simple process to achieve this goal. This chapter describes varied methods for gathering user requirements. It covers the following main topics:

- Characteristics of gathering user requirements

- Methods for gathering user requirements

  ○ Interviews

- ○ Survey questionnaires
- ○ Observations
- ○ Diaries/journal logs
- ○ Logs and data analytics
- ○ Analysis of work documents and procedures
- • Determining priorities
- • Outcomes of gathering user requirements

CHARACTERISTICS OF GATHERING USER REQUIREMENTS

The ILS project manager and staff should precisely define the various units within the organization or library, develop a clear understanding of the workflow of each unit, and identify the functions and the processes performed within each function. Paying attention to detail is essential to gaining a precise picture of the overall structure of the library and its parent institution. Staff should be proactive in gathering data from all identified constituencies and should raise as many questions as needed to develop a good understanding of the environment and workflow inside each unit and across the various units, as applicable. Examples of these questions are: What are the relationships between different units? What is the relationship between cataloging and information service or reference services? What is the relationship between information service and circulation? Appropriate data gathering should result in *baseline* data to be used in structuring the specifications for the proposed ILS. As was mentioned earlier, large libraries may apply a complex approach (more than one method) for gathering user requirements whereas small libraries may need to use a simple assessment method to this end.

METHODS FOR GATHERING USER REQUIREMENTS

Assessing user needs can be achieved through using quantitative and qualitative methods. Each of these methods employs specific techniques. The quantitative method aims at gathering numerical data whereas the qualitative method targets participants' ideas, comments, opinions, suggestions, and so on, about specific requirements or situations. The quantitative method includes techniques such as direct and indirect observations, transaction logs, and work documents containing statistical or numerical data (e.g., circulation reports, inventory data, and reference transactions).

The qualitative method covers interviews, diaries or journal logs, and work documents that describe the reality of a specific situation or action. In each method, you may choose one or more of the techniques involved. Ideally, the combination of both quantitative and qualitative methods is preferred because if well designed and analyzed, you will obtain richer and more accurate data that reflects better on the reality of the situation at hand.

Overall, the selection of specific methods and techniques will be based on the main purposes of inquiry; that is, what data to gather and how data will be used; experiences of personnel involved in data collection and analysis; and the consumers of these data (people who will read the results or the audience) (Creswell 2010). Additional factors include: (1) the ILS project timeline; (2) the cost of data collection and analysis (including personnel time); (3) the availability of library staff to interview or observe; (4) the availability of patrons to participate in the data collection.

Interviews

Interviewing is a skill that is gained through learning and practice. It is mainly a qualitative research method used to obtain or elicit information from target participants. Interviews can generate useful data for establishing user-centered requirements for an ILS. However, it can be time consuming as it requires planning, developing interview materials, obtaining the administration's consent to recruit and interview participants (patrons, staff members, administrators, and possibly stakeholders), gathering, transcribing, coding, and analyzing the data, and reporting the findings. The level of complexity involved in interviewing depends on the types of interviews conducted (structured, semistructured, or open-ended). The project manager should ensure that the interviewers are equipped with the necessary knowledge and skills of interviewing techniques. She may assist in developing the interview questions and script guide, pilot-testing the questions, coding the responses, analyzing the data, and possibly interpreting the findings, and also reporting the results.

Interviews are synchronous and often performed face-to-face. In cases where the interviewee cannot be present during the interview, the interviewer may conduct the interview over the telephone (Sharp, Rogers, and Preece 2011). However, the interviewer will lose the capture of cues in the interviewee's behavior (nonverbal communication) that may suggest discomfort or ambiguity or other affective states that cannot be sensed in telephone interviews (Shneiderman and Plaisant 2009).

Successful interviews are those that generate data that, once coded and analyzed, can provide good understanding of specific events that can be used to solve or improve specific situations. In his classic book on interviewing, Kvale (2007) outlines three main steps of an interview that are summarized as follows:

- *Before the interview*: Plan the time, prepare the setting, schedule an appointment with the participant, and practice to record and transcribe questions and answers.

- *During the interview*: Greet the participant, recall the purpose of the interview, ensure confidentiality, and proceed with the questions.

- *After the interview*: Summarize key points of the interview and obtain feedback from the participant, thank the participant, and ask whether he has any questions for you or comments. Review the notes taken during the interview, and reflect on the conduct of the interview process.

Kvale (2007) also describes the qualities of a skilled interviewer as one who is knowledgeable about the focus of the interview; capable of using a good structure; clear in asking questions; gentle (does not interrupt the participant while expressing his ideas); sensitive (attentive and good listener); open (responds nicely to questions asked by the interviewee), critical (challenges what is said), remembers what is said and integrates what has previously been said; and capable of interpreting the interviewee's comments or statements without changing their meanings.

Interviewing Staff and Administrators

Conducting the interview requires good planning and preparation. Consider these key factors when interviewing staff/administrators:

- Make an appointment with the interviewee in advance and explain the purpose of the interview.

- Introduce the interviewee to the purpose of data collection and inform her about the average time the interview may take.

- Ask the interviewee to sign a consent form. The project manager should provide guidance to the interviewer in advance about the legal aspects of data gathering in the organization.

- Develop an interview instrument with appropriate questions to ask of the staff member(s) to be interviewed. Consider using both closed and open-ended questions. Closed questions are those that can be answered as *Yes* or *No*. Open-ended questions are exploratory in nature and are used to elicit one's opinions or description of activities or tasks. They also provide the interviewees with the opportunity to make recommendations and/or provide comments.

- Use probes to elicit the data you are trying to gather, especially in cases when an answer to a question is vague or too concise that you cannot derive the information you are trying to capture. Be prepared to use a new line of inquiry when the interviewee provides comments or data that were not anticipated.

- Include questions that elicit information about the ILS features, functionalities, and capabilities they desire in a new system, likes and dislikes of the current system, and their level of satisfaction with it, and so forth. If the library does not have an ILS in place, consider asking questions about their level of satisfaction with the tasks they are performing, the main problems they experience in completing these tasks, and the barriers they perceive in meeting patrons' needs.

- Ask questions about the typical work tasks and activities staff/administrators perform on a daily basis, their perceptions of the effectiveness of performing these tasks and activities, and the difficulties or problems they experience in performing them.

- Seek staff/administrators' opinions about the different ILSs with which they are familiar; what they like and dislike about them, and how they feel about acquiring a new ILS or migrating to a new one, totally or partially.

- Do not preempt an answer by phrasing a question to suggest a particular answer.

- Elicit staff comments and/or suggestions at the end of the interview.

- Make the interview brief, yet informative in relation to the data to be gathered.

- Thank the staff member for her participation in data gathering. Ask her whether she has any questions or comments to add.

- Review the interview notes and reflect on the course of the interview.

Interviewing Patrons

Interviewing patrons is similar to interviewing staff/administrators in many respects. For example, the project manager or a project team member will also set goals for recruiting and interviewing patrons. The goals of gathering data from patrons should guide the development of the questions to include in the instrument. Similar techniques are also employed in interviewing patrons, including the following: introducing the purpose of data collection; communicating the average time the interview may take; requesting that the interviewee sign a consent form; using a script to guide the interview; asking both closed and open-ended questions; and using probes as needed.

Since patrons will mainly use the online catalog component of the ILS, interview questions should target the search and browse options and features, user expectations, and information needs, among others. If an online catalog is already in place and data is gathered to capture patrons' satisfaction/dissatisfaction with the current online catalog, the questionnaire should target the goals of data collection. Remember that user expectations of the online catalog have dramatically changed over the last few years because of patrons' use of Google, Yahoo!, Bing, Amazon.com, and similar services that provide easy access to information from one central location. This means that the open-ended questions should allow users to express their opinions and visions of the new catalog or interface.

Closed questions may be answered *Yes* or *No*, or may provide the patron with options to choose from. Sample closed questions are:

(1) How long have you been using the library's online catalog?

1–6 months _____ 6–12 months_____ Over 12 months_____.

(2) Have you used online catalogs other than the one we have in this library?

Yes____(if so, go to (3) No____.

(3) What are the names of the catalogs you have used? (Consider asking for the names of institutions where the patron used these catalogs, as most patrons may not know the exact names of the catalogs they have used.)

Open-ended questions allow participants to respond in their own words, using their own structure, giving them a greater sense of involvement and control during the interview (Valacich, George, and Hoffer 2011; Pickard 2013). Sample open-ended questions include:

(1) How often do you use the online catalog?

(2) What information do you typically look for in the online catalog?

(3) How do you look for information in the online catalog? (The interviewer might probe here: Do you search or browse?) (The interviewer should follow up with questions about searching and/or browsing.)

(4) How satisfied are you with the online catalog you have used in the past two years?

(5) What problems or difficulties have you experienced in using the online catalog?

(6) We are planning to improve the online catalog to make your experience more rewarding. What would you like the online catalog to do for you? What features or options could you think of? How should the online catalog look (e.g., screen)?

In interviewing patrons, make sure you:

• Elicit the patron's comments and/or suggestions at the end of the interview.

• Provide your contact information.

• Thank the interviewee for his participation in data gathering.

Recording the Interviews

To capture all accounts of the interview data, consider using an audio recorder. Typically, a digital recorder will allow you to import the recorded accounts or scripts into a computer for data transcription, coding, and analysis. Review the captured data as soon as possible to determine whether additional information—or a follow-up to clarify certain answers—is needed.

If you wish to take notes while recording the interview, make sure you do not distract the interviewee. You may want to ask the interviewee in advance if taking notes would be agreeable with him. Notes should focus on aspects of the interview that cannot be captured through the audio recording, including affective reactions and nonverbal communication. Give your full attention to the interviewee and listen carefully to his answers so that you are able to follow up on unexpected or vague responses.

Transcribing, Coding, and Analyzing the Interviews

After the interviews are completed, it is suggested that you transcribe the data as soon after the interviews as possible as you should be interpreting the data as you transcribe it noting patterns and themes as they emerge. At this step, you are processing the initial transcription of the data. Coding the data can be performed manually, but use of software is preferred especially if there is a high number of open-ended questions and the number of participants in the interview is more than 10 people. Examples of software tools for qualitative data coding are Atlas-ti (http://www.atlasti.com) or QSR NVIVO (http://www .qsrinternational.com). Examples of texts to consult on qualitative research techniques, data coding, and analysis are by Strauss and Corbin (2008) and Miles and Huberman (1994).

Survey Questionnaires

Unlike interviews, surveys are quantitative in nature and have instruments with questions that can be made accessible to a wide audience over the web. Survey instruments or questionnaires can be answered asynchronously (not interactively or in real time). Today, most if not all surveys are web-based, and software tools such as SurveyMonkey (http://www.surveymonkey.com), or IBM SPSS mrInterview (http://www.spss.com/software/data-collection/interviewer-web) are used to develop them. Web-based surveys are more efficient in that the completed questionnaires can be analyzed using descriptive statistics (percentages, mean value, median, and standard deviation) by the software used. Today, "many people prefer to answer a brief survey displayed on a screen instead of filling in and returning a printed form" (Shneiderman and Plaisant 2009, 151). Typically, survey questionnaires via regular mail may result in a 50 percent or higher return rate, whereas those filled over the web may yield less than 50 percent return rate (Sharp, Rogers, and Preece 2011). Therefore, be prepared to send more than one follow-up via e-mail to remind potential participants to fill out the questionnaire. Giving an incentive for completing the questionnaire may generate a higher return rate. This extra expense should be allocated in the project budget.

It is advisable that you develop good quality questions to gather the data needed, especially since you will not be interacting with the participants (no probes or follow-ups on unexpected answers). The questions should be well focused, clear, and free of technical jargon so that you are able to achieve those goals. A mix of closed and open-ended questions should be included as appropriate.

Conducting surveys requires use of adequate sampling methods, design of good quality questions, and appropriate data coding and analysis. The quality of responses is influenced in many cases by the quality of questions posed. While the guidelines and questions described in the interviewing section could be adapted for designing survey questionnaires, it is suggested that you consult basic books or guides on research methods. For example, the book by Connaway and Powell (2010), *Basic Research Methods for Librarians*, covers all types of methods with a focus on quantitative research. Another book to use is *Practical Research Methods for Librarians and Information Professionals* by Susan Beck and Kate Manuel (2008), which focuses on both qualitative and quantitative methods. For an overview of all types of research methods, consult the book by Alison Jane Pickard, *Research Methods in Information* (2013).

Observations

Observing people as they perform their jobs will capture data that interviews and questionnaires may fail to report. While interviews and surveys are based on data provided by the participants and reflect their own recall of certain procedures, subjective opinions, personal interpretation of certain events or issues, and observations provide more accurate and objective accounts of the participants' work contexts, tasks, and goals. When performed over a long period of time (i.e., continuously), observations can provide details about how people perform their tasks in everyday life. Observations may also be performed at random times. However, they may not reflect a holistic picture of reality. Observations are costly, time consuming, and difficult to code, analyze, and interpret. Therefore, they should be planned and carried out by knowledgeable and well-trained personnel. To save time and money, observations should be conducted for a limited time and with a limited number of participants. The timeline established for the observations should be flexible to accommodate unforeseen circumstances.

As with interviews and survey questionnaires, observations should be based on a set of goals. Establishing these goals should guide the method(s) of observation to employ, that is, direct observation and/or indirect observation. Using the 3W rule of thumb (3W)—*Who, Where,* and *What*—should help you design and set realistic goals for the observations. Robson (2002) provides a nine-element framework for observing participants in their work environment:

- Space (description of the physical space)

- Actors (who are being observed, and what are the participants' characteristics and work responsibilities?)

- Activities (what are the actors doing during the observation and why?)

- Objects (what physical objects are the actors using (e.g., computer)?

- Acts (what are the specific actions the participant is doing—talking, moving things around, etc.?)

- Events (what events are taking place other than those set in the goals of the observation?)

- Time (how is the time being used in relation to the activities performed?)

- Goals (what are the actors trying to accomplish?)

- Feelings (what affective reactions do the actors exhibit during the observation?)

These goals allow the observer to focus on the data being gathered. However, the observer should be able to modify or reschedule the observation as she learns about unexpected situations or events.

There are two main types of observations, direct and indirect. Each type has its own techniques, which are briefly described in the next section.

Direct Observation

Direct observation is obtrusive, meaning that the participant is aware of the observation. The observer may take notes of the activities performed and events taking place during the observation session. Multiple observation sessions may be needed to capture as much data as possible to reflect the work reality of the participant. Nonetheless, the more data you collect, the more time you will need to code, analyze, and interpret the information generated.

Conducting an obtrusive or direct observation may also be achieved by installing a usability software tool on the participant's computer. Such a tool will be set up to record all computer screen activities the participant performs. In order not to misinterpret actions the participant may exhibit during the observation (e.g., sighing, looking frustrated), the observer may set the software to record the participant's nonverbal communications along with verbalization of the actions being performed (think-aloud protocol). By doing so, the observer will be able to capture the participant's experience in using the online catalog. Morae software packages published by Techsmith (http://www.tech smith.com/morae.asp?CMP=KgoogleMtmhome&gclid=CNGZpJayqZ8CFR KfnAodOh2o1Q) are examples of usability software that allow for the observation of multiple participants simultaneously from afar and without causing distraction (Morae Observer). Recording the actions or activities performed can be accomplished by using Morae Recorder, so that when equipped with a digital camera and microphone, one is able to capture verbal and nonverbal communication in real time during the interaction. The coding and analysis of the collected data can be achieved by using Morae Manager. The observer may take notes during the observation and ask a participant questions about the interaction with the ILS. Morae may be used to collect data about the work activities and tasks staff and administrators perform online in the workplace. The software may also be used to gather data about patrons' interaction with the current ILS (if one is already in place).

Use of usability software can be more effective and efficient in collecting data about the interaction. However, it can be costly and time consuming, when multiple users are to be observed simultaneously, requiring use of a site license of the software for multiple client stations. In addition, the data generated from the recorded activities can be complex to analyze and interpret, especially if you are new to this kind of usability research. This kind of data gathering requires preparation of usability materials, including tasks to assign to participants, checklists of activities to follow during data collection, and possibly entry and exit survey questionnaires. Training in use of usability software, gaining adequate knowledge of usability research, and learning how to develop usability materials are essential for successful data gathering, coding, and analysis.

Indirect Observation

Indirect observation is unobtrusive, meaning that the participant is unaware of being observed or is asked to collect data using diaries of their activities on a regular basis. While direct observation has the potential to make the participant change her normal behavior (Valacich, George, and Hoffer 2011; Pickard 2013), indirect observation may capture normal behavior in a specific context. For example, one may observe how reference services staff interact with patrons and take notes during the observation. One may also observe a patron's interaction with the online catalog and take notes without making the patron aware of such observation. Another technique is to ask participants to keep diaries or journal logs of their activities based on the guidelines provided by the observer (see the "Diaries" section). Observations have drawbacks. Observing people without their knowledge could be unethical. To overcome this problem, seek the consent of the people you will be observing before collecting the data. Another problem is that indirect observation may generate data "out of context" as the observer is unaware of the goals and actions being performed by the participant. In addition, interpretation of the collected data may be inaccurate, as the observer may lack an adequate level of understanding of the participant's task goals. Moreover, the data may also be incomplete due to the fact that the observer failed to capture sufficient data. Due to these limitations, indirect observation should be employed to complement other methods such as interviews and surveys.

Diaries or Journal Logs

A better indirect observation data-gathering technique is the tracking of participants' activities, information behavior, needs, and the problems they experience, and so on through the use of diaries or daily journal logs. When employing this technique, one can set goals for the data gathering using diaries and provide the participants with clear guidelines for writing them. Diaries may be used when participants cannot be observed in person. They are inexpensive and require no or minimal expertise to write. However, diaries can be incomplete if the participants do not remember to write them on a daily basis. To capture data from various perspectives of the work activities of the participants, diaries should be written for a long period of time. If you are operating under time constraints, diaries may not be an advisable data-gathering technique. Another potential problem with using diaries is that they may generate accounts that do not match the specific goals of data gathering. Therefore, it is recommended that you develop a standard online or web-based form to transcribe daily logs so that you can standardize data entry and import the data into a database for analysis (Sharp, Rogers, and Pierce 2011; Pickard 2013).

Logs and Data Analytics

Traditionally, reference staff in many libraries keeps logs of reference transactions on a daily basis to gather statistics about traffic at the reference desk and the type of reference questions asked (directional, factual, research). While the level of traffic can help with adequate scheduling, the type of questions asked can provide directions for improving services. For example, if many patrons ask for directions—to the bathrooms, copiers, computer labs, and so forth—then a site map with improved signage in key areas could solve these problems and, in turn, diminish the number of directional questions posed by patrons. One difficulty that staff may experience in keeping logs of questions asked and assistance provided to patrons is the demand on staff time, especially during peak hours when they are busy. One should not expect that every type of question asked or assistance sought will be logged. Although one may not capture all the transactions performed on a daily basis, analysis of data collected over a long period of time could provide understanding of the key issues or problems patrons experience in finding services and in using specific tools such as the online catalog interface or discovery interface.

Data analytics can also be collected from circulation, cataloging, and other logs. Data analytics over a period of time can be extracted, parsed, coded, and analyzed not only in relation to traffic, but also to perform query analysis of patrons' search strategies, errors made, browsing strategies, navigation, successes, and failures unobtrusively (Connaway and Powell 2010). Such analysis can identify whether the problems experienced by patrons over a long period of time are system-bound or skills-related. System-bound problems will require system design improvements. If such improvements are not feasible due to the technical limitations of the system, then a replacement of the online catalog should be considered. Note that a decision of such magnitude should not only be based on one occurrence and one method of data collection. One should use mixed methods including logs and observations, or logs and interviews, or logs and observations and interviews in order to capture the user experience that could help in justifying the replacement of the existing online catalog interface.

Many ILS companies have integrated a web analytics feature in their current systems. Analytics are unobtrusive but ethical and can be used to address problems with the current ILS—especially in terms of the online catalog or discovery interface. However, using this technique will not reveal the patron's age, adequate level of knowledge in using the system, or goals and intentions. Note that data analytics can be employed to complement other data-gathering methods, resulting in richer and more holistic understanding of users based on both system- and user-driven data.

Analysis of Work Documents and Procedures

Gathering user requirements for a new ILS can be augmented through the examination and analysis of existing documents and work procedures (manuals, guides, flowcharts, etc.) to identify details about the its requirements (design features, capabilities, and operation). Additional documents to examine include, but are not limited to, the parent institution's mission statements, strategic plan, technology plan, policies, job descriptions, current practices, and cumulative reports produced by each unit or department. This analysis should provide you with overall understanding of the components the ILS in question should support.

DETERMINING PRIORITIES

One of the major benefits reaped from data gathering and analysis is the ability to use facts to prioritize functions or justify the need for an ILS, migration to a new ILS, addition of one or more modules to the current ILS (e.g., discovery interface), or migration to a cloud-based ILS platform. This is especially important when a library is experiencing budget constraints because it could allow the organization to reap the greatest cost-benefits from its investment in a new model or platform.

Acquiring an ILS with the three basic modules (circulation, catalog, and online catalog) has become the norm. In considering priorities, you will need to consider the impact of technological advances on existing software models to choose from, library management platforms to adopt, or the discovery interface to add to the ILS. Joining a specific consortium of libraries has also become a trend to save on system and personnel costs.

OUTCOMES OF GATHERING USER REQUIREMENTS

The data generated from gathering user requirements will vary based on the method(s) used. The data will need to be reviewed, refined, coded, and analyzed so that it can be used for developing specifications for the prospective

ILS. Table 3.1 includes each method, outcome, and tasks to perform for each. The data-gathering scheme presented in this table is adapted from the work by Sharp, Rogers, and Preece (2011).

Table 3.1
Data-gathering method, outcome, and task

Method	Data Outcome	Task
Individual interviews using audio recording	Audio records with or without analyst's notes	Transcribe audio record of each interview; code transcribed data; analyze transcribed data; write and report results.Clean up notes taken during interviews, code, analyze, interpret, write, and report the results.
Direct observation using notes	Lists of recorded notes	Review lists. Clean up, transcribe, code, and analyze notes. Interpret, write, and report results.
Direct observation using usability software with or without field notes	Digital recordings of interaction	Replay recordings, determine usefulness of captured data (i.e., completeness), export data onto an external hard drive, import data into usability software management program for coding and analysis. Review analyzed data; interpret, write, and report results. If notes are taken, review, clean up, code, and analyze as needed. Notes can be used to complement data from recordings, as needed. Write and report results.
Diaries/journal logs	Records of diaries or journal logs	Collect diaries or journal logs; determine usefulness, code, analyze, and interpret data. Write and report results.
Data analytics	Files of web data analytics	Review files and write computer script to parse data. Code, analyze, and interpret data. Write and report results.

SUMMARY

The second phase of the Library Automation Life Cycle (LALC) involves intensive data gathering of requirements to develop an understanding of the needs, information behaviors, expectations, satisfaction, and perceptions, among other things. Note that the first and second phases of the project can be done in parallel.

Users include patrons, staff, administrators, and possibly stakeholders. Qualitative and quantitative methods may be used to collect this data. Qualitative methods include techniques such as interviews, direct observations, and diaries or journal logs. Quantitative methods cover surveys, system-generated data (e.g., transaction and query logs) and statistical data aggregated over a period of time for certain operations or functions such as circulation, cataloging, and reference/information service. The generated data should be reviewed, refined, coded, and analyzed as appropriate to develop reports on the findings that can be used to inform you of the ILS priorities and specifications that could meet the needs of users and the overall library mission and goals in the 21st century. If you are new to the automation or work environment, it is essential to become familiar with the varied operations of the library, workflows, and functions to learn about the kind of data to gather. In addition, gaining knowledge about qualitative and quantitative data-gathering techniques is necessary for getting involved in gathering user requirements. The method(s) to apply will depend on the type of the library environment and personnel resources available. For example, large libraries may need to employ a complex approach to gathering user requirements whereas small libraries will most likely follow a simple process to that end. Data analytics is a quantitative, unobtrusive method of collecting information about user information behavior in the online catalog or discovery interface. Selected ILS companies are now offering a data analytics feature for the ILS. If your ILS has this feature, take advantage of it to learn about users and their patterns of using the catalog or discovery interface.

Overall, use of more than one method of data collection should result in developing better understanding of user requirements, not to mention overcoming the shortcoming inherent in each data-gathering method and its techniques. Effective data gathering, analysis, and interpretation should assist you in developing specifications for the ILS as a whole and the platform that best meet the library's staff and patron needs. Remember that phase 2 of the LALC complements phase 1 discussed in Chapter 2. Therefore, learning about automation through reading relevant literature (phase 1), for example, is essential for understanding the processes involved in phase 2.

REFERENCES

Beck, Susan E., and Kate Manuel. *Practical Research Methods for Librarians and Information Professionals.* New York: Neal-Schuman Publishers Inc., 2008.

Connaway, Lynn P., and Ronald R. Powell. *Basic Research Methods for Librarians.* 5th ed. Santa, Barbara, CA: ABC-CLIO, 2010.

Courage, Catherine, and Kathy Baxter. *Understanding Your Users: A Practical Guide to User Requirements Methods, Tools, and Techniques.* San Francisco, CA: Morgan Kaufmann Publishers, 2005.

Creswell, John W. *Research Design: Qualitative, Quantitative, and Mixed Methods Approaches.* Thousand Oaks, CA: Sage Publications, 2010.

Kvale, Steinar. *Interviews: An Introduction to Qualitative Research Interviewing.* Thousand Oaks, CA: Sage Publications, 2007.

Miles, Mathew B., and A. Michael Huberman. *Qualitative Data Analysis: An Expanded Sourcebook.* 2nd ed. Thousand Oaks, CA: Sage Publications, 1994.

Pickard, Alison Jane. *Research Methods in Information.* 2nd ed. Chicago, IL: Neal-Schuman, 2013.

Robson, Colin. *Real World Research: A Resource for Social Scientists and Practitioner-Researchers.* Malden, MA: Blackwell Publishers, 2002.

Sharp, Helen, Yvonne Rogers, and Jennifer Preece. *Interaction Design: Beyond Human-Computer Interaction.* 3rd ed. Hoboken, NJ: John Wiley & Sons, Ltd., 2011.

Shneiderman, Ben, and Catherine Plaisant. *Designing the User Interface: Strategies for Effective Human-Computer Interaction.* 5th ed. Boston: Pearson Eddison Wesley, 2009.

Strauss, Anslem I., and Juliet Corbin. *Basics of Qualitative Research: Techniques and Procedures for Developing Grounded Theory.* 3rd ed. Thousand Oaks, CA: Sage Publications, 2008.

Valacich, Joseph S., Joey F. George, and Jeffrey A. Hoffer. *Essentials of Systems Analysis and Design.* 4th ed. Upper Saddle River, NJ: Prentice Hall, 2011.

WEBSITES

Atlas-ti. http://www.atlasti.com.
IBM SPSS. http://www.spss.com/software/data-collection/interviewer-web.
Morae Software. http://www.techsmith.com/morae.asp?CMP=KgoogleMtm home&gclid=CNGZpJayqZ8C.
QSR NVIVO. http://www.qsrinternational.com.
SurveyMonkey. http://www.surveymonkey.com.

Chapter 4

LALC Phase 3

STRUCTURING USER REQUIREMENTS AND
SELECTING A SYSTEM

Various methods and techniques for gathering data to determine user requirements for an integrated library system (ILS) were described in Chapter 3. Once the findings from this data gathering have been reviewed and interpreted, you (and your project team) should identify the priority needs of patrons, staff, administrators, and possibly stakeholders and map them to the outcomes of the feasibility studies you had performed in order to determine which needs are most feasible technically, operationally, economically, legally, and politically. The generated needs should be rephrased and fleshed out into specifications to include in the Request for Proposal (RFP) document (see Appendix). Libraries, regardless of type and size, have many ILS software options and platforms from which to choose (proprietary and open source), making the structuring of user requirements basically similar for each option. This chapter describes the following main topics:

- Structuring user requirements
  - Prioritizing ILS software
  - The RFP document
    - Advantages of developing an RFP
    - Disadvantages of developing an RFP

- ○ General guidelines for preparing the RFP document

- ○ Content of the RFP

- ○ Instructions to the vendor

- ○ Contract negotiation to purchase the ILS

- ○ Summary

- • Selected ILS products

  - ○ Proprietary ILS for small libraries

  - ○ Open-source ILS for small libraries

  - ○ Proprietary ILS for large libraries

    - ○ Library Services Platforms (LSPs)

    - ○ Other ILSs

  - ○ Open-source ILS for large libraries

    - ○ Kuali Open Library Environment (OLE) (LSP)

    - ○ Other ILSs

  - ○ Social online catalogs

    - ○ Social online public access catalog (SOPAC)

    - ○ Library Thing.

STRUCTURING USER REQUIREMENTS

Structuring user requirements for a proprietary or open-source ILS is a major component of the ILS selection process. Due to the fact that ILS software is well established in the automation marketplace, use of system design processes to design and develop new ILS software is not applicable. However, while modifications to existing open-source ILS software can be made by staff with technical expertise, it is not considered as typical systems design that is used to design and create a system. For information about systems design processes and modeling techniques, consult books and related materials on this topic. An example is the book by Valacich, George, and Hoffer (2011) titled, *Essentials of Systems Analysis and Design*.

In a library's environment, user requirements are structured in a RFP, a document that describes a library's specifications for essential and desirable features in an ILS. Essential features are mandatory (*must have*) and desirable features are optional (*should have*). Once the RFP document is developed, reviewed, and approved by the administration, it is sent to prospective ILS vendors to review and provide responses to the specifications and components such as the terms and conditions described in the document. The ILS project team members who are knowledgeable about various aspects of library automation and the operations of their own units should be involved in developing the RFP document. Sometimes, the technology director or coordinator in a school district, for example, takes charge of developing this document. While this person may be qualified to manage the technology aspects of an ILS (e.g., network, software installation, and updates), the person may not possess adequate knowledge about the functionalities, tasks, and activities performed by each library unit (e.g., circulation, cataloging, and user information assistance). Being part of the project team is essential for articulating the needs and priorities of your own unit and/or all library units. The project team should review the sources covered in Chapter 2 to gain knowledge about the state of library automation industry, automation technologies, and trends, as well as identify the ILS vendors that serve their library environments. These sources are: *Library Journal: The Digital Shift* (http://www.thedigitalshift.com); Automation Marketplace authored by Marshall Breeding; *Computers in Libraries, Buyer's Guide* (July/August) or its online equivalent (http://bg.computersinlibraries .com); *American Libraries, Buyer's Guide* (http://americanlibrariesbuyersguide .com) and its "Automation" section (http://americanlibrariesbuyersguide.com/ index.php?category=Automation&category_id=799); Pamela Cibbarelli's *Helping You Buy ILS: Guide to ILS Vendors & Products* (http://www.info today.com/cilmag/CILMag_ILSGuide.pdf); and *Library Technology Reports.* The latter often publishes reports on hot topics related to library automation that can be helpful during the selection process. See also the list of selected major ILS proprietary and open-source software (OSS) products for small and larger libraries at the end of this chapter.

If a decision during the planning process (Chapter 2) was made to consider an OSS ILS, it is advisable that you document user and system requirements in an RFP in case the library is asked to bid on an OSS. These requirements will help you customize the software after installation to meet your needs. An OSS allows a library to have more control over the decisions it makes about the systems, sets its own priorities in relation to the functionalities and features desired in the ILS, saves money on software cost, and shares the improvements made to the software with the open-source distribution community. The OSS uses the GNU General Public License (GPL), which is available at (http:// www.gnu.org/licenses). Different types of OSS for libraries are described at the OSS for libraries website located at (http://oss4lib.org).

Regardless of whether the desired ILS is proprietary or OSS, the project team should also do the following:

- Select between three and six ILS–appropriate software to review.

- Visit the website of each of the ILS vendors or companies. Read about the software features and find whether there is a list of libraries that have recently purchased the software. If such information is not available, ask the company to e-mail it to you.

- Gather information about the ILS vendors or companies (headquarters, history, financial stability, latest financial report, latest news, etc.).

- Download a demo of the ILS software from the company's website, if available. Otherwise, request that a demo be sent to you.

- Go through each ILS demo and note the strengths and weaknesses of each module, your likes or dislikes, and so forth on a checklist (e.g., Excel sheet) you develop for each of the ILSs under consideration. The checklist may be divided into sections—one for each of the modules previewed such as the online catalog or OPAC, circulation, cataloging, discovery interface, and other add-on modules as applicable.

- Find written reviews about each of the ILSs under consideration.

- Identify neighborhood libraries that have recently purchased one of these ILSs to visit and obtain feedback from the librarians who have been using them. These libraries may have additional modules for which you did not obtain a demo and, therefore, you will be able to test these and the whole software in full operation with existing hardware. If patrons are using the online catalog on-site, obtain a permission to observe their interaction with it. Consider interviewing them informally about their experiences with the catalog. Take notes during the visit to supplement the checklist.

- Compare notes with other project team members about the ILSs, discuss gaps or conflict of opinions about their features, strengths, weaknesses, likes or dislikes, and so forth. Try to reach a consensus so that you can develop a consolidated master checklist of the features, strengths, and so on.

- Invite a sales representative from each of the ILS companies to your library site to demonstrate the software. Using the consolidated checklist and other notes you may have taken, prepare a list of questions to ask of each representative about the software. Demonstrations provided by representatives usually reflect the latest software enhancements, thus giving you up-to-date information that may have not been published.

- Take notes during the software demonstration as needed.

- Meet with the project team members to discuss the software demo, compare notes, and augment the checklist with new information as appropriate. The outcome of the demos should allow you and the project team to prioritize the ILS software based on functionalities, needs, and priorities.

Prioritizing ILS Software

Following the demos of about three to six ILSs and after a debriefing session with other project team members, you should be able to compare these ILSs module by module and rate each module using a rating scale (e.g., five points). The three ILSs that receive the highest overall positive ratings should be considered for further examination. In rating each ILS, consider the following:

- The percentage of features available in each module, strengths, and level of meeting users' needs (patrons, staff, administrators, etc.), as well as the needs and priorities of the overall mission of the library, goals, and strategic plan of its parent institution

- The availability of an add-on discovery interface or discovery service and its features and requirements, as well as the cost. If federated search tools are desirable, features provided in these tools should be assessed

- The overall software capabilities, customization through application programming interface (API), and scalability

- Compliance with the latest bibliographic standards including MARC 21, Fundamental Requirements for Bibliographic Records (FBRR), and Resource Description Access (RDA); another standard is 3M Standard Interchange Protocol, which is currently a National Information Standards Organization (NISO) standard and used for circulation functions (http://news.3m .com/press-release/company/3m-donates-standard-interchange-protocol-sip-national-standards-organization-n). If an acquisitions module is procured, it should be compliant with the Electronic Data Interchange (EDI) standard.

- The type of cloud-based hosting of the software, support provided, and cost

- The cost of the basic ILS software, each desired add-on module (integrated or stand-alone), and frequency of software updates

- The quality of service provided by the vendor (e.g., technical support, turnaround time for assistance, diagnostics and troubleshooting), and service availability

- The ILS vendor's plan for implementing cutting-edge applications in the next couple of years

- The online and hard copy documentation of the software, indexing quality, and organization

- The type and cost of training provided

- The cost of annual software technical support and maintenance for on-site or cloud-based hosting

In selecting an OSS, also give attention to the following factors:

- *Source code dimension*—inspect the source code, robustness of the coding, level of code reuse, and level of code documentation.

- *Design and schema*—inspect the database, data design, and the degree of flexibility it provides.

- *Open-source development community*—plan for the source code enhancement processes and the degree of participation in its development (Balnaves 2008). Also, consult SourceForge (http://sourceforge.net), a site devoted to finding, creating, and publishing OSS.

- Reputation of the software performance and reliability

- Ongoing effort in the development of the software, number of versions released, and the bugs or errors that have been fixed

- Open standards and interoperability with other software

- Active support community to answer questions and help with problems through blogs, listservs, and other media; for example, Code4Lib (http://www.code4lib .org) is an active blog to use for communication about OSS including ILS.

- Commercial support from firms that offer third-party assistance

- Documentation available from users that have developed it

- Skill set needed to work with the software

- Project development model describing the development process, contributors, and contribution criteria

- License and conditions for use and contribution to the ongoing development of the software

- Case studies of libraries that have selected OSS (see Singh, 2013).

Breeding discusses fundamental components that should be taken into consideration during the selection process of an OSS. These include:

- *Licensing and distribution*—should be based on the GNU GPL because it will ensure freedom in the way that the software is shared and modified.

- *Infrastructure components*—should be mature and reliable. These components include the server operating system (e.g., Linux); web server (e.g., Apache Web); database engines (e.g., MySQL, PostgreSQL for data functions); programming language (e.g., Perl); and staff client support (e.g., Java Swing).

- *Standards supported* (e.g., Unicode, Z39.50 for server and client, MARC 21, Dublin Core, etc.)

- *Scope*—support for local content, electronic record management, discovery interface, OpenURL link resolver, support for consortia and union catalogs, among others

- *Support*—commercial support firms to support the software

Note that Breeding's article was published in 2008 and since that time, developments in query languages, software and hardware hosting (in the cloud), web-scale library management systems, and other technologies and services have surfaced that libraries can use based on their needs.

In a 2011 study, Müller evaluated all ILS OSS and open license software using 40 criteria and analyzed 800 functions and features to identify which ILS are most suited to the needs of libraries. He also identified the strengths, weaknesses, and differences or similar features of each ILS. He found that of the 20 ILSs that qualified for analysis as open-source ILSs, only Evergreen, Koha, and PMB met the criteria, functions, and features. He recommended that libraries investigating open source distinguish between OSS and freely licensed software.

In retrospect, the gathered information should help you and the project team to prioritize ILS software that best meets your needs and develop the RFP document. The next section describes how to prepare such a document.

The RFP Document

The RFP is a document that contains essential and desirable specifications that an ILS must meet. In addition, this document includes but is not limited to background information about the library, description of existing ILS (in case the library already has one in place), guidelines for responding to the RFP, and library terms and conditions (see Appendix for an example of an RFP). Once signed by the designated parties, the RFP is sent to ILS vendors under consideration who will be asked to respond to it within a specific period of time (see the following section on how to prepare the RFP). Another method for obtaining responses to an RFP from ILS vendors is by calling for *open bids* that is advertised in specific sources or venues (e.g., over the Internet). Normally, an extended or a full RFP is provided in the advertisement.

The extended RFP process is not universally followed. Some libraries are developing request for information (RFI) along with a short list of requirements to share with ILS vendors. Based on vendor response to the RFI, libraries may develop the extended RFP document.

Unlike the traditional method, the *call for bids* may result in a large number of responses that the project team will need to review and evaluate before making the selection decision, thus requiring allocation of additional time to complete this task. Nonetheless, the call for bids may be required by many institutions or organizations for purchasing an ILS. The Contoocook Valley Regional School District, Peterborough, New Hampshire (http://conval .edu) is one of these institutions that posted an open bid for its RFP over the Internet.

Advantages of Developing an RFP

The RFP document provides a means for communicating the software needs and wants of the library. It allows you to compare and evaluate the ILS software under consideration feature by feature based on the criteria you have established and also to choose software that best meets these criteria. The RFP may be the first step toward issuing a contract for the ILS vendor that receives the highest score in each criterion and meets other criteria such as financial stability, ranking in the past three years, and so on. However, the RFP should indicate that a vendor's reply does not constitute a legal contract or binding agreement for purchasing the ILS software.

Many software vendors supply customers with their own sample RFPs or checklists. While useful, the RFPs or checklists of companies contain specifications that are tailored to their own software. Therefore, it is highly recommended that you develop your own RFP document.

Disadvantages of Developing an RFP

Generally, developing an RFP is time consuming. However, the amount of time taken to complete this task varies based on the detail and number of modules for which both essential and desired specifications are to be covered in this document. The more modules you cover in the RFP, the more time consuming the process will be. This means that if you do not have sufficient time planned for this process, you may not be able to produce a good quality RFP.

Fleshing out user requirements into good specifications can be intimidating to those involved in the project because it requires specific knowledge of the verbs to use, adequate commands of the English language including grammar, and the writing of meaningful specifications.

The RFP process is costly in terms of personnel time. However, the cost can be reduced provided that the writers or developers of the RFP are knowledgeable about ILS features and functional requirements, have researched the ILS literature, and have reviewed varied software packages. Using good quality sample RFP documents may also help in reducing time spent on preparing your own RFP document (see Appendix for a high-quality RFP document). For additional examples of RFPs, see Cohn and Kelsey (2010). Note that you will need to update and augment the information in these RFPs to reflect latest technologies. The quality of the RFP responses received from vendors will vary depending on who replies to the RFP (senior, experienced staff versus staff with little experience). To ensure a good quality response to your RFP, ask that vendors provide the qualifications of the person(s) that will respond to the RFP.

General Guidelines for Preparing the RFP Document

RFPs are developed based on what is appropriate for the library. They may vary in length and format based on the type of library, timeline of the project, personnel resources, and existing policies. However, certain elements such as content, use of appropriate verbs, and specificity in articulating the specifications are similar across all RFPs.

Following are general guidelines for preparing the RFP:

- Include a cover page, table of contents, introduction, purposes of the proposed ILS, and a description of the current ILS as applicable. Other parts to include are covered in the content of the RFP (see next section).

- Organize the specifications into sections. For example, one section is required for general specifications, one for essential or mandatory specifications, and one for desired or preferred specifications (if you have time to write these).

- Use the word *must* in describing essential specifications and the word *should* in describing desirable or preferred specifications. *Essential specifications* are those you cannot do without; *desirable* or *preferred specifications* are nice to have, but you can do without them for the time being.

- List the tasks the ILS should perform, rather than how it should do them.

- Define all of the codes, symbols, descriptors, and scales you use, and provide instructions about how to use these in the introduction of the RFP.

- Provide a space before or after each specification or a table with varied codes indicating availability, no availability, under development, and so on to make it easy for the vendor to reply by placing a check mark or circling the option that applies.

- Use the following verbs: *allow, display, design, perform, provide, detect, initiate, generate, search, calculate, maintain, can, capable of, prompt*, and the like, as applicable.

- Request that the ILS vendor rate each specification in the RFP on the rating scale you provided and explain any rating of four or lower on a five-point scale. Some RFPs ask the vendor to answer *Yes* or *No* for each specification. Use of a dichotomous scale may be misleading because marking the availability of certain specifications as a *Yes* may not reflect the degree of its strengths.

- Allow sufficient space at the end of each section for the vendor's response or comments.

- Request a copy of the company's latest audited financial statement, names, and qualifications of key personnel including but not limited to those who review RFPs as well as the ones who work in technical support.

- Request a list of libraries (especially those in your region and/or state) that have recently acquired or implemented the software.

- Ask about usability or other kinds of published studies about the software.

- Allow vendors a minimum of four to six weeks to respond to the RFP. Additional information may be requested from the vendor as applicable.

Content of the RFP

The first page of the RFP includes a cover sheet with the title of the RFP, the name of the person to whom it is submitted, the company name and address, the name and address of the contact person(s) in the library and organization, and the submission date. The second page is a table of contents. The pages that follow it may include these main sections in the following order:

- Instructions to the vendor
- Introduction to the library

- Purpose for procuring an ILS (and/or for migrating from an existing ILS, as applicable)

- Current technology environment of the library (describe existing ILS, as applicable, and other technology available)

- Terms and conditions

- Description of items to be supplied by the vendor

- Vendor response to terms and conditions

- Vendor answers to specific questions not covered in the RFP specifications, as applicable

- Request for price quotation

- Notice of intent to respond

- Software specifications (general, essential, and preferred)

Instructions to the Vendor

This section explains the structure of the RFP document. It defines the descriptors used (e.g., essential means *must* have; preferred means *should* have), rating system or scale (e.g., 1–5 or 1–10 or *Yes, No*), and codes used (e.g., A = available, N = not available, U = under development, F = future development).

Introduction to the Library

In this section, provide a brief background about the library, its goals and objectives, and how these goals and objectives relate to acquiring the ILS. Key findings from the studies conducted to gather user requirements may be included.

Purpose for Procuring an ILS

In this section, provide reasons for procuring the ILS, whether you already have one in place or planning to migrate, adding a discovery interface layer or acquiring other add-on modules to the basic ILS components, as applicable.

Library Current Technology Environment

In this section, describe the technology environment including but not limited to services such as subscription to online databases, eJournals, eBooks, and so on, and the hardware available including local area network capacity, number of client stations available, number of technical personnel and their qualifications, remote access to the existing ILS and/or databases and other software or applications the library provides, and also the software hosting preferred (on-site versus cloud-based).

Terms and Conditions

In this section, provide the terms and conditions of the contract to be signed in the event the vendor's software is chosen, contract negotiation terms, and any penalty to be incurred if any of the terms of the future contract be violated. A legal counsel should review the terms and conditions stipulated in the RFP before it is sent out.

Items to Be Supplied by the Vendor

In this section, include a list of items for the vendor to supply in replying to the RFP, including, but not limited to the following: a letter referencing the RFP; a brief and recent company background and status (reorganization, merger, or acquisition within the last three years; public litigation with clients or third-party vendors within the last three years related to the ILS or anything that could affect the services the vendor will be providing in the near future); current status in the ILS marketplace, especially in the small library arena; overview or executive summary about the latest versions of ILS modules under consideration; customer list and five references; and financial statements for the last three years.

Vendor Response to Terms and Conditions

In this section, stipulate how the ILS vendor should reply to the terms and conditions (e.g., by agreeing to the terms and conditions stipulated in the RFP).

Vendor Answers to Questions

In this section, indicate that the vendor should provide detailed answers to all questions included in the RFP.

Request for Price Quotation

In this section, include a price quotation for the vendor to complete. The form, developed by the RFP writers, may cover a description of each item needed, quantity, and cost (e.g., basic ILS, discovery interface add-on layer or module, cloud software hosting, e.g., SaaS, record conversion (Recon), generic barcodes, and barcode scanners as applicable). It is best to request a price guarantee (fixed price) for 30–60 days for the listed items.

Notice of Intent to Respond

In this section, include a form titled, "Notice of Intent to Respond," for the vendor to fill out and return to the library indicating whether a response to the submitted RFP is or is not forthcoming. Allow four to six weeks for the vendor to respond.

Software Specifications

This section lists the general, essential, and preferred specifications for each ILS module desired. These specifications constitute the core of the RFP document. An example of well-developed specifications is found in the Appendix.

Criteria for Evaluating Vendor Responses to the RFP

In this section, clearly articulate that the library (include its name) has the right to use its own set of criteria for evaluating vendor responses to the RFP and to assign a weight or percentage for each of these criteria. The evaluation criteria are normally disclosed in the RFP. An example is the six criteria shown in the 2012 RFP of the Contoocook Valley Regional School District, Peterborough, New Hampshire (http://conval.edu), which includes the following:

- Response to system requirements (30%)
- Cost effectiveness of services (30%)
- Implementation plan (15%)
- Training plan (10%)
- Vendor profile and client list (10%)
- Warranties, maintenance, support, and update (5%)

This RFP is posted on a Google Docs website: http://docs.google.com. It is organized in the form of a call for bidders asking to submit proposals for a library management system. The nine-page RFP can be found by searching Google Docs or Google using the name of the school district and the keyword, RFP. Note that this RFP is not ideal because it lacks some necessary information about the school district's server architecture, transactions volumes the proposed ILS should support throughout its life cycle (e.g., check-in, checkout, authorities added, patrons added) and also server and client security.

Boss (2010) notes that a choice among vendor submissions requires evaluating on several criteria, including the following:

- Conformity to the functional specifications
- Flexibility of the software

- Suitability of the proposed or recommended hardware

- Conformity to standards

- Vendor viability

- Vendor performance per existing customers

- Initial cost

- Five-year cost

- Performance guarantees and remedies for poor performance

These criteria should be assigned scores or percentages. Boss (2010) notes that no vendor's offering will score well in each of these criteria. Therefore, make sure that the vendor with the highest rating overall, which has also been top ranked in the past three years, is selected.

Evaluation of Vendor Responses to the RFP

Normally, the RFP document that the library prepares describes the rules a vendor should follow in responding to the RFP. These rules may also provide details of each of the evaluation criteria the library will use in evaluating a vendor's response. The more well-developed an RFP is, the easier and less time consuming it will be for a vendor to respond to its requirements. See Appendix for an exemplary RFP to use in preparing your own.

Reviewing each vendor's response to the RFP should be based on the criteria you have established, in addition to the software demos you should view after you receive a bid from a vendor: phone communication, or interview with the vendor (as applicable); the reading you have done about the ILS, market rankings, and reviews; company financial stability, reputation, and ranking in the past three years; libraries on the vendor's client list, as well as other materials you have gathered and synthesized.

Once you have made a choice for the ILS that best meets the library's needs and priorities, you should begin negotiating a contract for purchasing the ILS.

Contract Negotiation to Purchase the ILS

Boss (2009) makes the case for spending time negotiating the contract with a vendor to purchase the ILS. He describes the following major points: components of the contract, hierarchy of document, duration of contract, applicable law, unrestricted use, hardware sizing, user interface, price, maintenance schedule, delivery and installation, acceptance tests, remote diagnostics, source code, and assignment (http://www.ala.org/ala/mgrps/divs/pla/tools/technotes/negotiatingils.cfm). Webber and Peters (2010) also provide essential points for negotiating a contract for an ILS.

The contract must also include an implementation plan, a schedule for training personnel to use the software, and a payment plan. If you are not financing the purchase, consider paying for it in three installations: one-third upon signing the contract, one-third upon successful installation and performance testing, and a final payment upon successful performance over time. Ensure that the library's legal counsel review the contract before it is signed.

Acquiring an ILS for the first time or migrating to a new ILS takes lots of effort and is "taxing" in terms of the library budget. Because it is a long-term investment in financial and personnel resources, you should become as savvy as you can about the automation process, project management, and technologies impacting on library automation.

SUMMARY

Structuring user requirements is a first step toward selecting an ILS whether it is proprietary or open source. These requirements are reaped from gathering and analyzing user data in phase 2 of the Library Automation Life Cycle (LALC). Developing a RFP is the best way for fleshing out the requirements in the form of specifications the library needs in its ILS. Every library's RFP varies in terms of the specifications needed. However, there are certain general guidelines for preparing a good quality RFP that you should follow.

There are different methods for requesting ILS vendors to respond to your RFP. First, you may develop a Request for Information (RFI) with basic requirements and based on the vendors' responses, you develop a detailed RFP. Second, develop the full RFP with all specifications, send to designated vendors, and evaluate the responses based on which you will select the ILS. Third, prepare the RFP and post an open *call for a bid* in venues such as the Internet. Normally, the RFP document is appended to the call for a bid. Regardless of the method used and whether the target ILS is proprietary or open source, your RFP should include general, essential or mandatory, and desired or preferred specifications that reflect the functional requirements of the ILS, among other components.

Procuring an open-source ILS requires inspection of the source code, robustness of the coding, database schema, data structure, and the level of flexibility for making changes to the software. Additional criteria are the following: use of modern programming language and availability of modular, scalable service-oriented architecture; utilization by a growing base of libraries and availability of an actively involved developer community. On the personnel level, staff with technical expertise is required for supporting the open-source ILS. If such expertise is lacking, hosting the ILS in the cloud (fee-based) or hiring a technical expert is an option. If neither option is feasible, acquiring an open-source ILS may not be a wise option.

Though time consuming and costly, the RFP document will allow you to compare vendor responses to the specifications stipulated and consequently, make a wise, objective decision about the best software that fits your library needs and budget. Evaluating vendor responses to the RFP should be based on several criteria with assigned weight, score, or percentage reflecting on priorities. Boss (2010) lists these criteria: conformity to the functional specifications, flexibility of the software, suitability of the proposed or recommended hardware, conformity to standards, vendor viability, vendor performance per existing customers, initial cost, five-year cost, performance guarantees, and remedies for poor performance. The final evaluation should also include the company's top ranking in the automation marketplace for the past three years and its financial performance and stability for the past five years.

SELECTED ILS PRODUCTS

This section provides a description of selected proprietary and open-source ILS for small and larger libraries. These ILS products were selected based on sales and potential as new products as reported by Marshall Breeding's "Automation Marketplace 2012" (http://www.thedigitalshift.com/2012/03/ils/automation-marketplace-2012-agents-of-change/). Note that the list does not intend to advocate any ILS product or solution. Libraries need to research the literature to review other ILSs before making decisions on procuring a specific system.

ILS FOR SMALL LIBRARIES

This section describes select proprietary and open-source ILS software suitable for small school, special, and public libraries.

Proprietary ILS for School Libraries

Five ILS designed for school libraries are described in the following section.

Destiny Library Manager

Follett Software Company offers Destiny Library Manager, a solution for managing circulation, cataloging, searching (public access), reporting, and other management activities. Destiny Library Manager supports the management of textbooks and media collections, as well as a school district's subscription and free online databases and electronic resources in one integrated solution. In addition, "Destiny Library Manager is certified to meet the standards of the Schools Interoperability Framework (SIF), an industry-wide initiative that enables the software systems that manage education to seamlessly share information, saving time by eliminating redundant data entry" (http://www.follettsoftware.com/_files/fsc/file/cms/10533A_ProductBrch_Library_SnglPgs_FINAL_11_07.pdf). The system integrates with DestinyResource Management Solution modules. In the United States, "more than 20,000 schools and 1,400 districts across the country are using Destiny Library Manager" (http://www.follettsoftware.com/_files/fsc/file/cms/10533A_ProductBrch_Library_SnglPgs_FINAL_11_07.pdf). Follett also has Destiny Quest, a mobile discovery interface app, which is compatible with iPhone, iPod touch, iPad with iOS 4.2 or later version, and Android (http://www.follettsoftware.com/ezform.cfm?ezid=281&urlRef=destinyquestmobile). This app is available for libraries that have the Destiny automated system. Quest supports searching for library materials, checking out eBooks, holding items, viewing account information (fines, holds, checkouts, etc.), maintaining a list of books to read, and generating content through reviews and ratings for items read. A library that uses Destiny must make its Destiny accessible on the web and provide students with user names and passwords in order to enable Quest. This app is one of the very few discovery interfaces available for school libraries (http://www.follettsoftware.com/destiny-quest). Additional solutions offered by Follett are: Textbook Manager (for managing textbooks); Media Manager (for managing nonprint media); Digital Content Solution—One Search (provides unified access to library collections and subscription to free and online databases in search results based on one single search); Student Manager and Asset Manager (integrated inventory tracking system for all types of equipment, media collection, hardware, and other resources held by a library or district-wide).

Alexandria

Alexandria integrated library system is offered by COMPanion Corporation. This ILS is designed for K–12 libraries. It has public access with federated searching, circulation, cataloging, acquisitions, textbook management/tracker, and administrative management. It supports a centralized union catalog (in a LAN) and a distributed union catalog (in a WAN). Alexandria's mobile app is compatible with iPhone, iPod, and iPad. COMPanion offers a multidata station (MDS) where more than one library can have its own database housed on a central server by the Alexandria Controller application. The latter can update and backup all of the databases at once to one location. This is a service that hosts and backs up the data while giving a library control over managing its own database on-site (http://alexwebdemo.companioncorp.com/home).

Alexandria supports collection development, reading programs (e.g., Lexile), the SIF school framework to share student data, and SIP2 protocol for self-checkout and inventory. Moreover, it integrates with search tools such as NetTrekker (a search tool developed by Book Systems Inc., for searching across thousands of reviewed educational materials categorized by reading levels) and the information literacy skills model the Big6 Skills. Alexandria does not have a discovery interface for its K–12 system. In addition to schools, Alexandria provides ILSs designed for public, private, special, and university libraries (http://alexwebdemo.companioncorp.com/home).

Atriuum

Atriuum is a web-based ILS offered by Books Systems Inc. It has an online public access module that supports federated searching based on the SURFit federated searching tool. Atriuum's modules include cataloging and circulation in the basic ILS. Add-on modules are authority control, acquisitions, serials, and Booktracks. The latter is a web-based textbook management solution that tracks and manages textbooks, equipment, eReaders, and instructional materials at local and district-wide levels (http://www.booktracks.net). Atriuum also integrates NetTrekker. In addition, Book Systems offers KidZ-viZ, a public access catalog designed specifically for pre-K through third grade (http://www.booksys.com/v2/products). Book Systems is also known for its cataloging tool, eZcat, which is used to download and import MARC 21 records into a library's own cataloging database (http://www.booksys.com/ezcat-software).

In addition to Atriuum, Book Systems supports Concourse, its Windows-based integrated library system. Concourse has public access, circulation, and cataloging modules (http://www.booksys.com/concourse-library-automation). See also Atriuum for public libraries described under the section "Public Libraries."

LibraryWorld

LibraryWorld is a web-based ILS that services all types of libraries: school, public, academic, private, medical, and legal. It provides a full range of applications including cataloging, circulation, serials tracking, online patron access, and management. At the standard level, LibraryWorld's web-based hosting solution is offered for $425 a year. This supports up to 100,000 records and up to 40,000 patron records. It also accommodates up to 2,000 attachment files in pdf and jpeg formats. Library collections larger than 100,000 items will need to inquire about pricing. LibraryWorld mobile app supports iPhone and iPad and is available for free download from Apple Appstore, http://www.libraryworld.com/cgi-bin/lw3.pl?command=show_page&pagename=home_apps.html. LibraryWorld does not seem to employ federating searching or a discovery interface.

Library.Solution

The Library Corporation (TLC) (http://www.tlcdelivers.com) offers Library.Solution with different products targeted for schools and other small- to medium-sized libraries. These products include *ILS2 Kids*, a friendly, visual, interactive online catalog designed for young users in primary grades. It includes a spell-checker with suggestions and corrections, a predefined list of popular book titles, a category wheel with subject categories of interest to young users, and book covers that can be magnified to view detailed information about each book http://www.tlcdelivers.com/tlc/pdf/LS2%20KIDS_for_LS.pdf. Another online catalog is the *LS2 PAC* that is based on Web 2.0 features, including but not limited to the following: Relevance-ranking of results; user tagging, reviews, and ratings; item mapping showing its location on the shelves; and RSS feeds based on a user's profile. The mobile app, LS2 Mobile, is available to customers for free download at http://www.tlcdelivers.com/tlc/pdf/LS2%20Product%20Sheet.pdf. Additional modules include circulation (LS2 Staff) and Online Selection and Acquisition (OSA). The latter supports collection development and links to book vendors' collection titles along with views of MARC records. Online ordering of selected materials is supported, and libraries can view the MARC record of an item and import directly into their own cataloging databases. ITS.MARC is a flagship MARC record service provided by the Library Corporation and can be integrated with OSA.

The Library Corporation also offers Library.Solution for Schools, a union catalog for sharing resources. In addition, it provides solutions for public, special, and academic libraries. Additional information about products and services that the Library Corporation provides is available on its website.

Proprietary ILS for Special Libraries

Four selected ILS designed for special libraries are covered in this section.

EOS.Web

EOS International provides a suite of EOS.Web library solutions and knowledge management products in the special library arena including legal, medical, and enterprise libraries, and also information centers. EOS. Web is a web-based basic ILS designed for small libraries. It includes two basic modules: OPAC Discovery and cataloging. A library may choose one of these three modules to add to the basic system package: circulation, acquisitions, or serials.

Other EOS.Web products include electronic resource management, interlibrary loan (ILL), and digital asset management. The newest solution is EOS.Web Digital that is specifically designed for 100 percent digital electronic libraries or libraries transitioning to total digital content. For additional information about EOS International products and services, visit http://www.eosintl.com.

Inmagic Inc.

Inmagic Inc. has a suite of content management and ILS products for different types of special libraries including but not limited to legal, medical, and corporate. It basically offers two lines of products: social knowledge networks and social libraries. The former is a suite of solutions that include the following: Inmagic Presto AssociatioNet (for associations and nonprofit organizations); Presto for Financial Services (for corporate libraries and research centers); Proposal KnowledgeNet for Engineering (for streamlining the RFP bidding process, improving its quality, and managing its content); and Inmagic Presto (for competitive intelligence with a focus on information sharing across business and professional communities).

The social libraries solution covers Presto for Social libraries, DB/Text Library Suite, DB/Text Works, Genie, and DB/Text Web Publisher Pro. Inmagic Presto for Social Libraries is designed to manage a library's workflow, content publishing, and information sharing through its built-in social capabilities (blogs, wikis, ratings, and tag clouds). It provides search and discovery across collections of diverse content. The DB/Text Library Suite is a web-based ILS that is anchored by Genie ILS application that supports all functionalities of library operations, including but not limited to public access, cataloging, acquisitions, circulation, and serials.

Inmagic solutions's DB/Text Web Publisher Pro has a set of tools with the capabilities to publish and edit content, create interactive forms, develop, and customize reports, among other things. Additional information about Inmagic's solutions is located at http://www.inmagic.com/product-brochures. Inmagic is a well-established company in the special library arena. In October 2012, Inmagic was acquired by Sydney Plus International.

SydneyPlus

SydneyPlus International provides solutions for special libraries including business (Fortune 1000 companies), law firms, museums and archives, and government institutions through its SydneyPlus Library Automation System and Knowledge Management solution. The automation component is targeted for special libraries and has two versions, one web-based requiring a web browser and one Windows-based that can be used without a browser. Sydney-Plus supports public access through its .Net OPAC, circulation, cataloging, acquisitions, serials, and materials booking. SydneyPlus offers a cloud hosting solution of the ILS (http://www.sydneyplus.com). The company's suite of knowledge management solutions supports research, business development, and managerial reporting and control for all sizes of organizations, sectors, and geographic locations. On October 9, 2012, SydneyPlus International released its e-resource management module aimed at helping knowledge professionals in the management, cataloging, and routing of electronic resources. SydneyPlus International acquired Inmagic Presto in October 2012 http://www.sydney plus.com/SydneyPLUS/portal.aspx?p_aaaaostab=1.

Cuadra STAR

Cuadra Associates Inc. produces STAR Knowledge Center for Libraries (SKCL), a web-based ILS that targets special libraries. Cuadra Associates has products that support different types of libraries including archives management, collections management, knowledge management, records management, and media management. SKCL is used to manage collections of all types including libraries, archives, museums, and publishing houses. SKCL supports a spectrum of resources found in special libraries, including technical reports, internal documents, websites, and digital materials (http://www .cuadra.com/products/library.html). STAR is the core technology that underlies all of Cuadra's knowledge management solutions. It was designed to serve multiple information management needs in libraries, information centers, archives, museums, records centers, and publishing organizations. STAR provides robust capabilities for managing both traditional and electronic information (http://www.cuadra.com/technology/star.html). Cuadra STAR provides hosted services for all of its applications using Access Service Provider (ASP) hosting service.

Proprietary ILS for Public Libraries

Four selected ILSs designed for small public libraries are described in this section.

Apollo

One of the ILSs designed specifically for small- and medium-sized public libraries is from Biblionix (http://www.biblionix.com). Apollo is available as a web-based ASP and SaaS service. The features include an online catalog with federated searching, circulation, and cataloging modules, in addition to consortia capability. Cascaded Style Sheet (CSS) and Extensible Hypertext Markup Language (XHTML) can be used to customize Apollo. A library can integrate eBooks (using OverDrive software) and its subscription databases into Apollo. In April 2012, Biblionix released its mobile app, Apollo-To-Go, for no additional charge to its customers. Patrons can search, reserve, renew, and manage their accounts using a smartphone or mobile devices such as iPhone, iPad, and Android mobile devices. Detailed information about Apollo's specifications is available at http://www.biblionix.com/products/apollo/apollo.pdf.

Agent VERSO

Auto-Graphics Inc. produces AGent VERSO, a complete ILS suite with a next-generation public access interface (AGent Iluminar), cataloging, circulation, acquisitions, digital content resource management, serials, authority control, and administrative reporting. Besides the acquisitions, serials, digital content management, and MARCit, the kids' catalog add-on modules, the mobile app, iLib2Go, can be purchased to support user's access to the online catalog from mobile devices, item checkout, item booking, and interlibrary loan. AGent VERSO is offered as a cloud service using SaaS or as a stand-alone model. Its resource sharing supports use of the ILS in consortial library settings http://www4.auto-graphics.com/documents/VERSObro chureWEB.pdf.

Atriuum

Book Systems Inc. (http://www.booksys.com) offers Atriuum for small public libraries. See also Atriuum for school libraries previously described. This ILS is web-based and the public access catalog, SURFit, supports Web 2.0 technology and a federated search tool that retrieves information for a user's search query from a variety of sources including but not limited to books, library subscription online databases, open content databases, Google Books, and other book project that are available in the public domain (e.g., Project Gutenberg), and resources available for access through the Discovery Channel, among other media (http://www.booksys.com/sites/default/files/documents/Atriuum_SURFit%20_Flier.pdf). Like the public access module, cataloging and circulation modules constitute the core ILS. The cataloging module supports access to millions of MARC records available from the Library of Congress and other compatible databases http://www.booksys.com/sites/default/files/documents/Company%20Overview%20032013%20%28small%29.pdf.

Atriuum offers Librarian Desktop, a toolbar that librarians can customize based on their workflows. Atriuum software can be hosted on-site or in the cloud using ASP delivery model. Note that the ASP traditional remote hosting varies from the SaaS "true" cloud computing model. See "Software Architecture" in Chapter 7 for additional information about these delivery models (http://www.booksys.com/sites/default/files/documents/Company%20Overview%20032013%20%28small%29.pdf).

Book Systems' flagship product is eZCatPro, a web-based tool that supports access to millions of MARC 21 records from the Library of Congress and other MARC databases. Libraries can use eZCatPro to find matched record for books, videos, audios, computer files, and other types of materials. This subscription service supports in-house retrospective conversion (Recon) of materials performed in-house or acquired after the conversion has been completed (http://www.booksys.com/v3/products/atriuum/publics/). Book Systems is known for NetTrekker, another flagship product designed for K–12 for searching and retrieving "appropriate" information from the Internet to a user's search query. This software tool works with a library's online catalog interface and alongside SURFit to retrieve appropriate, relevant information suitable for K–12 clientele (http://www.booksys.com/sites/default/files/documents/Company%20Overview%20032013%20%28small%29.pdf).

Book Systems also has KidZviZ, a point-and-click online catalog designed for younger children to support reading skills in an easy-to-navigate environment. KidZviZ is empowered with visualization tools that allow children to associate terms or concepts learned in the classroom with relevant images (http://www.booksys.com/sites/default/files/documents/Company%20Overview%20032013%20%28small%29.pdf). Another product from Book Systems is Concourse, a "traditional" Windows-based ILS that supports online public access, cataloging and authority control, as well as circulation, self-checkout, inventory, and reporting (http://www.booksys.com/sites/default/files/documents/Company%20Overview%20032013%20%28small%29.pdf).

Libary.Solution

Library.Solution is produced by TLC (http://www.tlcdelivers.com) and targets public libraries (see also Library.Solution for Schools described previously). The ILS includes online catalog (LS2 PAC), a multi-application platform that merges library automation with full functionality of Web 2.0 features (relevancy ranking, tagging, recommender services, reviews, library's RSS feeds, etc.). LS2 PAC supports maps that show the location of items within a library, offers Google Analytics integration, and federated searching (http://www.tlcdelivers.com/tlc/what-we-do/library-automation/ls2-pac.asp).

LS2 PAC is a mobile app that supports remote access to the online catalog and integrates sources from social media tools such as LibraryThing, NovelList Select, and Goodreads (http://www.tlcdelivers.com/tlc/pdf/LS2pac.pdf).

The circulation module, LS2 Sta?, is full-featured interface that runs on tablets, laptops, or any mobile device. It can also be paired with a Bluetooth scanner to perform a full range of circulation tasks from anywhere inside or outside of the library. LS2 Staff is optimized for touch screen and handheld devices and provides direct access (using a single screen) to the library's online catalog. TLC offers a suite of cataloging tools including the Library of Congress, the British Library, and the National Library of Canada. It offers ITS.MARC, a cataloging resource with millions of MARC records accessible over the web. Its BiblioFile cataloging software is available for desktops and includes the records available from ITS.MARC and other databases.

The Cataloger's Reference Shelf is TLC's digital library of MARC manuals and all cataloging software products (http://www.tlcdelivers.com/tlc/

what-we-do/cataloging.asp). TLC also provides Authority Works, a front-end solution that supports the processing and authority verification and also updating of records in real time. Works support authority files from notable sources, including but not limited to The Library of Congress and the integration of these files into a library's own authority records and files (http://www.tlcdelivers.com/tlc/pdf/authorityworks.pdf). Another solution TLC offers in Library.Solution is floating collections, which allows borrowers to check out a book at one library branch and return it to another, thus supporting materials to "float" within the system (http://www.tlcdelivers.com/tlc/pdf/Floating_Collections.pdf).

LS2 Kids is the online catalog interface designed for children (see the section on schools for a description). TLC provides hosting solutions for public and school libraries.

Open-Source ILS for Small Libraries

This section describes the two well-established open-source ILS available for small libraries.

Koha

Koha is the first free and OSS library automation package (ILS). "Development is sponsored by libraries of varying types and sizes, volunteers, and support companies from around the world" (http://koha-community.org/home/#more-1). It was developed in 1999, and the first installation went live in 2000. Koha is an ILS with online public access, circulation, cataloging, acquisitions, and serials. The public access module supports federated searching rather than a discovery interface. Koha is a well-established ILS and has an online community, wiki, documentation, newsletter, project dashboard, announcements, and events (http://www.koha-community.org). Koha is available in many languages and has been implemented by many small- and medium-sized libraries worldwide. It has versions for small libraries and also college and academic libraries and supports consortia and individual libraries. It can be implemented on-site or in the cloud using one of the firms that supports it. It is compatible with Overdrive eBooks software application, SIP2, 3M EnvisionWare; it works with EzProxy dual authentication source for remote database access and is compliant with web technologies including XHTML, CSS, and Javascript (http://www.liblime.org). The latest version, 3.10.0, was released on November 23, 2012 and includes 160 enhancements and 455 bug fixes, according to the Koha community website (http://www.koha-community.org). A version of Koha is also available for academic libraries. Currently, Koha is serviced by three companies, Liblime (http://www.liblime.org), ByWater Solutions (http://bywatersolutions.com), and Equinox (http://www.esilibrary.com/esi).

OPALS

For all types of small libraries, Open-Source Library Automation Systems (OPALS) is a web-based ILS system that was cooperatively developed by six school libraries in New York for sharing resources. OPALS is supported by Media Flex (http://www.mediaflex.com) and can be hosted locally or in the cloud. Based on Media Flex's website as of October 2012, the annual cooperative support and update fee for OPALS is $500; annual hosting fee is $250; set up, configuration, and data migration fee (nonrecurring) is $250. The company also offers automation supplies and equipment (http://mediaflex.net/search_product.jsp?category=A&page_no=1). Based on *lib-web-cats* (http://www.librarytechnology.org/diglib-processquery.pl) there are 964 libraries using OPALS including elementary, middle, high school, and special libraries. OPALS supports public access (with federating searching), circulation, cataloging (with XML MARC and MARC 21 database structure), ILL, and a union catalog. Features employed in each of these modules, as well as system configuration and hardware requirements, are described on the OPALS website (http://www.mediaflex.net/showcase.jsp?record_id=52).

Small libraries can benefit from joining this consortium of libraries to gain full accessibility of OPALS features and functionalities at a reasonable cost.

Open-Source ILS for Public Libraries

Evergreen

Evergreen is the most well-established open-source ILS suitable for small public libraries in consortia and for individual large public libraries. Evergreen was designed by The Georgia Public Library Service (GPLS), the lending network for PINES. In 2005, following the evaluation of several ILSs, open source and proprietary, GPLS decided to design and develop Evergreen software using open-source technologies. Evergreen is described as a highly scalable software application for libraries of any size. It supports full functionalities of circulation, cataloging, and public access through its discovery interface. Recent releases include version 2.0, consisting of the acquisitions module and enhancements to circulation and the online catalog or discovery interface (http://evergreen-ils.org/dokuwiki/doku.php?id=feature_list_2_0). Future release is version 2.3 that will include the kids' catalog, among other features. Libraries in the United States, Canada, Australia, New Zealand, Czech Republic, Netherlands, India, and Mexico use Evergreen (http://evergreen-ils.org/dokuwiki/doku.php?id=evergreen_libraries). Based on *lib-web-cats*, there are 1,300 libraries using Evergreen. The software is freely licensed under the GNU GPL (http://evergreen-ils.org/dokuwiki/doku.php?id=faqs:evergreen_faq_1).

SOFTWARE FOR LARGE LIBRARIES

The current automation marketplace offers different options for all types of libraries and especially large ones. These options include the next generation ILSs or LSPs (also known as web-scale), ILSs with discovery interfaces, and open-source ILSs.

The following section describes the next generation ILSs, LSPs, selected proprietary and open-source ILSs suitable for public, special, and academic libraries. Libraries are encouraged to research additional platforms or ILS software to gain better understanding of the software models available in today's automation industry.

Library Services Platforms (LSPs)

LSPs are next generation ILSs that are "based on service-oriented architecture with web-based interfaces designed for deployment through SaaS" (Breeding 2013). The main difference between the traditional ILSs and LSPs is that ILSs were developed around print collections. As digital collections have increased in many libraries, notably academic and research ones, older ILSs could not be reconfigured to effectively and efficiently manage both print and digital collections. In addition, older ILSs do not take advantage of the latest technologies and architecture such as cloud computing (Grant 2012). Leading companies of LSPs are OCLC (WorldShare Management Services), Ex Libris (Alma), Innovative Interfaces (Sierra), Kuali Ole, and VTLS Open Skies. Serials Solutions is expected to release Intota Library Management System by late 2014. Open Skies may also be released at that time.

Selected LSPs are described in the following text. For additional information about other LSPs, refer to Grant (2012).

Alma

Alma was developed by Ex Libris in collaboration with a group of college and university libraries to create a unified resource management system that replaces current ILSs and allows for effective management of the full spectrum of library resources, including those in electronic and digital formats (Wang and Dawes 2012). The development of Alma began in 2009, and participating libraries provided input into the design, testing, and implementation of incremental releases.

Alma is a cloud-based next-generation library management system that supports the whole collection life cycle from selection and acquisition to access for all types of materials including print, digital, and electronic (http://www.exlibrisgroup.com/category/AlmaOverview). Alma is built on an open platform architecture that supports customization through API. Its unified functionality especially in relation to print, digital, and electronic collections allows libraries to streamline the management of library workflows (http:// www.exlibrisgroup.com/category/AlmaOverview). Alma's Meta Data Management System supports the sharing of metadata of bibliographic records among libraries (e.g., contribution of records, editing, enhancing, and downloading). Alma's material selection and acquisitions are integrated within both Alma core modules and the add-on discovery interface, thus, allowing patrons and staff to suggest new items for addition to a library's holdings (Wang and Dawes 2012).

As a unified library management solution, Alma "will replace a number of Ex Libris systems currently used by the library: the Aleph integrated library system, the SFX OpenURL link resolver, the Verde electronic resource management system, and the DigiTool digital asset management system" (Breeding 2012).

WorldShare Management Services

WorldShare Management Services (WMS) was developed by OCLC (http://www.oclc.org),1 a nonprofit organization that provides access to and shares bibliographic information, full text articles, digital and other resources to its member libraries (more than 74,000 in 170 countries). OCLC was founded in 1967; its member libraries produce WorldCat, the largest online database of library metadata worldwide (http://www.worldcat.org). WMS is totally web-based and is designed to streamline library operations while providing cooperative library management service for acquisitions, cataloging, circulation, license management, as well as "a powerful discovery and delivery experience for library users." "WorldCat data and services connect and provide access to 982+ million articles, videos, books, photographs, maps and other library materials, as well as 20+ million metadata records describing open access, digital materials." It is a unified system for identifying, selecting, acquiring, and managing library materials in all formats. Shared, real-time data supports cooperative collection building (http://www.oclc.org/en-US/worldshare-management-services/features.html).

OCLC's WorldCat Local is the discovery service for WMS. One search provides library users with instant access to all types of library materials (e.g., eBooks, subscription databases, eJournals, music, videos, and books), in addition to materials in group and consortia catalogs from libraries worldwide. WorldCat Local integrates with a library's circulation and delivery services (ILL), allowing users to find items of interest and place a request for items not available in a library's local collection. It has over 33 million items from Google Books, HathiTrust Digital Library (http://www.hathitrust.org/), JSTOR (http://www.jstor.org), and OAIster database of digital resources (https:// www.oclc.org/oaister.en.html). This discovery service provides access to "753+ million articles in full text, 14+ million eBooks from leading aggregators and publishers, 46+ million pieces of evaluative content (tables of contents, cover art, summaries, etc.) included at no additional charge, and 233+ million books in libraries worldwide." WorlCat Local's knowledge base enables a built-in OpenURL resolver and populates A to Z lists. It supports staff- and user-generated lists of customized books for special events or programs (http://www.oclc.org/en-US/worldcat-local/quickstart.html).

On March 13, 2013, OCLC announced the availability of its new World-Share ILL service in the United States. This service "will provide an integrated delivery solution with new and expanded features for libraries. The service will combine discovery and delivery of electronic, digital and print materials within a single interface. It will also support evolving workflow changes in libraries, such as the option to purchase needed items rather than borrow them" (Breeding 2013). Refer to http://www.librarytechnology.org/diglib-fulldisplay.pl?SID=2014010170159912&code=bib&RC=17749&Row=2&.

Sierra Services Platform

Sierra Services Platform is produced by Innovative Interfaces Inc., a company with leading solutions in the library automation industry. Innovative provides solutions to academic, public, special, and K–12 libraries (http://www.iii.com). It offers the following: Millennium ILS (see next section for a description); Encore Synergy, the discovery interface for Sierra; Electronic Resource Management (ERM), INN-Reach, and ArticleReach for resource sharing; Digital Asset Management Content Pro for managing archives, special collections, and other digital materials; a Decision Center for collection building and management; Millennium Via for K–12 schools; and SkyRiver bibliographic utility for shared cataloging. The latter has become part of Innovative Interfaces' suite of products on March 4, 2013.

Sierra's Service-Oriented Architecture (SOA) design is built on PostgreSQL database technology. Sierra is designed with four layers: Database Layer, Business Logic Services Layer, Presentation Layer, and Open Access Layer. In addition, Sierra provides a comprehensive library of APIs for third-party and library-developed applications to support interaction with web properties and social networking sites, integration, creation, and collaboration with numerous applications and devices (http://sierra.iii.com/technology-update). Sierra's deployment options are cloud-based, local, and SaaS.

Unlike Millennium, which is a closed system, Sierra offers a unified approach for delivering all staff tasks through a single client. Sierra has a unified desktop app that allows for switching from one function to another; that is, from circulation to cataloging or acquisitions to cataloging in seconds, thus, saving time by eliminating the need to navigate between modules to complete certain tasks. In addition, Sierra streamlines administrative tasks through its drag-and-drop functions from any area of the system and provides a consolidated approach to user and role management. Moreover, the dashboard provides a single point of access for library staff to customize everyday workflow activities and run different applications and tools. Furthermore, Sierra Database Navigator (DNA) provides libraries with documentation describing the underlying data structure of the system, which supports the querying and reporting activities performed in the database (http://blog.sierra.iii.com).

Intota

Intota is a web-scale management system provided by Serials Solutions (http://www.serialssolutions.com). It supports a single, unified solution for the entire resource life cycle for libraries, including selection, acquisition, cataloging, discovery service (Summon 2.0), and fulfillment, regardless of format (http://www.serialssolutions.com/en/services/intota). Summon 2.0 is built around a single, unified index of different types of resources that returns a unified set of results for a search query. In addition, it offers many features, including, but not limited to, Topic Explorer, Scholar Profiles, Automatic Query Expansion, Database Recommendations, and Real-Time Reference Help. For additional features of Summon 2.0, visit http://www.serialssolutions.com/en/services/summon/summon-2.0.

Intota contains a knowledge base of authoritative metadata that saves on the cost of data acquisition. As a unified solution, it simplifies the tasks by enabling staff to easily manage all types of materials in a single workflow. In addition, it offers an assessment tool that illuminates how the collections are being used and how items under consideration for purchase fit within the library's existing collections.

Intota is an open, flexible system that is built on standards with published APIs. Intota's complete product is expected to be released by the end of 2013. It will be deployed as a multitenant SaaS (http://www.serialssolutions.com/assets/resources/Intota-Datasheet_Imagine.pdf).

Proprietary ILS for Large Public Libraries

Symphony

Symphony ILS is provided by SirsiDynix, one of the leading companies in automation solutions and services that are targeted for public, academic, special, and K–12 libraries (http://www.sirsidynix.com). Symphony supports the varied operations of libraries including circulation, cataloging, acquisitions, serials, digital asset management (portfolio), reserves, outreach, and media booking.

Symphony has been installed in several public and academic libraries and consortia. In 2012, SirsiDynix was the leader in ILS installations of Symphony in these libraries (Breeding 2012). Symphony is founded on a multitier architecture that supports interoperability across diverse hardware platforms, operating systems (e.g., Unix, Microsoft Windows, and Linux) and databases (e.g., Oracle10/11, MicrosoftSQL Server 2008, and SirsiSynix's own c-ISAM database). Symphony is an open system with a robust API-rich ILS that combined with RESTful web services (the expansion of REST is Representational State Transfer) and provided a high level of customization options into the library's own ILS. RESTful is a way for exposing web APIs to allow for ease of use of web services and enhance customization of the ILS (http://www .layer7tech.com/solutions/securing-restful-web-services?gclid=CNbc2sfKmL YCFQQEnQodrmoAAw).

Symphony is available as a cloud service using the SaaS delivery model and as an on-site service for hosting the software locally (http://www.sirsidynix .com/sites/default/files/dl/symphonybookfullpage_0.pdf).

Symphony supports MARC 21, MARCXML, and non-MARC formats in a single database. It is standards-compliant and works with relational database systems such as Oracle. Symphony offers mobile apps for staff for managing both circulation and inventory of materials in real time and offline modes. The mobile app for user remote access to the online catalog is BookMyne. Symphony version 3.4.1 supports text messaging of notifications to library users, holdings of MARC records in multilingual formats, and Solaris x86 operating system (http://www .sirsidynix.com/sites/default/files/dl/symphonybookfullpage_0.pdf).

Polaris

Polaris is a product of Polaris Library Systems. Its customer base includes public, academic, private, and few school libraries (http://www.polarislibrary .com). Polaris ILS offers cataloging, circulation with ExpressCheck, acquisitions, serials, a discovery suite, and Fusion digital collection management solution. Polaris PowerPAC is the discovery interface that supports one search box for searching all types of materials. It was redesigned in Polaris version 4.1 "with content carousels, recently viewed titles and the ability to feature new titles, events" (http://www.polarislibrary.com). The community profiles integrates with PowerPAC and provides *Feature It*, a function for promoting relevant library resources and community/organizations events in the context of search results, similar to the "You might also like," features. Within community profiles, ContentXChange allows a library to extend its services, and community organizations can post a "content carousel" of library books, materials, and events that connect visitors back to the library. PowerPAC supports faceted searching by material type and reading level, among other facets. The eBook integration function supports the integration of eBooks into PowerPAC. Polaris offers Mobile PAC, a mobile application for accessing the online catalog on cell phones and mobile devices.

In March 2012 Polaris launched the Polaris Developer Network to provide open access to its API. Following an agreement with 3M Library Systems on July 24, 2012, Polaris began offering self-checkout and RFID systems in addition to integrating eBooks with the 3M Cloud Library eBook Lending Service. This service supports access and management of both print

and electronic materials in one single interface (http://www.polarislibrary
.com/?s=3M+partnership).

On January 24, 2013, Polaris announced its plan to release Polaris Social
PAC (http://www.polarislibrary.com/polaris-revolutionizes-the-ils-with-
social-pac/), a social networking feature from the ChiliFresh, a patron review
search engine that integrates with any ILS including PowerPAC (http://www
.chilifresh.com/html/how_it_works.php). This social feature offers library
users a socially connected online catalog experience.

Carl.X

Carl.X is a next-generation ILS that is based on Web 2.0 technologies. It
is produced by TLC (http://www.tlcdelivers.com), a provider of a complete
suite of ILS products and services for different types of libraries.

Carl.X is an open, scalable, UNIX- and SQL/Oracle-based solution that is
suited for large public libraries and consortia (https://www.tlcdelivers.com/
wp-content/uploads/2013/02/CarlX.pdf). The staff client features integration of and access to all modules through a single client, allowing staff to use
circulation, cataloging, acquisitions, serials, and other library units. Staff can
customize many features in the system, including, but not limited to, real-time
processing of activities, global update from within the staff client, floating collections, seamless interaction with third-party vendors, and ad hoc reporting.

CARLweb is a customizable, multilingual web-based online catalog with
Unicode-based architecture that supports any language, including those with
non-Roman characters. This OPAC offers powerful search capabilities, integrates with, and provides access to library materials in different formats such
as eBooks, photos, audios, and videos. APIs maximize the customization of
the OPAC interface to meet the needs of libraries and their user communities.

Other products that TLC offers include LS2 PAC, LS2 Kids, and LS2
Mobile. See a description of each of these products under the section, Proprietary ILS for Small Public Libraries.

Proprietary ILS for Large Academic Libraries

Aleph

Aleph is one of the automation products provided by Ex Libris (http://
www.exlibrisgroup.com) to suit the needs of academic, research, and national
libraries, as well as library consortia worldwide. Aleph's suite consists of
different modules including a web-based online catalog, cataloging, acquisitions, serials, circulation, digital asset management (DigiTool), ERM (Verde),
and preservation of digital information (Rosetta).

A library may choose to use the traditional online catalog interface or
acquire Primo, the next-generation discovery interface that is based on Web 2.0

technologies. Primo is an integral component of Primo Central Index, which provides a single search box for searching and discovering local and external print, digital, and electronic resources. Primo employs a relevance-ranking algorithm to retrieved results on search queries (http://www.exlibrisgroup .com/category/PrimoOverview).

Aleph, based on open architecture, is customizable, scalable, interoperable, and it supports heterogeneous consortium environments by offering options that can be used in libraries running a variety of ILSs, digital repository applications, and metasearch licensing arrangements. Aleph supports the Unicode standard for multiscript text, allowing users to interface with Primo in their preferred language. Primo Mobile App is available for iPhone and Android smartphones (http://www.exlibrisgroup.com/files/Products/ Aleph,Voyager/Aleph/Aleph_A4_low.pdf).

Ex Libris has released its bX usage-based services, a suite of services that uses data mining and analytics strategies to capture user patterns in finding information such as journal articles, publications in conference proceedings, and other scholarly materials. The bX Recommender software solution provides users with recommendations for relevant articles other users had consulted, similar to "users interested in this article also used these articles" (http://www .exlibrisgroup.com/category/bXUsageBasedServices). Finding full text articles electronically is facilitated by clicking on the SFX link resolver that is integrated in Primo to determine local availability of designated journal subscriptions or to request document delivery of the articles (http://www.exlibrisgroup.com/ ?catid={039F7CC2-68A2-4365-ADD8-39E7ABB4111B}#{3F20D29E-F0A2-4DD3-87D5-BF83A668F87A}). All SFX features are supported by the SFX Knowledge-Base, a central data repository with information about electronic journals, conference proceedings, eBooks, and other types of scholarly materials.

Millennium

Millennium is one of the flagship products provided by Innovative Interfaces (http://www.iii.com). Millennium ILS is a fully integrated system and consists of varied modules including the online catalog, Web PACPro discovery interface, circulation, cataloging, acquisitions, serials, ERM, digital asset management, collection management (with a Decision Center based on Dynamic Library Intelligence software), as well as a resource-sharing solution that includes INN-Reach and ArticleReach consortial borrowing systems.

WebPAC Pro is based on Web 2.0 technologies and can interconnect with the other discovery service platform, Encore Synergy, which integrates with the Sierra Services Platform (http://www.iii.com/products/webpac_pro.shtml). AirPAC is Millennium's mobile app for accessing the online catalog and delivering information to smartphones. Like the WebPAC Pro discovery interface, AirPAC uses RightResult, a relevance-ranking technology for ranking retrieved results on search queries by relevancy (http://www.iii.com/products/airpac.shtml).

Innovative also markets a Millennium solution for public libraries and another for the K–12 arena, the Millennium Via K–12. The latter is a solution designed to streamline library operations in large school districts while allowing individual libraries to present and manage their unique resources and services (http://www.iii.com/products/viak12.shtml).

Following the integration of SkyRiver Technology Solutions, Innovative announced in March 2013 that it withdrew the claims of the antitrust lawsuit it filed with SkyRiver against OCLC in 2010. SkyRiver is a bibliographic utility that offers cataloging services for libraries; it is currently one of Innovative's product suites (http://www.skyriver.com).

Symphony

Symphony is an ILS that is used by many public libraries and consortia. Please see a description of this system under Proprietary ILS for Large Public Libraries.

OPEN-SOURCE ILS FOR LARGE LIBRARIES

This section describes selected open-source ILS available for large public and academic libraries.

Evergreen

Evergreen is a well-established open-source ILS that is suitable for large public libraries and consortia. For a description of this system, see ILS for small libraries, open-source ILS for public libraries.

Kuali OLE

Kuali OLE is at the forefront of open-source LSPs. It has its roots in the OLE Project, a project funded by The Andrew W. Mellon Foundation to build a flexible, service-oriented, enterprise-ready library management system for academic and research libraries (http://www.kuali.org/ole). Kuali OLE has 10 university library partners including a consortium of Florida libraries (http://www.kuali.org/ole/partners).

Kuali OLE supports the wide range of resources and formats of scholarly information. It is interoperable with other enterprise- and network-based systems. Its service layers consist of the following: select and acquire (for acquisitions functions); descriptive metadata (based on MARCML and Dublin Core standards—for cataloging functions); faceted discovery (based on Solr search and faceting—for searching the online catalog); Kuali Financial System (for financial functions); Apache Jackrabbit (content repository); Kuali Rice (version 2.0 includes Enterprise Middleware—identity management, workflow, messaging, triggers, rapid application development, service registry, and rules engine); and Patron Services (for circulation functions). Additional layers and sublayers will be released in 2014 and beyond.

Early implementations of Kuali OLE (in Lehigh University and University of Chicago libraries) are scheduled for 2013–2014; mid-implementations (in Indiana University, University of Pennsylvania, Duke University, and North Carolina State University libraries) are scheduled for 2014–2015; and later implementations (in University of Maryland and Florida Consortium libraries) are scheduled for 2016 (Camden, Mouw, and McNamara 2012) (http://www .kuali.org/sites/default/files/ole/ALCTS%20Kuali%20OLE%20ALA2012 .pdf). The release of Kuali OLE version 0.8 is scheduled for the second quarter of 2013; version 1.0 release is targeted for the fourth quarter of 2013. A detailed timeline on each release is provided at http://www.kuali.org/ole/timeline.

Other Open-Source ILS

Libraries should examine additional open-source ILS software to determine their suitability. Examples are: OpenBiblio (http://obiblio.sourceforge.net), originated in Spain; PMB PhpMyBibli (http://www.pmbservices.fr/), originated in France; Emilda (http://freecode.com/projects/emilda), originated in Finland; Invenio (http://invenio-software.org), originated in Europe; NewGenLib (http://www.verussolutions.biz), originated in India; and LearningAccess ILS (LA ILS) (http://www.learningaccess.org/ils-system), originated in the United States. For additional information about these and other ILSs, see Vasupongayya, Keawneam, Sengloilaun, and Emmawat 2011. An additional source to consult is BibLibre, a company located in Marseille, France that provide OSS to all types of libraries and help them choose the software that best meet their needs (http://www.biblibre.com/en).

Social Online Catalogs

There are two main social interfaces of interest to all types of libraries. One is a social discovery platform that is built by a community of libraries (SOPAC) and another by a community of end users (LibraryThing). These are briefly described in the following text.

Social OPAC (SOPAC)

SOPAC (http://thesocialopac.net) is an open-source social discovery platform for library bibliographic data that was developed by John Blyberg. The software is maintained by Blyberg and hosted by the Darien Library in Darien Connecticut and supported by the SOPAC's core development group. SOPAC is based on Drupal content management platform and two software libraries, Locum and Insurge. Locum is an open-source programming language PHP that allows SOPAC to interface with a library's ILS and maintains an external index of its holdings. According to Blyberg, Locum is "a stand-alone abstraction layer that functionally separates any application that is buit on top it from the business logic of whatever underlying system is in place" (http://791linkeddata.blogspot.com/2011/04/sopac-social-online-public-access.html). Insurge manages and supports the social functions of the underlying ILS, stores and uses the data supplied by the end user (e.g., tags, reviews). Developers can configure their own versions of SOPAC, customize the search and retrieval features including the filtering of results based on different available options such as relevancy and user reviews. SOPAC integrates with any library's holdings data. An updated version of SOPAC, SOPAC2, is expected to be released by the end of 2013. SOPAC software is available for download from its official website located at http://thesocialopac.net.

LibraryThing

LibraryThing (http://www.librarything.com) is a social networking site that revolves around personal collections collected by people rather than bibliographic data shared by libraries in SOPAC. It is considered an online book club that was created by Tim Spaulding to connect people through their book collections. Posting one's own book collection requires establishing an account. Once a book is posted and is found, LibraryThing will automatically post an image of the book's front cover, date of publication, International Standard Book Number (ISBN), other editions available, places for purchasing the book online, tags, a star rating, a Dewey decimal number, and the date the book was acquired (http://www.pcmag.com/article2/0,2817,1992863,00.asp). One can catalog his own books using Amazon.com, the Library of Congress, and 690 libraries worldwide. One can also import book information from any external sources. LibraryThing is available in more than 30 languages. As of October 20th, 2013 LibraryThing had 1,500,000 book users. The subscription fee is $10 a year or $25 for lifetime membership (http://www.librarything.com). Libraries may benefit from using LibraryThing to identify books favored by users of certain maturity levels that they may need to add to their own library collections. In addition, they may explore user tagging and metadata sources to use in cataloging such as the Library of Congress and other libraries. Moreover, libraries may use LibraryThing in an advisory capacity to recommend books to read based on users' shared interests.

NOTE

1. In 2010, SkyRiver Technology Solutions filed an antitrust lawsuit against OCLC, claiming that OCLC was "unlawfully monopolizing bibliographic data, cataloging service, and interlibrary lending markets and was attempting to monopolize the market for integrated library systems by

anticompetitive and exclusionary agreements, policies and practices" (http://www.librarytechnology.org/docs/14917.pdf). On March 4, 2013, Innovative Interfaces decided to withdraw the claims of the lawsuit against OCLC, and SkyRiver became one of its suite of products (http://www.librarytechnology.org/diglib-fulldisplay.pl?SID=20140101828857421&code=bib&RC=17718&Row=1&).

REFERENCES

Balnaves, Edmund. "Open Source Library Management Systems: A Multidimensional Evaluation." *Australian Academic & Research Libraries*. March 1, 2008. http://www.highbeam.com/doc/1G1–179348488.html. Accessed January 10, 2013.

Boss, Richard W. "Harley from PTFS-LibLime: What It Is-and Isn't." *Online: Exploring Technology and Resources for Information Professionals*. March 24, 2010.http://newsbreaks.infotoday.com/NewsBreaks/Harley-From-PTFS LibLime-What-It-Is-and-Isnt-67309.asp. Accessed January 14, 2013.

Boss, Richard W. "Negotiating Contracts with Integrated Library Systems Vendors." *PLA Tech Note*. 2009. http:www.ala.org/ala/mgrps/divs/pla/tools/technotes/negotiatingils.cfm. Accessed August 2, 2013.

Breeding, Marshall. "Automation Marketplace 2012: Agents of Change. 2012. http://www.thedigitalshift.com/2012/03/ils/automation-marketplace-2012-agents-of-change. Accessed February 10, 2013.

Breeding, Marshall. "Curtin University in Australia Selects Ex Libris Alma for Unified Resource Management." 2012. http://www.librarytechnology.org/diglib-fulldisplay.pl?SID=20140101900329589&code=bib&RC=17434&Row=1&. Accessed March 15, 2013.

Breeding, Marshall. "Major Open Source ILS Products." *Library Technology Reports*, November/December (2008): 16–31.

Breeding, Marshall. "New WorldShare Interlibrary Loan Service Simplifies Library Workflows, Expands Delivery Options." 2013. http://www.librarytechnology.org/diglib-fulldisplay.pl?SID=2014010170159912&code=bib&RC=17749&Row=2&. Accessed April 1, 2013.

Camden, Beth Picknally, James Mouw, and Frances McNamara. Kuali OLE: Developing and Implementing a Community Source LMS. 2012. http://www.kuali.org/sites/default/files/ole/ALCTS%20Kuali%20OLE%20ALA2012.pdf. Accessed April 1, 2013.

Cibbarelli, Pamela. *Helping You Buy ILS: Guide to Products & Vendors*. 2010. http://www.infotoday.com/cilmag/CILMag_ILSGuide.pdf. Accessed January 10, 2013.

Cohn, John M., and Ann L. Kelsey. *The Complete Library Technology Planner: A Guidebook with Sample Technology Plans and RFPs on CD-ROM*. New York: Neal-Schuman Publishers Inc., 2010.

Ex Libris. Aleph. n.d. http://www.exlibrisgroup.com/files/Products/Aleph, Voyager/Aleph/Aleph_A4_low.pdf. Accessed March 15, 2013.

Ex Libris. bX. 2012. http://www.exlibrisgroup.com/category/bXUsageBased Services. Accessed March 15, 2013.

Ex Libris. "Primo Overview." 2012. http://www.exlibrisgroup.com/category/PrimoOverview. Accessed February 10, 2013.

Ex Libris. SFX. 2012. http://www.exlibrisgroup.com/?catid={6C372F94–751E-4FE0-B6ED-64CE35B085DB}. Accessed March 15, 2013.

Grant, Carl. 2012. The future of library systems: Library services platforms. Information Standards Quarterly, 24, no. 4, 4–15. http://www.niso.org/apps/group_public/download.php/9922/FE_Grant_Future_Library_Systems_%20isqv24no4.pdf.

Innovative Interfaces, Inc. AirPac. 2013. http://www.iii.com/products/airpac.shtml. Accessed March 16, 2013.

Innovative Interfaces, Inc. "Millennium Via K-12 libraries." 2013. http://www.iii.com/products/viak12.shtml. Accessed March 16, 2013.

Innovative Interfaces, Inc. "WebPAC Pro." 2013. http://www.iii.com/products/webpac_pro.shtml 2013. Accessed March 16, 2013.

Kuali. "Open Library Environment." 2013. http://www.kuali.org/ole. Accessed April 1, 2013.

Kuali. "Open Library Environment. Partners." 2013. http://www.kuali.org/ole/partners. Accessed April 1, 2013.

Kuali. "Open Library Environment. Timeline." 2013. http://www.kuali.org/ole/timeline. Accessed April 1, 2013.

The Library Corporation. Carl.X. n.d. https://www.tlcdelivers.com/wp-content/uploads/2013/02/CarlX.pdf. Accessed March 25, 2013.

Müller, Tristan. "How to Choose a Free and Open Source Integrated Library System." *OCLC Systems & Services: International Digital Library Perspectives*, 27, no. 1 (2011): 57–78. http://www.emeraldinsight.com/1065-075X.htm. Accessed March 16, 2012.

Polaris Library Systems. "Polaris Library Systems Enters Strategic Partnership with 3M Library Systems." 2012. http://www.polarislibrary.com/?s=3M+partnership. Accessed March 29, 2013.

Polaris Library Systems. "Polaris Social. 2012. http://www.polarislibrary.com/polaris-products/polaris-integrated-library-system/. Accessed April 1, 2013.

Serials Solutions. "Intota: Imagine a Better Way." 2012. http://www.serialssolutions.com/assets/resources/Intota-Datasheet_Imagine.pdf. Accessed April 4, 2013.

Serials Solutions. "Introducing Summon 2.0." 2013. http://www.serialssolutions.com/en/services/summon/summon-2.0. Accessed April 4, 2013.

Singh, Vandana. "Open Source Integrated Library Systems." 2013. http://opensourceils.com. Accessed January 15, 2013.

SirsiDynix. "SirsiDynix Symphony Integrated Library System." n.d. http://www.sirsidynix.com/sites/default/files/dl/symphonybookfullpage_0.pdf. Accessed March 30, 2013.

SOPAC. SOPAC, The Social OPAC Online Public Access Catalog. 2011. http://791linkeddata.blogspot.com/2011/04/sopac-social-online-public-access.html. Accessed on September 6, 2013.

3M Company. 3M Donates Standard Interchange Protocol (SIP) to National Standards Organization (NISO): 3M Library Systems Collaborates with NISO to Enhance Future Library Self-Service Technologies. 2012. http://news.3m.com/press-release/company/3m-donates-standard-interchange-protocol-sip-national-standards-organization-n. Accessed April 19, 2013.

Valacich, Joseph S., Joey F. George, and Jeffrey A. Hoffer. *Essentials of Systems Analysis and Design.* 5th ed. Upper Saddle River, NJ: Prentice Hall, 2011.

Vasupongayya, Sangsuree, Kittisak Keawneam, Kittipong Sengloilaun, and Patt Emmawat. Open Source Library Management System Software: A Review. *World Academy of Science, Engineering and Technology,* 53 (2011): 850–65. http://waset.org/publications/8208/open-source-library-management-system-software-a-review. Accessed April 1, 2013.

Wang, Yongming, and Trevor A. Dawes. The Next Generation Integrated Library System: A Promise Fulfilled? *Information Technology and Libraries,* 31, no. 3 (2012): 76–84.

Webber, Desiree, and Andrew Peters. *Integrated Library Systems: Planning, Selecting, and Implementing.* Santa Barbara, CA: ABC-CLIO, 2010.

WEBSITES

American Libraries, Buyer's Guide. http://americanlibrariesbuyersguide.com. "Automation." American Libraries Buyer's Guide. http://americanlibrariesbuyersguide.com/index.php?category=Automation&category_id=799.

BibLibre. http://www.biblibre.com/en.

Book Systems. http://www.booksys.com.

ByWater Solutions. http://bywatersolutions.com.

ChiliFresh. http://www.chilifresh.com/html/how_it_works.php.

Code4Lib. http://www.code4lib.org.

Collective Access. http://collectiveaccess.org.

Computers in Libraries, Buyer's Guide. http://bg.computersinlibraries.com.

Contoocook Valley Regional School District, Peterborough, New Hampshire. http://conval.edu.

The Digital Shift. http://www.thedigitalshift.com.

Emilda. http://freecode.com/projects/emilda.

Equinox. http://www.esilibrary.com/esi.

Evergreen Doku Wiki. http://evergreen-ils.org/dokuwiki/doku.php?id=faqs:evergreen_faq_1.

Ex Libris. http://www.exlibrisgroup.com.

Follett Software Company. http://www.fsc.com.

GNU. http://www.gnu.org/licenses.

Google Docs. http://docs.google.com.

HathiTrust Digital Library. http://www.hathitrust.org.

Innovative Interfaces. http://www.iii.com.

Invenio. http://invenio-software.org.

JSTOR. http://www.jstor.org.

King County Library System, Issaquah, Washington. Request for Qualifications for Supplemental Evergreen System Development. http://www.libraryworks.com/library_bid_rfp_alert/030711/Evergreen.htm.

Koha. http://koha-community.org/home/#more-1.

Kuali OLE. http://kuali.org/ole.

Layer7 Technologies. http://www.layer7tech.com/solutions/securing-restful-web-services?gclid=CNbc2sfKmLYCFQQEnQodrmoAAw.

LearningAccess ILS (LA ILS). http://www.learningaccess.org/ils-system.

LibLime. http://www.liblime.com.

The Library Corporation. https://www.tlcdelivers.com.

Library Technology Guides. http://www.librarytechnology.org.

Lib-Web-Cats. http://www.librarytechnology.org/libwebcats.

NewGenLib. http://www.verussolutions.biz/web.

OAIster. https://www.oclc.org/oaister.en.html.

OCLC. http://www.oclc.org.

OCLC. WorldCat. http://www.worldcat.org.

OCLC. WorldCat. Quick Start. http://www.oclc.org/en-US/worldcat-local/quickstart.html.

OCLC. WorldShare Management Services. http://www.oclc.org/en-US/worldshare-management-services/features.html.

OPALS. http://www.mediaflex.net/showcase.jsp?record_id=52

OpenBiblio. http://obiblio.sourceforge.net/.

Open Source Watch. http://www.oss-watch.ac.uk/resources/procurement-infopack.xml.

OSS. http://oss4lib.org.

PMB. http://www.pmbservices.fr/

Polaris Library Systems. http://www.polarislibrary.com.

Serials Solutions. http://www.serialssolutions.com.

Sierra Blog. http://blog.sierra.iii.com.

Sierra Services Platform. http://sierra.iii.com.

SirsiDynix. http://www.sirsidynix.com.

SkyRiver Technology Solutions. http://www.skyriver.com.

SOPAC. http://thesocialopac.net.

SourceForge. http://sourceforge.net.

3M Company. http://www.3M.com.

Chapter 5

LALC Phase 4

SYSTEM IMPLEMENTATION. PART I. PREPARING THE COLLECTION FOR THE INTEGRATED LIBRARY SYSTEM

Collection preparation is part of the integrated library system (ILS) implementation phase. It consists of various activities including collection weeding, inventory, shelflist analysis (if a shelflist exists), retrospective conversion (Recon), and collection barcoding. The steps taken in preparing the collection will affect later stages of implementation and also impact on how the ILS will be used and managed. Note that while most libraries are already automated and have an online catalog, there are libraries in rural areas and private libraries in urban areas that are not fully automated or have old versions of automation software in use and may migrate to new software in the near future. During this phase, a library will need to consider the components of implementation described in this chapter that are most meaningful and applicable to its own situation.

Once a decision has been made about the ILS of choice or during the waiting period for vendor responses to the Request for Proposal (RFP), the project manager develops a plan for preparing the collection for automation. Running this plan in parallel should expedite the implementation of the ILS. Note that facility planning is described in Chapter 6 and that this chapter focuses only on collection preparation. It describes the following main topics:

- Collection weeding
- Weeding circulation and other records

- Collection inventory

- Shelflist analysis

- Retrospective Conversion (Recon)

- Bibliographic standards

- Barcodes, radio frequency identification (RFID), and barcoding

COLLECTION WEEDING

Every library should have a weeding policy or a set of criteria to use in judging which materials are to be weeded, replaced, or repaired, as well as what to do with materials that are withdrawn from the collection. The weeding policy is part of a collection development or selection policy. The American Library Association (ALA) has a resource list titled *Weeding Library Collections: A Selected Annotated Bibliography for Library Collection Evaluation* (http://www .ala.org/tools/libfactsheets/alalibraryfactsheet15) that can be helpful in drafting your own collection development policy including weeding and taking inventory. For example, in using your library's weeding criteria, items in the collection that do not meet one or more of the criteria outlined in the policy should be weeded and disposed of based on the policy.

Weeding the collection in accordance with the policy or based on the guidelines provided by a specific ILS vendor or firm will save on the cost of converting each of the weeded items into a MARC 21 format. "MARC is the acronym for MAchine-Readable Cataloging. It defines a data format that emerged from a Library of Congress-led initiative that began nearly forty years ago. It provides the mechanism by which computers exchange, use, and interpret bibliographic information, and its data elements make up the foundation of most library catalogs used today. MARC became USMARC in the 1980s and MARC 21 in the late 1990s" (http://www.loc.gov/marc/faq.html#definition).

Weeding Circulation and Other Records

Every library maintains circulation records, acquisitions records, and other records that will need to be reviewed and weeded based on the library's weeding policy before implementing the ILS. If your library does not have an ILS and you are using circulation cards, you will need to purge the records for patrons who are no longer affiliated with your parent's institution. Material checkout cards for these patrons will also need to be weeded if these materials have been returned. Normally, libraries recall checkout items before weeding so that they can account for missing or lost items and make decisions about these before performing Recon. The manual weeding and purging of patron records may be time consuming depending on the number of registered or enrolled patrons. However, if your library has an ILS, the weeding of circulation records will be less time consuming. As was mentioned earlier, the library should have a circulation policy covering the weeding of patron records. Acquisition records of library materials such as purchase orders, subscriptions, claims, vendor performance, accounting, and so forth should be reviewed and weeded especially if an ILS acquisitions module is being considered. The acquisitions policy should contain procedures for weeding records that are no longer current or needed. Similarly, all other records for which processes will be automated for the first time—or exported from the current ILS to another one—should be reviewed to ensure a smooth transition to the new ILS environment.

COLLECTION INVENTORY

Traditionally, all libraries relied on their shelflists in performing collection weeding and inventory. As most libraries are already automated and no longer keep a shelflist or card catalog, the inventory is performed using a handheld device to scan library materials on the shelves, which generates a report of existing and missing materials, in addition to gaps in the collection. However, if your library is undergoing automation, manual inventorying of the collection will be performed. In order to save time, both weeding and inventorying the collection can be performed simultaneously. After the inventory is completed, a decision is made with regard to the kinds of materials to be destined for Recon. Ideally, all materials that are destined for Recon should have shelflist cards. In the absence of such cards, it is recommended that you work with the ILS vendor under consideration to learn about the handling of the bibliographic information of materials destined for Recon.

Performing the collection inventory can be time consuming, and the time taken to complete it will depend on the size of the collection and the number of staff members involved in this activity.

SHELFLIST ANALYSIS

Shelflist analysis is performed to examine the completeness and accuracy of the catalog cards that will be sent for Recon. If your library has a shelflist, prepare this list based on the guidelines provided by the ILS vendor. Typically, each shelflist card should contain the International Standard Bibliographic Number (ISBN) and the Library of Congress Card Number (LCCN) besides the bibliographic information. In addition, it should indicate item holdings such as the number of copies or volumes, as applicable, in the library.

In the absence of the shelflist, an ILS vendor may suggest that you copy the title page of each item in the library, transcribe the ISBN and LCCN, and include the number of copies or volumes, as applicable, held by the library so that a barcode is created for each of the copies or volumes. The vendor may also ask that you complete a questionnaire or form about the collection in order to create a profile that will be used to guide the Recon process. An example of such a questionnaire is provided by MARCIVE Inc. at http://home.marcive .com/index.php?option=com_content&view=article&id=33&Itemid=45.

RETROSPECTIVE CONVERSION (RECON)

Recon is a process consisting of creating a MARC 21 record for each collection item held by the library. There are various options for pursuing Recon including outsourcing, in-house, and hybrid. Each option has advantages and disadvantages. Selecting an option depends on the size of the collection, nature of the collection, timeline for completing the ILS project, cost, staffing, and knowledge of staff performing the Recon.

Outsourcing Recon

In this option, a contract is signed with an ILS company to provide the MARC 21 records for the items in a library's collection. The company will assign staff to search for the information that represents each library item against the MARC databases in use. Each item is searched in one or more of these databases to find a "match." All matched items will be downloaded and exported onto an external drive to be sent to the library. In the case of "no match," and based on the library's specifications stipulated in the contract, a MARC 21 record will be keyed in (created from scratch) by the company for a given item. Typically, the cost of created records is higher than that for matched ones. For unique items such as special collections, the probability for finding matches is lower than that for other items. Learning about the nature of your collection is very important because it will influence the percentage of match rate and the cost of Recon. For example, a library's collection may consist of books, media, and local history items. The cost for Recon will vary across these types of items.

Choosing a Recon Outsourcing Vendor

Many companies provide data conversion and MARC 21 record services. Backstage Library Works, Brodart, Follett Software Company, The Library Corporation, MARCIVE, and Online Computer Library Center (OCLC) are just a few. In selecting a specific company or vendor to outsource Recon, consider the following:

- The MARC 21 database(s) (e.g., Library of Congress) used to find MARC 21 records

- The size of the MARC 21 databases used and the type of records included (e.g., print, nonprint). A vendor's MARC 21 database should contain a minimum of 4 million records when used to provide records for small libraries and more than 8 million records for larger libraries.

- The qualifications of staff responsible for the Recon project. The more skilled staff members are at applying bibliographic standards (i.e., MARC 21, AACR2R, etc.), the higher the accuracy rate will be. The accuracy rate should not fall below 98 percent. Note that these standards are being replaced with Bibliographic Framework (BIBFRAME) and Resource Description and Access (RDA), respectively. Consider asking the Recon vendor how the implementation of these standards will impact the records created based on the old standards in the near future. See Bibliographic Standards section for additional information.

Table 5.1
Selected Recon companies

Company Name and Address*	Company Name and Address
Brodart Automation 500 Arch St. Williamsport, PA 17705 Phone: (800) 474-9816 E-mail:support@brodart.com URL: http://www.brodart.com	The Library of Congress Cataloging Distribution Service Customer Services Section Washington, DC 20541-4912 Phone: 1 (800) 255-3666 (202) 707-6100 E-mail: cdsinfo@loc.gov URL: http://www.loc.gov/cds
Follett Software Company 1391 Corporate Dr. McHenry, IL 60050 Phone: (800) 323-3397 URL: http://www.fsc.follett.com	MARCIVE, Inc.P.O. Box 47508 San Antonio, TX 78265-7508 Phone: (800) 531-7678 E-mail: info@marcive.com URL: http://www.marcive.com
SkyRiver (Innovative Interfaces) Innovative Interfaces 5850 Shellmound Way Emeryville, CA 94608 Phone: (510) 655-6200 E-mail: info@iii.com URL: http://www.iii.com/products/ skyriver.shtml	OCLC Headquarters 6565 Kilgour Place Dublin, OH 43017-3395 Phone: (614) 764-6000 (800) 848-5878 E-mail: oclc@oclc.org URL: http://www.oclc.org
The Library Corporation Research Park Inwood, WV 25428 Phone: (800) 325-7759 E-mail:info@tlcdelivers.com URL: http://www.tlcdelivers.com http://www.itsmarc.com	SLC (Special Libraries Cataloging) Services 4493 Lindholm Rd. Victoria, BC V9C 3Y1 Canada Phone: (250) 474-3361 E-mail: mac@slc.bc.ca URL: http://www.slc.bc.ca

*All URLs were last accessed on December 15, 2013.

- The quality of MARC 21 records. Full MARC 21 records are desired. Media specialists or information professionals should compare samples of MARC records from various vendors before making a final decision on which vendor to use.

- The cost of providing each completed MARC 21 record (matched)

- The cost of keying in or creating a full (or brief) MARC 21 record from scratch (not matched)

- The cost of enriching a MARC 21 record such as adding a table of contents, summaries, reviews, or additional subject headings, as applicable

- The turnaround time for completing Recon

- The vendor's experience, reputation, and reliability

The procedure for finding matched records include: searching for each item in your collection against the MARC 21 database(s) in use to find a match. Such a match is found using ISBN and/or LCCN—ISSN for serials such as journals, annuals, magazines, and so on. This process is followed until all items have been matched with MARC 21 records. The items are saved and exported onto an external drive or e-mailed using a secure file transfer protocol. In the case no matches are found in the database for certain items, a MARC 21 record will be created from scratch for each of the items, saved, and exported onto the same or another external drive or transferred electronically to the library.

Once the ILS software is installed and working properly, the MARC 21 records will be imported into the cataloging module to create and index the records in the database module.

Advantages of Outsourcing Recon

Outsourcing Recon has the following advantages:

- It saves time, thus allowing the information professional to attend to user and other services or activities on site.

- It provides faster completion of the Recon project over in-house Recon. First, because the company's Recon staff are well versed in the procedure, and second, because several full-time staff may be assigned to work on the project. This is not likely to happen if Recon is performed in-house.

- The turnaround time for completing the Recon project can be predicted. This helps the project manager to establish a schedule for implementing this component of the ILS.

- It may generate a higher match rate than in-house Recon especially since a Recon company may use multiple MARC 21 databases to find matches.

- It saves time on creating MARC 21 records from scratch for items that have "no match" in the databases.

- It allows linking smart barcodes to their respective items during the Recon process based on the library's specifications at no or minimal cost.

- It saves time on linking authority records to their respective items during the Recon process, thus saving time for creating cross-references after implementing the ILS.

Disadvantages of Outsourcing Recon

Outsourcing Recon has the following disadvantages:

- The Recon project may not be completed on time as scheduled.

- There is always a possibility of mismatches and errors in the MARC 21 records; thus, the cleanup of these records is recommended after being imported into the ILS.

In-House Conversion Process

The in-house Recon is similar to the outsourced Recon with the exception of access to fewer MARC 21 databases especially for small libraries that cannot afford using OCLC. The options for performing Recon in-house include:

- Subscription to a fee-based MARC web service

- Use of MARC 21 records available on the web at no charge

- Creation of MARC 21 records using a MARC software tool

Many ILS vendors or companies provide access to their web-based MARC databases for a fee. Once you subscribe to such a service, you will be able to search one or more MARC 21 databases to find matches. Use of these services should go beyond finding matches to include the ability to edit, save, and export these MARC 21 records directly into the ILS cataloging module (after the software has been installed) or to save these records onto an external drive to import later into the ILS. The fee you will pay for this kind of service will be based on the type of MARC 21 records to use (print, nonprint, pre-1965, etc.), the number of records contained in the database (normally, 4 million records is the minimum for a small library and 8 million for larger ones), and the length of the subscription to the service.

BookWhere from WebClarity Software Inc. (http://www.webclarity.info) is an example of a fee-based web service that provides copy cataloging of MARC 21 records. Based on the description provided on the company's website, BookWhere is "the most comprehensive and user friendly copy cataloging tool available for building and maintaining your library catalog. With the largest selection of accessible library databases in the world, BookWhere can easily locate the quality MARC cataloging records you need."

Another service is ITS.MARC from the Library Corporation (http://www.itsmarc.com), which provides access to more than 29 million MARC records that are compatible with many ILSs, as described on the company's website. ITS.MARC databases include LC MARC English, LC MARC Foreign Language,

Asian MARC, Canadian MARC, A/V Access, British MARC, Media MARC, School MARC Sears, and School MARC LC. Searching the Z39.50, OCLC, and the Library of Congress MARC databases is also available. A 30-day free trial can be downloaded from the company's website. ITS.MARC also has Bibliofile, a set of 20 different MARC databases that can either be downloaded from the website or ordered on CD. A list of these databases is available in the FAQ section located at http://www.itsmarc.com/BiblioFileFAQ.asp. There is a 30-day free trial of the database and a training video that requires a user ID and password.

eZcat from Book Systems is another well-established software and service for finding MARC 21 records. eZcat allows use of multiple databases simultaneously (Library of Congress and over 400 other publicly listed libraries) to retrieve cataloging data for different types of library materials (books, video, audio, computer files, etc.). The Book Systems website describes that eZcat Pro has the same features as eZcat with the additional features of editing, printing, batch processing, and exporting of MARC records (http://www.booksys .com/ezcat-software). A free demonstration of the software is available upon request from Book Systems.

A larger and more well-established source of cataloging data is OCLC. Its WorldCat is the "world's largest online catalog of library content" in various formats. Libraries that are members of OCLC can access cataloging data for varied purposes including Recon. Membership in OCLC is constituted through the contribution of a library's holdings to WorldCat, whether this contribution is made as an independent institution or as a member of a consortium, state, or national library. While there is no separate membership fee to join OCLC, a subscription to WorldCat or other services that contribute intellectual content are required (http://www.oclc.org/en-US/membership/become-a-member.html). On May 4, OCLC's holdings reached 2 billion records (http:// www.oclc.org/en-US/home.html?redirect=true). If your library cannot afford OCLC membership, other options should be pursued.

SkyRiver is a recent service that is used by many libraries to find cataloging data. In February 2013, SkyRiver became one of the suites of products and services provided by Innovative Interfaces (http://theskyriver.com/overview). SkyRiver is a resource sharing network with 40 million MARC records that is offered on an annual subscription flat rate and for unlimited use. This cataloging service is ILS-independent and integrates with local ILSs. It accommodates "all levels of RDA adoption, including hybrid AACR2/RDA as well as full RDA support. The transition to RDA is eased with an intuitive template to ensure RDA coding accuracy and contextual linking to the RDA Toolkit" (http://theskyriver .com/wp/wp-content/uploads/2012/08/SkyRiver-Brochure14.pdf).

Web-Based Free MARC Services

Web-based online catalogs for varied types of libraries can be searched to locate MARC 21 records for specific items. Saving these records on PC or external drive is not possible. However, you may copy and paste a record into a word processing application or print the record. Manual input of the cataloging data into the local ILS cataloging module would be the approach to follow for creating the record. If you are not comfortable inputting this data, consider using MARC Magician offered by Mitinet Library Services. Magician can format the data input into a MARC 21 format. It can also be used for creating MARC 21 records from scratch (http://www.mitinet.com/Products/MARC Magician.aspx).

The Library of Congress Z39.50 Gateway (http://www.loc.gov/z3950) supports searching for MARC records across hundreds of college and university online catalogs. A search in any of the online catalogs in the gateway will result in a bibliographic record that can be viewed in both a full and brief tagged display (with MARC tags). Like the web-based online catalogs, saving MARC records is not possible, making the copying and pasting into a word processing application the only option for capturing MARC data.

Using shared union catalogs or consortia websites is another way to obtain MARC data. An example is the *Big Country Library System* (BCLS) union catalog (http://www.bclstx.org). Searching this system for a book by Stephen King, for example, retrieves multiple entries and clicking on one of them will retrieve the item in a normal view (brief citation) that can be expanded into a display of the MARC record. Copying and pasting the record into an application program or printing it out are the only options.

Another pathway to locate MARC 21 data is by searching *lib-web-cats* (library websites and catalogs), a directory of libraries worldwide that is managed by Marshall Breeding on his Library Technology website (http://www.librarytechnology.org). Searching the directory provides a listing of links to the library's website and online catalog. Clicking on the online catalog link takes you to the library's catalog search page to input information for a specific item. Once the bibliographic data for the item is displayed, click on the link to the MARC record to view the metadata. The directory provides additional information about a given listing including the geographic location, address, library type, current and previous library automation systems used, and the size of the library's collection (http://www.librarytechnology.org/libwebcats). Becoming a member of SOPAC will provide additional venues for finding MARC records.

Creating MARC Records

There are situations when you will need to create MARC records for purposes other than Recon. One of these is creating MARC records from scratch for an item that does not have a MARC record in the databases you have used in-house during the Recon process. Similarly, if a record for an item was not found by the Recon vendor, a staff member at the vendor's location will create the record by inputting the data based on cataloging rules. This type of data input is called original cataloging. Using MARC Magician or similar tools will save time in cataloging and, as was mentioned previously, will format the input data into a MARC 21 format. A MARC record can also be created using copy cataloging such as Cataloging in Publication (CIP) provided by the Library of Congress on the back of the title page of the majority of books published in the United States or owned by the Library. CIP is brief in nature and intends to provide guidance in cataloging an item from scratch especially when a MARC record for that item is not available. Manual data input requires an adequate level of knowledge of cataloging rules (AACR2R, RDA, MARC 21 standard, and other bibliographic standards associated with cataloging). As was mentioned earlier, MARC Magician can be used to create records from scratch (http://www.mitinet.com/Products/MARCMagician.aspx). Magician allows for the creation, editing, and correction of MARC records based on the AACR2R rules and MARC 21 standard. Based on the description provided by Mitinet, MARC Magician automatically checks the records for structural accuracy and corrects errors in different fields including but not limited to punctuation, description of item (GMD), filing codes in the indicator fields, and control fields with incorrect codes. It provides features such as online tips and examples for using most fields and subfields in a MARC record. Magician creates all fields, tags, and codes for specific types of materials, and formats cataloged data into an accurate MARC 21 record. In addition, this software supports saving and importing formatted records into a library's online catalog. Magician can be instrumental for creating MARC records for new collection items the library acquires after the Recon has been completed, or for creating MARC records for local history items for which MARC records do not exist.

Advantages of In-House Recon

Performing Recon in-house has the following advantages:

- The information professional's firsthand knowledge of the collection may generate a higher accuracy rate than the vendor's Recon provided that the professional possesses the level of knowledge needed to manage the Recon project effectively.

- Using fee-based MARC web services for finding matching MARC 21 records is possible from any remote location where an Internet connection is provided. Being away from the office may reduce interruption and yield higher accuracy rate.

Disadvantages of In-House Recon

The disadvantages of in-house Recon outnumber the advantages. Some of the disadvantages follow:

- Recon may take a long time to complete, especially if the library is understaffed. The larger the size of the collection, the longer it will take to complete the conversion of records into the MARC 21 format.

- Service to users may be hampered when much of staff time is devoted to Recon.

- Constant interruption during Recon may increase error rate, which in return will affect the quality of the MARC 21 records.

- Training in cataloging, understanding MARC format, and use of MARC databases may be time consuming. Hiring volunteers without background knowledge or training may impact on the accuracy rate and the timeline for completing Recon.

- The larger the size of the collection, the greater is the cost especially in terms of personnel time and resources.

- Technical problems such as hardware, software, power, or Internet failure will delay the conversion.

Making a decision as to the Recon option to pursue should be informed by the outcome of a cost analysis performed for both outsourcing and completing the Recon in-house so that you are able to justify the Return on Investment (ROI) of each option. See Tables 5.2 and 5.3 for an example of cost analysis.

Hybrid Conversion Process

This process involves having part of the collection converted by an ILS vendor or company and part of it converted by media center or library staff. For example, nonprint materials may be converted in-house if the library possesses a small collection of these, and print materials may be outsourced to the vendor. The same procedures for Recon described previously are followed. The advantages and disadvantages of this Recon process combine those of both the vendor and in-house conversions. However, the match or hit rate for in-house Recon tends to be lower than the outsourced one. In addition, the quality of and consistency in the MARC 21 records may differ if the database(s) used in-house are not procured from the outsourcing vendor that performed Recon for the print collection.

COST ANALYSIS

Performing a cost analysis allows you to determine the most cost-effective and efficient approach to use for the Recon project and justify the best ROI for the library. The cost analysis is described in the following section. It will vary across libraries and, therefore, it is provided here as a guideline. You should adapt it to your own library environment to estimate and compare the cost of each conversion option. Note that in addition to the cost analysis, you should consider the advantages and disadvantages of each option and the expected time to complete the Recon project.

Cost Analysis for Outsourcing Recon

Estimating the cost of vendor conversion should be based on the following: the number of books to be converted, number of MARC fields to be enhanced (optional), number of audiovisual materials to be converted, smart barcodes, barcode setup fee, spine labels, matching of authority records (optional), output of MARC records via Secure File Transfer Protocol (SFTP), output to CDs or other external devices, and shipping the shelflist cards.

Scenario

Let us assume you have a collection of 5,000 items: 4,750 books and 250 nonprints. The ILS Recon vendor under consideration charges $0.50 per each book and $0.75 per each nonprint item. Let us also assume that you want only one field in the MARC record (tag 520) enhanced and the vendor charges $0.05 per enhancement. The estimated cost shown in Table 5.2 for the Recon of this collection assumes that the collection had 100 percent match rate (to keep the analysis simple). Otherwise, there is a higher charge per item for creating a MARC record from scratch.

Table 5.2
Cost analysis for outsourcing Recon

Description*	Quantity	$Unit price	$Extended price
Conversion (90% of 5,000 items)	4,750	0.50	2,375.00
Conversion of AV items (10% of collection)	250	0.75	187.50
One field enhancement	4,750	0.05	237.50
Onetime setup fee for smart barcodes	N/A	125	125
Smart barcode labels	5,000	0.05	250
Spine labels	5,000	0.01	50
Output of MARC records	1 CD	15	15
Shipping and return of shelflist cards	1 box	50	50
Miscellaneous	Varies	50	50
Total	—	—	$3,339.50

*This analysis is based on a small collection of 5,000 items and cost of conversion provided by an automation company that serves small libraries.

Cost Analysis for In-House Recon

Assuming you are considering the in-house conversion option for the 5,000 items and that you have decided to use a fee-based web service from an ILS vendor, the cost of Recon should include: labor cost (time taken by a professional or trained staff); fees for using and importing MARC records from automation companies' web databases; cost of barcode software (for smart barcodes); barcode machine and barcode printer; cost of barcode labels, spine labels, and miscellaneous items. The labor cost will vary based on who will be doing the conversion (professional or trained staff member). As illustrated in Table 5.3, the cost of conversion by a professional is twice as much as the cost by a trained staff member.

Cost Analysis Estimate for Conversion by a Professional and a Technical Staff Member

Assume that the size of a library's collection is 4,750 books and 250 non-print items. In addition, assume that the professional staff member makes twice as much as the technical staff member who will be trained to do the conversion, and that it will take both staff members the same amount of time to convert an item (this assumption is subject to the level of training of the technical staff member and is assumed so for the purpose of simplicity in calculating the cost). As shown in Table 5.3, the cost of Recon for one year by a professional staff member is $23,300, compared to $11,750 by a technical staff member. The quality of the conversion may be compromised if the staff member is not well trained in performing it and if the level of knowledge of MARC standard or AACR2R is inadequate.

The cost estimate for in-house conversion is based on 10 months of work. However, due to the degree of uncertainty that characterizes the searching for a MARC record, editing, enhancing, saving and/or importing it into the ILS, it is advisable that you calculate the *expected time* to complete the conversion. The next section shows how to perform this task.

Expected Time to Complete the Recon Project

To estimate the expected time to complete the Recon project, use the Program Evaluation Review Technique (PERT). This technique uses optimistic, pessimistic, and realistic time estimates to complete a task (Valacich, George, and Hoffer 2011). This technique is based on the following equation:

$$ET = O + 4r + p/6$$

ET = Expected time for completing an activity

O = Optimistic time for completing an activity (the minimum time to complete the activity)

r = Realistic time for completing an activity (the most likely time to complete the activity)

p = Pessimistic time for completing an activity (the maximum time to complete the activity)

The realistic time (r) is weighted four times more than the optimistic time (O) and the pessimistic time (p) because the expected time (ET) should be closer to the realistic time.

Table 5.3
Cost analysis for in-house Recon by professional and technical staff

Recon by Professional	Cost	Recon by Technical Staff Member	Cost
a. Pay rate/month	4,000.00	a. Pay rate/month	$2,000.00
b. Hourly rate ($4,000/ 160 hrs per month)	$25.00/hr	b. Hourly rate ($2,000/ 160 hrs per month)	$12.50/hr
c. Hours for Recon (20 hrs/week x $25) weeks	$500	c. Hours for Recon (20 hrs/week x $12.50)	$250
d. Hours for Recon for 44 weeks* (20 hrs/ week x 44 weeks x $500/week)	$22,000.00	d. Hours for Recon for 44 weeks* (20 hrs/ week x 44 weeks x $500/week)	$11,000
e. MARC service subscription per year	$500.00	e. MARC service subscription per year	$500.00
f. Barcode production software	$250.00	f. Barcode production software	$250.00
g. Barcode labels	$50	g. Barcode labels	$50
h. Spine labels	$50	h. Spine labels	$50
i. Miscellaneous	$50	i. Miscellaneous	$50
Total (items di)	$22,900.00/ year*	Total (items di)	$11,450.00/ year*

*It is assumed that the professional will have time off from work for vacations, holidays, and other kind of absences. Therefore, the hours are based on 10 months of work a year. This cost analysis should be adapted to a specific library environment.

How to Apply the Equation?

Let us assume that the optimistic time (O) to search, edit, enhance, save and/or import a MARC record by a professional will take 5 minutes, a realistic time of 7 minutes, and a pessimistic time (p) of 10 minutes. The ET to convert an item into a MARC format will be as follows:

$$ET = 5 + 4(7) + 10 = 43/6 = 7.16$$

If the expected time to convert one item takes 7 minutes and 0.16 seconds, then the expected time to convert 5,000 items will be (5,000 x 7.16 = 35,800 minutes or approximately 597 hours). If the professional devotes 20 hours per week to Recon, the expected time to complete the conversion project will be nearly 30 weeks (597 hours/20 hours per week = 29.85 weeks). This expected time does not involve the time it takes to learn how to use the MARC database service, the barcode production software, generation of barcodes or affixation of spine labels. If this equation is used to project the expected time to complete the Recon project by a professional, the cost for in-house conversion described in Table 5.3 should be based on 30 instead of 44 weeks, bringing the cost of Recon by a professional to $15,000.

By taking all factors into consideration (cost analysis, advantages/disadvantages of each option, and the expected time to complete the project), you should be able to make a wise decision on the option you choose and provide a strong rationale for this decision.

BIBLIOGRAPHIC STANDARDS

Traditionally, the format and content of cataloged records stored in the ILS are based on the AACR2R and MARC 21 standards. Transitioning from AACR2R to the RDA standard for cataloging is underway by libraries. The Library of Congress' Network Development and MARC Standards Office is developing a framework for working with MARC data in a XML environment. The Library of Congress has also initiated the BIBFRAME transition initiative to determine a transition path for the MARC 21 exchange format to more web-based, Linked Data standards. BIBFRAME.ORG is a central hub for this effort. These standards and the initiative are described in this section.

MARC 21

MARC 21 is a format for bibliographic data that is "designed to be a carrier for bibliographic information about printed and manuscript textual materials, computer files, maps, music, continuing resources, visual materials, and mixed materials. Bibliographic data commonly includes titles, names, subjects, notes, publication data, and information about the physical description of an item" (http://www.loc.gov/marc/bibliographic). A MARC 21 record is composed of three elements: (1) the record structure; (2) the content designation; and (3) the data content of the record.

(1) The record structure is based on two standards: The International Standard Organization (ISO 2709) Format for Information Exchange; and the American National Standards Institute/National Information Standards Organization (ANSI/NISO Z39.2) Bibliographic Information Interchange.

(2) The content designation is a set of codes used to identify and characterize the data elements within a record and support the manipulation of that data for each MARC format.

(3) The content of the data elements that comprise a MARC 21 record is defined by a minimum of three standards, including the International Standard Bibliographic Description (ISBD), Anglo-American Cataloguing Rules Second Revised Edition (AACR2R), the Library of Congress Subject Headings (LCSH), or other cataloging rules, subject thesauri, and classification schedules used by the organization that creates a record. The content of certain coded data elements is defined in the MARC formats (e.g., the leader, field 007, field 008).

Table 5.4
Most frequently used MARC 21 tags

Tag	Field Name
010	LCCN
020	ISBN
100	Personal name main entry
245	Title proper and statement of responsibility
250	Edition (or version number of a computer file, a map's scale, etc., as applicable)
260	Publication information
300	Physical description
440	Series
500	Notes (e.g., general note, index, references)
520	Annotation or summary
650	Topical subject heading (repeatable field)
700	Personal name added entry (repeatable field)
800	Series added entry
856	URL address (repeatable field)
900	Local field (e.g., local call number, barcode number, price, vendor information)

The components of the five MARC 21 communication formats (e.g., bibliographic data, authority data, and holdings data) are described in detail at http://www.loc.gov/marc/bibliographic/bdintro.html.

MARCXML

MARCXML is a framework that is being developed by The Library of Congress' Network Development and MARC Standards Office to allow for working with MARC data using Extensible Markup Language (XML), a web coding language. This framework provides more flexibility for libraries to work with MARC data such as creating relationships or connections across various elements in MARC records to enhance user information discovery experience. The framework includes components such as schemas, style sheets, software tools, and utilities. These components are described at the MARCXML website, located at http://www.loc.gov/standards/marcxml/.

Bibliographic Framework Transition Initiative and BIBFRAME

The Library of Congress and a community of libraries have undertaken The BIBFRAME Transition Initiative or BIBFRAME to determine the plan for migration of the MARC 21 format to web-based, Linked Data standards; to accomplish this migration, a Linked Data model, vocabulary, and necessary tools are needed (http://bibframe.org). The Library of Congress has selected Zepheira for building the model and tools. This company provides solutions to many organizations to use Semantic Web standards, Linked Data models, and schemas to connect over the web (http://zepheira.com).

BIBFRAME.org is the central hub for this Framework Initiative. A demonstration area, a draft BIBFRAME vocabulary, and transformation services are provided on this hub's website at http://bibframe.org. The transformation services support the migration from existing MARC 21 data by translating the data to the BIBFRAME model. For a description of the Framework's Linked Data Model and supporting services, view the Library of Congress document located at http://www.loc.gov/bibframe.

Functional Requirements for Bibliographic Records (FRBR)

FRBR is a conceptual entity-relationships model developed by the International Federation of Library Associations and Institutions (IFLA) to represent a more effective approach to user access and retrieval of information in online catalogs and databases. The model consists of three groups of entities: (1) the work itself or intellectual endeavor; (2). the person or body responsible for the intellectual endeavor; and (3) the subjects of the endeavor including concepts, objects, events, or places. In the context of the model, these relationships depict the links between and among entities in a record, allowing users to obtain additional information by making connections between the entity found and other related entities (http://archive.ifla.org/VII/s13/frbr/frbr_current5.htm). FRBR is separate from AACR2R or ISBD. The FRBR model serves as the foundation of RDA (see description of the latter in the next section).

Additional detail about FRBR is provided in IFLA's final report located at, http://www.ifla.org/files/assets/cataloguing/frbr/frbr_2008.pdf.

Anglo-American Cataloging Rules, Second Revised Edition (AACR2R)

Traditionally, describing items to encode in MARC 21 format is based on the Anglo-American Cataloging Rules, Second Revised Edition (AACR2R). The latter consists of a set of rules for describing various types of materials in a MARC 21 record. Published in 1967, the rules were revised in 1978 and 1988. Adherence to the rules is important for maintaining consistency in cataloging and providing effective information access and retrieval. AACR2R is being replaced by the RDA standard. ILS vendors are providing tools to allow libraries to transition from AACR2R to RDA.

Resource Description and Access (RDA)

RDA was implemented on March 31, 2013 by the Library of Congress. MARC 21 records with RDA cataloging are established for both bibliographic records and authority records. The RDA Access Toolkit website has examples of how to apply RDA for different types of records and how to encode the records in MARC 21 format (See Table 5.5).

The RDA format consists of three main components: RDA REF (e.g., 2.3.2) which is similar to a tag in a MARC record; data element (e.g., title proper), which indicates the type of data to input into the REF area; and data recorded (i.e., the description information of the element). For example, the RDA elements for a book begin with ref 2.3.2, which is assigned to the element (title proper), meaning that the title of the book should be encoded in ref 2.3.2. This is illustrated as follows:

Data REF	Data Element	Data Recorded/Description
2.3.2	**Title proper**	**Automation made easy.**

For additional information about cataloging items in different formats and encoding the information in a MARC 21 record, view the RDA Access

Table 5.5
RDA refs and data elements

RDA REF	Data Element
2.3.2	Title proper
2.4.2	Statement of responsibility relating to title proper
2.5.2	Designation of edition
2.8.2	Place of publication
2.8.2	Place of publication
2.8.4	Publisher's name
2.8.6	Date of publication
2.12.2	Title proper of series
2.13	Mode of issuance
2.15	Identifier for the manifestation (e.g., ISBN of hardbound)
2.15	Identifier for the manifestation (e.g., ISBN for paperback)
3.2	Media type
3.3	Carrier type
3.4	Extent of text
3.5	Dimensions
4.3	Contact information (e.g., publisher's URL)
6.9	Content type
7.16	Supplementary content (e.g., includes bibliography and index)
17.8	Work manifested (i.e., author's name, title of book)
19.2	Creator (i.e., the author's name)
18.5	Relationship designator (i.e., author's name)
25.1	Related work

Toolkit located at http://www.rdatoolkit.org/examples/MARC, and click on "Examples." This website has very useful content related to RDA and MARC standards. It is noteworthy that knowledge about AACR2R makes learning the RDA easier than you think. Similarly, knowledge of how to apply MARC 21 standard will facilitate the encoding of RDA elements into a MARC 21 record.

At the core of these frameworks and standards is Linked Data. In June 2012, OCLC began using Linked Data to describe an item's bibliographic information metadata. "Built on general Web technologies, Linked Data uses URIs (Uniform Resource Identifiers) to identify entities or concepts . . . and RDF

(Resource Description Framework) to describe links between structured data" (http://www.oclc.org/data.html). RDF is one of the recommendations by the World Wide Web Consortium (W3C) to create metadata in Semantic Web data models. OCLC uses Schema.org markup, a collection of markup schemes or languages employed in websites that use structured data (http://schema.org).

Another important recommendation is the Simple Knowledge Organization System (SKOS), which is a model for sharing and linking knowledge organization systems such as thesauri-using ontologies, taxonomies, classification schemes, and subject headings to enable data sharing across various applications. The SKOS model makes the export of data from current knowledge organization systems into the Semantic Web possible and at a low cost (http://www.w3.org/TR/skos-reference).

BARCODING THE COLLECTION

Barcoding is the process of placing a barcode on each item in the database. A barcode identifies a specific item and allows it to be checked in and out by using a barcode scanner or by keying the barcode number into the ILS.

Barcodes

A barcode contains both bars and spaces. A row of numbers appears under the code to indicate the meaning of the bars and spaces. Many barcode standards are available for different uses. For ILS, the two most common standards are Codabar and Code 39 (http://www.makebarcode.com/specs/barcodechart.html). ILS and other barcode vendors may employ different symbology within these standards. Ask the barcode vendor about the type and meaning of the symbology that is compatible with your ILS.

Types of Barcodes

Standard or classic barcodes used in libraries have been either smart or dumb. Smart barcodes are linked to their respective items during Recon. It is called smart because by looking at the barcode, one can identify the title of the item it belongs to, its author, and call number, as well as the name of the institution or library to which it belongs. After these barcodes are generated and linked to their respective items, they are organized by call number and sent to the library that requested them. Each of these barcodes should be affixed only to its respective library item, unlike a dumb barcode that can be placed on any item.

Dumb barcodes are generic; they do not identify any item's title, call number, or author. When generic barcodes are purchased, they only have the name of the institution or library. A dumb barcode can be affixed to any item during the barcoding process. Linking a dumb barcode to an item may occur as the item is checked out, or when an item is cataloged in-house using MARC 21 format. Each MARC 21 record has a tag for entering an item's barcode.

Radio Frequency Identification (RFID)

"RFID is a combination of radio-frequency-based technology and microchip technology. The information contained on microchips in the tags affixed to library materials is read using radio frequency technology. A reader (a.k.a. sensor, scanner, or interrogator) looks for antennae on the tags and retrieves information from the microchips through them" (Boss 2011). RFID tags are used for theft detection of library materials and for handling material checkout and check-in more efficiently. For example, use of RFID tags allows the checkout and check-in of a stack of items at once, thus, saving staff and patron time.

RFID tags are more expensive than barcodes. According to Boss (2011), a book RFID tag costs $0.20 and a media tag $0.65. Boss estimates that a library with 40,000 items should budget for $27,000 to $35,500 in an RFID system. The cost of the system has plummeted since that time, but it can still be costly for some libraries on small budgets. New libraries being built will most likely prefer to invest in an RFID system over an electromagnetic (EM) security system.

Advantages of RFID

RFID offers many advantages over the traditional barcoding technologies system. These include a fast checkout and check-in of library materials, simplified patron self-checkout of materials, higher reduction in security exit sensors false alarms, speedier inventorying of library materials and item searching, reduction in the amount of time required sorting library materials for reshelving, and longer life for RFID tags over traditional barcodes (Boss 2011).

Disadvantages of RFID

Despite the many benefits of RFID systems, they have following disadvantages over traditional systems. As described by Boss (2011), RFID is more expensive than barcodes or EM strips, or radio frequency (RF) systems. In addition, RFID tags are not compatible across systems and are subject to interference by hackers who can block the radio signal or interface one tag in a way that it cancels another tag to block the signal; it can be removed if exposed unless they are placed inside the front cover of books, or placed in multiple places, or disguised as bookplates. A major disadvantage is that these tags are perceived by library and other users as susceptible to invading their privacy.

The perceptions that RFID tags can be a threat to a patron's privacy are attributed to patron information that the tags can be read from a distance after the patron has checked out library materials and taken them to places such as homes or offices. Boss (2011) argues that the vast majority of these tags store only the item ID, usually the same number that previously has been stored on a barcode. The link between borrower and the borrowed material is maintained in the circulation module of the ILS. The additional information stored on an RFID tag contains only information about the item such as holding information and call number and rarely author or title information. Boss adds that since the RFID tags can only be read from a distance of 24 inches or less using special readers or sensors with limited power of 10 watts as required by law, it is, therefore, not possible for someone to read tags from the street or an office building hallway. However, he notes that RFID systems may be a potential threat to a patron's privacy where the use of the encrypted "smart card" is as a patron ID card. This card can function as a debit card when a patron pays for library services and the patron's account information could be hacked by others. Additional information about RFID is provided at http://www.ala.org/pla/tools/technotes/rfidtechnology.

Acquiring Standard Barcodes

Standard or traditional barcodes are acquired through ILS vendors or are generated in-house using a barcode production software tool that is compatible with the ILS. Before making a decision to purchase smart barcodes or generate them in-house, perform a cost analysis to determine the most cost-effective method.

Barcodes must be compatible with the ILS in place. Before ordering barcodes, develop specifications for them and keep them on file. If you outsource Recon, you will obtain the converted records in MARC 21 format along with their respective smart barcodes. These barcodes will be customized based on your specifications (title, author, call number, and name of the institution or library). Additional specifications should include the barcode standard (Codabar or Code 39), ease of scanning, lamination or protective coating, and durability. Keep the barcode range on file so that each time additional barcodes are ordered, the barcodes are kept in correct sequence.

Procedures for Barcoding the Collection with Standard Barcodes

Barcoding is a very time-consuming process. The larger the collection, the more time it will take to barcode it. The availability of adequate staffing and the development of a good plan may reduce barcoding time. For example, before the process begins, it must be determined which materials will be barcoded. For example, will materials in the vertical file be barcoded?

Following are procedures that may facilitate barcoding:

- Make an effort to close the library to the public to avoid interruption and to expedite the process.

- Recall checked-out items.

- Divide the shelves into sections, and barcode one section at a time. If adequate staffing is available, one or more staff members may be given responsibility for barcoding one or more sections.

- Use the smart barcodes first because they are arranged by call numbers and, possibly, by prefixes (e.g., fiction, biographies).

- Verify each item's call number against the call number on the barcode. If the call numbers match, place the barcode on the item in the designated area. (See the following section about placing barcodes.) Make sure all smart barcodes have respective items in the collection.

During barcoding, you may encounter errors in barcode labels (e.g., in call numbers or titles) and find that several barcodes are missing. If these or other problems occur, contact the vendor for replacement. If this problem is detected for barcodes generated in-house, then the barcodes will have to be regenerated.

Placing Standard Barcodes on Print Materials

The place on the item a barcode is placed is determined by how items are scanned during inventory and by the type of material (e.g., print, audio disc, videotape) being barcoded. To choose the best placement, first simulate the collection inventory process by selecting sample items to scan. Determine the barcode placement that will make scanning easiest and fastest.

The following are some of the many options for barcoding print materials:

- Place the barcode on the front book cover in the top right or top left corner, vertically or horizontally.

- Place the barcode on the outside of the back cover in the top right or top left corner, vertically or horizontally.

- Place the barcode inside the back cover in the top right or top left corner, vertically or horizontally.

- Place the barcode inside the front cover in the top right or top left corner, vertically or horizontally.

- Place two identical barcodes, one inside and one outside the cover, in the top right or top left corner, vertically or horizontally. If the library cannot afford purchasing two barcodes per item, staff may place one barcode in the preferred area and transcribe the barcode number inside the item using a permanent marker.

- Avoid placing a barcode on an item's spine or where important information will be covered.

Placing Standard Barcodes on Digital and Other Media

Barcoding digital media, such as DVRs, DVDs, Blu-Rays, computer software, audio compact discs, CD-ROMs, audiotapes, and videocassettes, requires careful consideration because barcode scanning may damage the encoded information.

To barcode media items with accompanying pieces (e.g., guides, manuals, booklets), follow these suggestions:

- Place a barcode on the outside of an item's container, cover, or jacket, preferably in the upper left corner.

- Transcribe the barcode number on each accompanying piece (e.g., booklet, guide) using a permanent marker.

- Label each accompanying item above or below the barcode number to alert circulation staff that the item is part of a set.

- Transcribe the barcode number on the item's label using a permanent marker.

Protecting Standard Barcodes

Scanning barcodes causes them to deteriorate over time unless they are laminated or covered with protectors. In addition, barcodes are subject to vandalism. Make sure that barcodes are safeguarded against both types of damage. If the barcode labels have good protectors, then users will find them hard to remove.

Tagging Materials with RFID

Like the options of placing barcodes on print materials, there are varied options for placing RFID tags. Typically, the inside of the back cover of an item is used. However, for added security, placing the tags inside the front cover under a bookplate or with a logo printed on the tag is recommended (Boss 2011). Tags should be placed three inches above the bottom of the page to avoid possible interference from the metal shelves when doing the collection inventory.

Libraries that are migrating from an EM or RF system will need to devise a plan for converting materials to the RFID system and to purchase one or more conversion stations for completing the conversion. Materials may be converted during or after checkout. In this case, both the barcode and RFID tag readers should be used in tandem until all materials are converted. The conversion process can be time consuming. The time it will take to complete this process depends a number of factors, including, but not limited to, the number of items to be converted, the number of conversion stations used, the amount of information added to tags, the number of personnel doing the tagging, and the amount of training and level of skills the personnel possesses in tagging materials.

Newly built libraries that have acquired an RFID system will most likely complete the tagging project faster than libraries that are migrating to RFID since there are no existing barcodes to scan. The amount of information added to tags is a factor to consider in completing the tagging project. Consult with your RFID vendor about positioning the tags on items and the whole implementation process of the RFID system.

Other Barcodes Used in Libraries

Quick Response (QR) codes are being used by many libraries to provide access to digital content from a user's smart phone. These codes do not replace item barcodes; rather, they are used to connect users to a specific library web page or content. QR codes were developed in Japan in the 1990s for use in logistics, retail, inventories, and for tracking information for products, among other things. QR codes are 2D rich matrix that encode information and require a generator or a barcode reader such as Kaywa code (http://qrcode.kaywa .com/). A comprehensive list of additional code reader software is located at http://www.mobile-barcodes.com/qr-code-software. Differences among QR code generators reside in their decoding, tracking, and encoding abilities. Availability for free versus a fee is an additional difference (Cordova 2011). In order to read a QR code, a smartphone should be equipped with a QR code reader. The phone's camera acts like a scanner, and once the code is scanned, a URL, contact information, SMS, or similar links to information is immediately displayed on the phone. To download scanner applications for varied mobile devices and operating systems (OS) and to gain additional information about QR codes, visit the Albertson's Library located at http://guides.boisestate .edu/qrcodes.

SUMMARY

The implementation of the ILS covers multiple activities including weeding the collection and circulation records, inventorying the collection, Recon, and barcoding or tagging materials. The amount of effort and time spent on these activities apply to libraries in different ways and depends on whether these libraries already have an ILS in place and migrating to another one or whether they are implementing an ILS for the first time.

While weeding and inventorying the collection should be based on a library's collection development and weeding policy, Recon can be achieved using different approaches. Recon is process for finding matched MARC 21 records for each item in the collection. MARC 21 is a bibliographic standard for encoding cataloging data so that a computer can read and store it in the ILS. There are three options for completing the Recon project: outsourcing to an ILS vendor or company, performing the work in-house, or using a hybrid approach that combines the outsourcing and in-house options. Making a decision on the best Recon option is not an easy task. Nonetheless, assessing the advantages and disadvantages of each option, performing a cost analysis for each option, and calculating the expected time to complete Recon in-house using the PERT formula should allow you to make the best decision.

Basic knowledge of bibliographic standards is necessary for understanding the metadata of bibliographic records. Standards and initiatives, namely MARCXML and the BIBFRAME Transition Initiative, tools, and supporting services provided by the Library of Congress and the library community will allow the migration of the data from the MARC 21 format to a web-based Linked Data model based on the Semantic Web technologies. BIBFRAME will provide users with a more effective means for navigating the information in a bibliographic record and obtaining additional information based on making connections between and among data entities and their relationships. Libraries will be transitioning from AACR2R to the RDA cataloging standard using the FRBR model as the foundation.

Other Semantic Web technologies are being implemented for describing metadata include, but are not limited to Resource Description Framework (RDF) (for describing entities and concepts), Schema.org (a collection of markup schemes), and SKOS (for sharing and linking data across various applications). These technologies are recommended by the W3C.

Barcoding the collection using traditional or standard barcodes consists of placing a barcode on each item for which the bibliographic data has been converted and a MARC 21 record has been created. Normally, a "smart" barcode is linked to an item during the creation of the MARC 21 record. "Dumb" barcodes are generic and can be used to barcode the collection before, during, or after the creation of MARC 21 records. While smart barcodes identify the items they are associated with, dumb barcodes do not.

Libraries that acquire an RFID security system instead of traditional systems such as EM or RF will use RFID tags to barcode the collection. RFID is more costly than the traditional barcoding systems; however, it is more effective and efficient and can save users and staff time checking out materials, among other things.

The depth and breadth of preparing the collection for an ILS will vary among libraries. However, the basic principles are the same. As you embark on a new ILS or a migration project, it is important to consider the various activities involved in implementing the ILS based on your own library environment and priorities.

REFERENCES

American Library Association. RDA Toolkit: Resource Description and Access. "MARC Record Examples of RDA Cataloging." 2010. http://www .rdatoolkit.org/Examples/MARC. Accessed February 12, 2013.

American Library Association. RDA Toolkit: Resource Description and Access. "RDA Background." 2010. http://www.rdatoolkit.org/background. Accessed January 29, 2013.

American Library Association. Weeding Library Collections: A Selected Annotated Bibliography for Library Collection Evaluation. "ALA Library Fact Sheet 15." 2009. http://www.ala.org/tools/libfactsheets/alalibrary factsheet15. Accessed January 22, 2013.

BIBFRAME Model Overview. 2013. http://bibframe.org. Accessed May 20, 2013.

Big Country Library System (BCLS). *Union Catalog*. 2011. http://www.bclstx .org/. Accessed May 22, 2013.

Book Systems. eZCat/eZCat Pro. http://www.booksys.com/ezcat-software. Accessed May 19, 2013.

Boss, Richard W. *RFID Technology for Libraries*. 2011. http://www.ala.org/pla/ tools/technotes/rfidtechnology. Accessed May 20, 2013.

Breeding, Marshall. *Lib-web-cats: A Directory of Libraries throughout the World*. 2012. http://www.librarytechnology.org/libwebcats. Accessed May 21, 2013.

Cordova, Memo. "The Quick Response (QR Code): Graphic Potential for Libraries." *The Idaho Librarian* 61, no. 1 (2011).

IFLA. *Functional Requirements for Bibliographic Records. Final Report*. 2009. http:// www.ifla.org/files/assets/cataloguing/frbr/frbr_2008.pdf. Accessed May 18, 2013.

Koha. http://www.koha.org. Accessed February 20, 2013.

The Library Corporation. *ITS.MARC*. 2011. http://www.itsmarc.com. Accessed January 24, 2013.

Library of Congress. *Bibliographic Framework Initiative*. 2013. http://www.loc .gov/bibframe. Accessed May 20, 2013.

Library of Congress. *MARC and FRBR*. n.d. http://www.loc.gov/marc/marc-functional-analysis/frbr.html. Accessed May 19, 2013.

Library of Congress. *MARC Frequently Asked Questions (FAQ)*. http://www .loc.gov/marc/faq.html#definition. Accessed February 6, 2013.

Library of Congress. *MARC Standards*. 2013. http://www.loc.gov/marc. Accessed May 22, 2013.

Library of Congress. *MARCXML Schema*. 2012. http://www.loc.gov/standards/ marcxml. Accessed May 22, 2013.

Library of Congress. *RDA in MARC*. 2013. http://www.loc.gov/marc/RDAin MARC.html. Accessed May 20, 2013.

Library of Congress. *Understanding MARC Machine-Readable Cataloging*. 2009. http://www.loc.gov/marc/umb. Accessed January 21, 2013.

Library of Congress. *Z39.50 Gateway*. 2011. http://www.loc.gov/z3950. Accessed May 20, 2013.

MakeBarcode.COM. *Barcode Comparison Chart*. 2011. http://www.makebarcode .com/specs/barcodechart.html. Accessed May 15, 2013.

Mitinet Library Services. *MARC Magician*. 2011. http://www.mitinet.com/ Products/MARCMagician.aspx. Accessed May 20, 2013.

OCLC. *OCLC Linked Data.* 2013. http://www.oclc.org/data.en.html. Accessed May 22, 2013.

Schema.org. *What Is Schema.org?* n.d. http://schema.org. Accessed April 21, 2013.

SkyRiver Services. 2013. http://theskyriver.com/services. Accessed May 20, 2013.

Valacich, Joseph S., Joey F. George, and Jeffrey A. Hoffer. *Essentials of Systems Analysis and Design.* 5th ed. Upper Saddle River, NJ: Prentice Hall, 2011.

W3 Consortium. *SKOS Simple Knowledge Organization System Reference. W3C Recommendation 18 August 2009.* http://www.w3.org/TR/skos-reference. Accessed April 24, 2013.

WebClarity Software Inc. *BookWhere.* 2011. http://www.webclarity.info. Accessed January 24, 2013.

WEBSITES

Albertson's Library. "QR Codes." http://guides.boisestate.edu/qrcodes.

International Federation of Library Associations. http://www.ifla.org/en/node/949.

ITS.MARC. Bibliofile. http://www.itsmarc.com/BiblioFileFAQ.asp.

Kaywa code. http://qrcode.kaywa.com.

Library of Congress. http://lcweb.loc.gov.

MARCIVE Inc. http://home.marcive.com/index.php?option=com_content&view=article&id=33&Itemid=45.

Mobile Barcodes.com. http://www.mobile-barcodes.com/qr-code-software.

OCLC. http://www.oclc.org.

OCLC WorldCat. http://www.oclc.org/worldcat.en.html.

Schema.org. http://schema.org.

SKOS. http://www.w3.org/TR/skos-reference.

SkyRiver. http://theskyriver.com.

Chapter 6

LALC Phase 4

SYSTEM IMPLEMENTATION. PART II. INSTALLATION, TESTING, FACILITY, TRAINING, AND TRACKING SYSTEM USE

Following or during the collection preparation, acquisition, or creation of the MARC 21 records during Retrospective Conversion (Recon), and barcoding or tagging the collection, you should begin planning for the installation of the integrated library system (ILS) design of the library facility. This chapter describes various activities performed during this phase of the ILS project. It covers the following main topics:

- Installation

- Testing

- Proprietary ILS

- Open-source ILS

- Configuring the ILS

- Site/facility preparation

- Maintenance

- Training

- Tracking system use

INSTALLATION

Installing the ILS varies across different types of libraries and the process to use depends on the decision you have made during planning and system selection; that is, whether the ILS software will be hosted on premises (on-site) or in the cloud using software-as-a-service (SaaS) or other hosting solution. For on-site hosting, there are four types of software installation: direct installation, parallel installation, single-location installation, and phase installation. Using one or more of these options will be based on the library's needs and priorities. For hosting the ILS by a provider, the latter will be responsible for managing all aspects of the software including installation.

On-Site Installation

Following is a description of each of the four installation options.

Direct Installation

Direct installation is performed when your library is acquiring an ILS for the first time. The ILS software is installed on a network server and access to the software is provided over the library's network.

Parallel Installation

This type of installation is normally used if your library already has an ILS and has migrated to a new one. Both the old and new ILSs can be run in tandem over a period of time (six months to one year) to ensure a smooth migration from the old to the new ILS.

Single-Location Installation

A single-location installation is also known as "pilot" installation. It is recommended in situations where a library is part of consortium of libraries that use a specific ILS. Before going totally live with the ILS, a specific library is selected as the pilot site for the installation. A demo site is created, and the ILS software is installed on a server to be tested for proper operation.

Phase Installation

Phase or incremental installation focuses on the primary modules your library need and can afford. Additional modules can be added as the library's budget allows.

TESTING ON-SITE HOSTED ILS

Three approaches can be used to test the ILS software hosted on-site:

Incremental Testing

This testing is performed at the module level as a component of the larger ILS. The project manager and staff determine what to be tested in the selected module to evaluate its performance and proper operation. During testing, in general, document the errors and problems found in writing using a "test" sheet created for each module. Minor errors or problems may be resolved in-house whereas serious errors and problems should be communicated to the ILS vendor to resolve.

Integrated Testing

This testing may include more than one module or component of the larger ILS. Examples are the circulation module paired with the online catalog (or a third-party *discovery interface* as an add-on) and cataloging; or cataloging and acquisitions; or circulation, cataloging, and the *discovery interface*. Errors are documented and resolved in-house or communicated to the ILS vendor to resolve.

Full Testing

This ILS testing covers the entire ILS to ensure that it is working properly in its entirety and is in line with the specifications and requirements agreed upon with the ILS vendor. Full testing may also include data security and reliability of the ILS.

The ILS should not become available for use before all errors and problems are worked out and staff members are well trained in using it. To test the proper operation of each module before importing MARC 21 and other data, for example, catalog a few titles (in the cataloging module), enter selected patron records, and circulate a few items (in the circulation module), prepare purchase orders (in the acquisitions module), customize selected features (in the management or utilities or the like module), and search for the items you have cataloged in the online catalog or discovery interface, as applicable. Perform other activities in each of the modules including but not limited to sorting records, editing, deleting, and printing records. If peripheral hardware such as barcode scanners are in place, install them to scan item barcodes for checkout and check-in, issue fines, and print mock-up overdue notices. Create a "test" sheet for each module; log what you have tested, and describe the outcome so that errors and problems can be compiled easily. Screenshots of major errors should be included in the test report and communicated to technical staff, if they can be resolved locally; otherwise, the report should be relayed to the ILS vendor to resolve the errors and problems detected during testing.

Once the problems and errors are worked out, *acceptance testing* is performed. The purpose of this testing is to gain confidence that the software, hardware, and peripherals are working properly together and ensure that the ILS is functioning in its entirety to your satisfaction. The next step is to customize the ILS and import the data such as bibliographic records (MARC 21), patron data, acquisitions data, and other data, as applicable.

TESTING FOR OPEN-SOURCE ILS

The nature of testing a hosted ILS varies depending on the type of ILS firm that hosts the software. Testing can be performed by starting a virtual web server for a fee with the ILS service provider and operating it over a period of time as needed (Corrado and Moulaison 2012). Testing can also achieved by using the "sandbox" feature the service provider makes available for access on the web.

To fully test the installed ILS, you should have provided the service provider with copies of the bibliographic data (MARC 21 records), patron records, circulation transaction records, authority records, acquisitions records, item/copy records, and other records from the current ILS, if one is already in place, or export and import the data using a spreadsheet program or database so that you are able to create electronic files that can be converted for loading and testing in testing in the new ILS. This process is needed for records other those that will be converted into a MARC 21 format (e.g., patron records). See the data import section for additional information. In addition, you will need to configure the ILS (set up the library's parameters, policies, etc.) based on your library's workflow and policies. See the next section.

Another type of testing that you should consider is one that many libraries perform during the migration from a current ILS to a new one. This involves extracting sample data from various modules to send to the service provider for testing. The provider may do more than one test of the data loads to ensure correct mapping of all data fields for all types of record. Upon acceptance of the test data, the final data loads are installed in the ILS. You should be able to test these loads using the sandbox to ensure that the data is accepted before going live with the new ILS. Additional information about data extraction, testing, and migration is provided in Chapter 8.

CONFIGURING THE ILS

Each library will need to customize its ILS to brand it in the library environment and its parent organization. Customizing the ILS after software installation consists of setting up system parameters based on the library's workflow needs and policies. These parameters include, but are not limited to creating circulation policies, patron categories, item types, overdue rules, holds rules, and academic calendar. Specifically, defining patron privileges, circulation periods, fines, holds, calendar, and overdue rules are defined in the circulation module. Indexing fields in MARC 21 records, authority headings and fields, display of records in the online catalog or discovery interface (e.g., tagged, labeled, card catalog format), advanced search features, and so forth are defined in the cataloging module. Features such as user tagging, user reviews, banner, colors, search box or boxes, among other things, are customized in the discovery interface or the online catalog as applicable.

Use the ILS manual for instructions on how to set the parameters of your ILS. Note that proprietary ILS is not as customizable as its open-source counterpart. If the ILS software is based on the open system platform, a computer analyst or programmer or technical expert will be able to interface with the parent system using the application programming interface (API) to modify beyond the standard configuration parameters. Use of API requires technical expertise and training. In the case open-source ILS is hosted on-site, the technical expert will take responsibility for all customization. Consulting with the ILS software online community and attending workshops that are normally held by the selected ILS companies at major national conferences (e.g., American Library Association (ALA) annual and mid-year conferences, and Special Library Association annual conference) will add value to your learning about the ILS.

Upon the completion of the ILS configuration, data are imported (downloaded) and/or inputted into the ILS as applicable. Methods for performing these activities are described in the following section.

Data Import into the ILS

Data import will vary based on the library's environment (acquiring an ILS for the first time versus migrating to a new ILS). The amount of data to be imported also varies across libraries. Data sets to import include bibliographic records, circulation records, and other records that support the operation of other modules as applicable. A description of data import into cataloging and circulation modules follows.

Cataloging and MARC 21 Data

If an ILS is procured for the first time, the data converted into a MARC 21 should be ready for import or download onto the network server on-site if this hosting solution has been selected, saved, and indexed (access points for headings are created—author, title, subject, etc.) according to the parameters set up during configuration. Once the discovery interface is ready for use, user access and retrieval of these records becomes available. In addition, the authority records will also be imported, saved (in the authority module), and linked to their respective MARC 21 records. In the case of cloud hosting, copies of data files sent to the service provider will be imported into the ILS, and the library will have a virtual access to the data via a web browser.

Circulation and Patron Data

Unlike cataloging data, the import of the circulation data such as patron records is not cut-and-dry because the data may have been kept in a format that is not compatible with the ILS (manual or paper-based). This situation occurs in a nonautomated library environment. Creating patron records from scratch in the circulation module is time consuming. Staff, students, and other patrons must have circulation records containing last name, first name, address, telephone number, social security number, and e-mail, as well as other borrower's information (e.g., fines and overdues) that should be ported into the ILS after implementation.

The format of patron records must be exported into spreadsheet software or a database so that they can be imported into the ILS circulation module. Webber and Peters (2010) suggest that you sort these records alphabetically or count records by borrower type, city, or zip code, and consider what fields are needed in a borrower's record (e.g., last name, first name, street address, phone, parent information, e-mail address, and birth date). The export of patron data and its import into the ILS will save you a tremendous amount of time that would otherwise be spent on creating patron records manually. Consult with the ILS firm before you import patron records into the ILS. In a cloud hosting environment, the ILS service provider will provide you with guidelines on how to extract the circulation data and advise you about the software application to use for this process.

Other Data

The volume of data to export and import into the ILS will depend on the spectrum of components acquired in the ILS. That is, basic ones (circulation, cataloging, public access) and add-ons (acquisitions, serials, etc.) Data import for these add-on modules should also be exported into specific computer applications (e.g., Excel) to allow for its import into the ILS. As was mentioned earlier, the data export and import should have been discussed in advance with the ILS vendor and addressed in the specifications of the RFP. In the case of data export and import into an open-source ILS, the technical expert in consultation with library staff and possibly the ILS open-source community should be able to carry out these important tasks.

SITE/FACILITY PREPARATION

The acquisition of a new ILS may require purchase of new pieces of hardware that meet the specifications of the software. The spectrum of preparing the facility may vary based on whether the ILS is hosted on-site or in the cloud. This section covers hardware and furniture.

Hardware

The ILS company or firm provides the minimum hardware specifications needed for computers and peripherals.

Computers

Computers are needed to allow users' access to the library's webpage, online catalog or discovery interface, and use of other electronic resources. Increased use of mobile devices including smartphones, iPhones, and tablets may reduce the need for public access computers in many libraries. The online catalog interface or discovery interface or discovery service should be ready for use on these mobile devices. The number of public access computers to purchase will depend on the type of the library, policy for using mobile devices on the library's premises, average number of users that access the library's online catalog interface or discovery interface through the organizational website or library's website, and budget. Analysis of these factors should support your decision making as to the number of computers to purchase in support of public access to the catalog's interface.

Staff Clients

Staff clients are more powerful than public access computers in terms of storage, speed, and functionality. These clients are needed to support the management and operations of the ILS. Web servers are also needed in the event the ILS is hosted on a library's premises. However, the number of these servers will decrease if the ILS software is hosted in the cloud through a service provider. Note that the library also has the option to host hardware in the cloud using the infrastructure-as-a-service (IaaS) model (see Chapter 7) to save on the cost of purchasing and troubleshooting hardware problems. In a cloud-based hosted ILS, the hosting provider will stipulate the minimum specifications for these clients.

Printers

Wireless and power-plugged printers may be purchased based on demands and the use patterns of the online catalog interface on the library's premises. These demands differ by type of library, user community served, and use of mobile devices to access and retrieve information. Increased access through mobile devices will reduce the number of printers needed for public access. Therefore, meeting these demands should be based on analyzing the use patterns in your library.

As to staff demands for printers, the number and type of printers will also depend on the size of the library and use patterns of printers for sharing management reports in hard copies versus digital formats.

Furniture

Public access computers need specific kind of furniture to accommodate wire management, electric needs, and the wires for keyboards and monitors (Baule 2007). Computer chairs also need be based on certain specifications for height and width to accommodate the age of the users or patrons, especially in K–12 settings. When purchasing furniture, pay attention to all users, including those with special needs. Furniture, especially chairs, should be ergonomically designed, safe, and comfortable. The design of the physical facility should support people with disabilities by conforming to the 2010 Americans with Disabilities Act (ADA) Accessible Design (Department of Justice 2010).

The circulation and reference service desks should be of certain height depending on the age of patrons served. For example, the height for serving young patrons (K–7) is lower for both sitting and standing work surfaces than the height for older patrons (K–8 to K–12). The work surface should be ADA-compliant to support serving patrons with special needs. Poorly designed furniture can result in poor health and induce or increase stress, especially in people who use it on a daily basis.

ILS Documentation, Maintenance, and Support

System documentation may be in the form of a manual containing information about software installation, site setup, customization, and search features, indexing, linking authority records, troubleshooting, and so forth. The manual can be accessed in both hard copy and online formats.

The manual for a proprietary ILS will not include the internal coding or diagramming techniques employed in developing the software. In contrast, the manual for an open-source ILS will include coding, diagramming techniques, internal design of the database, and programming language(s) used, among other things. This information allows the technical expert to modify the ILS source code to customize the software.

MAINTENANCE

The maintenance of the ILS software and hardware require continuous maintenance especially if it is hosted on-site. Maintenance covers environmental care, data backup, data security, and database cleanup.

Environmental Care

Hardware, including computers, staff clients, servers, hubs, and other devices supporting the operation of the local network should be located in a cool, clean, and secure area. Cables, wires, servers should be isolated from moisture, mold, and water. Servers should be placed in a safe and environmentally controlled room away from traffic and patron access. Servers should be supplied with an uninterruptible power supply (UPS) device to protect the system against blackouts, surges, and other problems. For additional information see Chapter 7.

Data Backup

Every library must develop a backup strategy for the ILS as part of a library security and/or network plan. Data backup is the creation of a copy (or more than one) of the ILS data files to use in case of data loss caused to hard disk crash, fire, theft, power outage, and accidental deletions. Having a backup plan will eliminate the need for reentering the data. Data stored in the ILS hard disk should be backed up on external hard drives, and/or other devices and stored off-site. If a server is available in the library or in the building, the data are also backed up on the server. Back up data files daily and the entire system once or twice a week. Label the devices used to back up the files, date, and store them in a safe place off-site. It is recommended that you use the ILS manual for instructions on how to back up the data files, and how to restore or recover lost data. Data backup can be also performed by an ILS vendor for a fee. For example, *CyberTools for Libraries* (http://www.cyber toolsforlibraries.com) provides a fee-based data hosting for libraries that need external backups for their data files. Based on the description on its website, all hosted data files remain the property of the library and are shadowed in real time through access to the server residing at the company's hosting site. The data are protected against unauthorized access, and library staff remains in control of updating and copying the data and performing other data management activities. In addition, CyberTools performs daily backups of the data on multiple servers. This cloud hosting solution includes only ILS data files rather than the whole ILS.

If the library data files are to be moved to the cloud, the service contract or agreement should contain provisions for data backup, security, privacy, disaster recovery, network outage procedures, level of service availability, rates of service, data availability in the event the provider goes out of business or is bought, and back up for network connectivity in case a server goes down (Wale 2011).

Network and Computer Security

If the library's ILS is hosted on-site, data and other servers should be protected by a firewall to obstruct unauthorized access. The InfoPeople website (http://infopeople.org) has a resource list on computer and network security. Measures for securing the network include but are not limited the following:

- House the servers in a secure area.
- Install antivirus software.
- Restrict access to the directory structure using files and directories permissions.
- Review server logs periodically.
- Make regular backups.

Security measures are needed to protect the library's computers, staff clients, and servers. These include, but are not limited to, requiring user authentication, installing antivirus software, and educating and also reminding staff about the importance of security (http://infopeople.org/resources/security).

Antitheft Gates

Security measures should be taken to protect the library's collection and prevent theft of library materials. As theft is on the rise in libraries in the United States, many libraries install security gates to prevent or reduce the risk of material theft. Patrons passing through the gates with items that have not been desensitized during checkout will set off the alarm. Library security gates and accessories supporting electromagnetic (EM), radio frequency (RF), and radio frequency identification (RFID) systems vary. For example, two popular RFID security gates are the application family identifier (AFI) and electronic article surveillance (EAS) (Haley, Degnan, and Haefliger 2008). Each of these systems or gates is described in the *Library Security Primer*, published by Brodart Library Supplies (http://www.libraryworks.com/LW_Best%20Practices/BP_Library_Security_Primer_0807.aspx). RFID security systems are more costly than other systems. They require the purchase of RFID tags, readers, and a dedicated server, among other components (Boss 2011). See Chapter 5 for additional information about RFID requirements. Besides Brodart, there are other companies that offer security systems and accessories such as Galord, Minitex, Tech Logic, and 3M (see Table 6.1).

It is advisable that you compare the specifications (specs) and cost of three security systems to determine the one that best meets the library's needs and budget. Security personnel must monitor the library facility on a regular basis to prevent theft, vandalism, and other problems.

Database Cleanup

The ILS databases, such as cataloging and circulation, may require review to detect major errors that could cause information retrieval problems or create disputes with patrons over borrowing privilege. If Recon is outsourced to an

Table 6.1
Selected vendors of security systems and accessories

Company	System Type	Address	URL*
Bibliotheca	RFID	Bibliotheca RFID Library Systems AGErlenstraße 4a 6343 Rotkreuz, Switzerland Phone +41 41 726 99 55	http://www.bib liotheca.com
Brodart Library Supplies	RFID, EM, RF	P. O. Box 3037, Williamsport, PA 17705, 888-820-4377	http://www .brodart.com
EnvisionWare Home	RFID	EnvisionWare Inc., 2855 Premiere Parkway, Suite A, Duluth, GA 30097-5201, 800-216-8370	http://www .envisionware .com
Gaylord Library Supplies	EM, RF	P. O. Box 4901, Syracuse, NY 13221, 800-448-6160	http://www.gay lord.com
Libramation Home	RFID	Libramation Inc., RFID Specialists, 12527-129 Street NW, Edmonton AB, Canada T5L-1H7 780.443.5822, 888-809-0099	http://www .libramation .com/
Minitex	RFID, EM	Minitex, 15 Andersen Library, 222 21st Avenue South, Minneapolis, MN 55455-0439, 800-462-5348, 612-625-9527	http://www .minitex .umn.edu/ Products/3M/ Systems.aspx
Tech Logic Home	RFID	1818 Buerkle Road, White Bear Lake, MN 55110, 800-494-9330	http://www .tech-logic .com
3M Worldwide	RFID, EM, RF	Building 224-2E-40, St. Paul, MN 55119, 800-328-0067	http://www.3m .com/us/ library
VTLS Home	RFID	VTLS Inc. Corporate Headquarters 1701 Kraft Drive Blacksburg, VA 24060, 800-468-8857	http://www .vtls.com

* URLs last accessed on December 15, 2013.

ILS vendor that provides good quality records, then the cleanup of these records would most likely be minimal. Similarly, if Recon is performed in-house by knowledgeable staff using good quality MARC 21 databases, the cleanup could be nominal. However, if Recon is completed in-house by trained volunteers or support staff members who are not well versed with the MARC 21 or other bibliographic rules and formats, the cleanup would be maximal. Some errors caused during Recon (e.g., incorrect indicators, missing added entries) will prevent users from retrieving certain information from the library's online catalog interface or discovery interface. Consider using MARC Magician (MARCIVE).

The circulation database contains borrower's data, and in the event the data were not weeded before implementing the ILS, errors in patron records could cause problems. For example, if a patron had returned a borrowed item but the circulation module reflects that the item is still checked out to the patron and is past due, the patron could be billed for overdue. This problem could result in a dispute with the patron if it is not corrected quickly. Maintaining the integrity of the bibliographic and other data in the ILS is an ongoing process to which staff should attend.

TRAINING

Training is essential because staff and patrons will need to learn how to use the system effectively and efficiently.

Staff

Typically, in libraries with a small number of staff, training includes the entire staff. The form of training and cost should be stipulated in the contractual agreement with the ILS proprietary or open-source company. In larger libraries, one staff member from each unit attends on-site training offered by the company and becomes a trainer for other staff users. The number of days of training will vary based on the spectrum of modules implemented in and the complexity of the ILS. For example, if you acquired the three basic ILS modules (circulation, cataloging, and online catalog) for a small library, two days of training for a system manager may be sufficient. However, if you purchased all modules available in a complex ILS designed for a large academic library, additional days of training will be needed. Training in use of the ILS is provided by proprietary and open-source automation companies. Webinars for system training may be available at a lower cost. Libraries need to weigh whether on-site or remote training best meets their needs.

Patrons

Patrons are usually trained by library staff. Training in use of the ILS online catalog or discovery interface should be part of the library's user instruction or digital information literacy skill program. The depth and breadth of training differ by type of library and the ILS it has acquired. For small libraries such as schools, *Standards for the 21st-Century Learner* (http://www.ala.org/ala/mgrps/divs/aasl/guidelinesandstandards/learningstandards/AASL_Learning Standards.pdf) and *Standards for the 21st-Century Learner in Action* (http://www.ala.org/ala/mgrps/divs/aasl/guidelinesandstandards/learning standards/standardsinaction.cfm) developed by the American Association of School Librarians (AASL) in 2007, provide skills benchmarks for incorporating information literacy standards into the school library program. Similarly, *Information Literacy Competency Standards for Higher Education*, developed by the Association of College and Research Libraries (ACRL) in 2000, focus on making students information literate and provides indicators to measure their performance in meeting each standard (http://www.ala.org/acrl/standards/informationliteracycompetency#stan). These standards are being revised by an ACRL task force during 2013–2014. (http://www.ala.org/acrl/standards/informationliteracycompetency). User training in use of the online catalog should be embedded in every library's user instruction or information literacy program based on national or statewide information literacy standards.

Learning in the 21st century will demand new ways of thinking, innovation, and creativity. Educating patrons in effective use of the online catalog or discovery interface should foster learning, spark creativity, and equip them with the digital skills needed to thrive in the ever-changing digital information environment.

TRACKING SYSTEM USE

One of the primary benefits of the ILS is the generation of a variety of reports to use for managing library operations. For example, gathering transaction data from the circulation module can inform the library manager about collection age, items that circulate the most in a specific subject area, peak transaction activity, and in-library use of materials (if a scanning device is purchased for this purpose), among other things. Reports can be generated based on these data to evaluate the strengths and weaknesses of existing collections by discipline, which can serve as an impetus for requesting funds to enhance the collection in weak subject areas. Peak transaction activities will indicate the need for scheduling additional staff to serve patrons more effectively and efficiently.

The online catalog or discovery interface or discovery service can be used to examine users' search behavior. ILS web analytics can be used to generate detailed reports about users' interaction with the interface or service. These analytics are unobtrusive in that data are collected about users without observing them and provide data sets about user behavior and interaction with the interface that can be much larger than the data obtained from survey questionnaires or interviews (Jansen 2009). Once the log data are parsed, cleaned up, coded, and analyzed, you can obtain a profile of users' information behavior. This includes, among other things, the length of search sessions, type of search strategies, type of queries, length of queries, URLs visited, errors committed, successes, and failures in finding information. The generated data can inform the development of information literacy programs and the level of training that should be provided to enrich the user's information discovery experience. Additional information about evaluating the ILS is covered in Chapter 9.

SUMMARY

The first phase of ILS implementation consisted of a number of activities that one can follow to prepare the library's collection for automation (Chapter 5). In the present chapter, other processes of implementation are described including different software installation models, testing methods, facility preparation including hardware and furniture.

ILS installation varies based on the software model chosen (on-site hosting versus cloud hosting). If an on-site hosting solution is desired, the ILS software can be installed using varied methods: direct installation, parallel installation, single-location installation, or phase installation. Use of one or more of these methods depends on whether the library is automating for the first time or is migrating from an existing ILS to a new one. If the ILS is hosted in the cloud, the hosting company will install the software on one or more servers and provide virtual access to it over the web. A cloud hosting solution could be a good option for small libraries that have a small number of staff and/or lack technical experts on staff. A library may choose to host the ILS software in the cloud using SaaS, or hardware using IaaS, or both solutions. In either case, the library should have a contractual service agreement with the hosting provider that stipulates the provider's responsibilities, nature of service to be provided, and cost. While cloud hosting offers benefits, it can be costly. In addition, there are risks associated with data security and data privacy. Service discontinuation by the provider is another risk. A thorough research of ILS cloud service providers should guide your decision in selecting the best hosting service that meets your library's needs.

Installing the software assumes that compatible hardware is available. This includes public access computers, staff clients, servers, and needed peripheral devices such as inventory devices, self-checkout circulation devices, and printers, among other things. The type of these hardware pieces and number to purchase will differ by the type of the library, use patterns including use of mobile devices (smartphones, tablets, etc.) to access the catalog's interface inside the library, policy for using these devices on premises, and the chosen hosting model of the ILS software.

Following the ILS installation on-site, the general parameters of the ILS are set up (e.g., banner, colors, passwords, and security). Data is imported and/or created in each module and tested for proper operation.

Staff should be trained extensively in how to use the ILS so that they are able to train patrons in using the online catalog interface or discovery interface. Staff should integrate use of the catalog or discovery interface into the library's user instruction or information literacy program. Staff training can be costly. However, webinars on use of the ILS can be less costly. The type of training to choose should be based on the chosen ILS and your library's needs and cost. Staff training by the ILS whether company or open-source firm should be stipulated in the ILS purchase contract.

Data backup for each module should be performed on a regular basis. Antivirus software and firewalls should be in place to protect the security of servers, staff clients, and public access computers running over the network. It is advisable that you maintain a copy of data backups outside of the library premises to use in case of emergency. If the ILS is hosted in the cloud, the service provider will be responsible for data security, system backup, and data privacy.

Tracking use of the online catalog's interface or discovery interface can be achieved through web analytics. Many ILS proprietary companies offer this add-on software application to generate detailed reporting on patron's interaction with the ILS.

REFERENCES

American Association of School Librarians (AASL). "Standards for the 21st-Century Learner." 2007. http://www.ala.org/aasl/standards-guidelines/learning-standards. Accessed January 1, 2013.

Association of College and Research Libraries (ACRL). *Information Literacy Competency Standards for Higher Education*. 2000. http://www.ala.org/acrl/standards/informationliteracycompetency#stan. Accessed September 7, 2013.

Baule, Steven. M. *Facilities Planning for School Library to Technology Centers*. 2nd ed. Worthington, OH: Linworth Publishing Inc., 2007.

Boss, Richard W. "RFID Technology for Libraries." 2011. http://www.ala.org/pla/tools/technotes/rfidtechnology. Accessed January 22, 2013.

Corrado, Edward M., and Heather L. Moulaison. "The Library Cloud: Pros and Cons." *The Digital Shift*. 2012. http://www.thedigitalshift.com/2012/03/software/the-library-cloud-pros-and-cons. Accessed June 25, 2013.

Haley, Connie K., Kathleen Degnan, and Kathleen Haefliger. *Library RFID Technology Update*. 2008. https://sites.google.com/site/chaley102/Home/library-rfid-technology-update. Accessed January 23, 2013.

InfoPeople: Moving Libraries Forward. "Network Security." http://old-infopeople.org/resources/security/networks. Accessed April 3, 2013.

Jansen, Bernard J. *Understanding User-Web Interactions via Web Analytics. Synthesis Lectures on Information Concepts, Retrieval, and Services*. Bonita Springs, FL: Morgan & Claypool, 2009.

U.S. Department of Justice. Americans with Disabilities Act. *2010 ADA Standards for Accessible Design.* http://www.ada.gov/2010ADAstandards_index .htm. Accessed March 16, 2013.

Wale, Carla P. "Cloudy with a Chance of Open Source? An Examination of Open Source Integrated Library Systems and Cloud Computing." 2011. https:// lib.law.washington.edu/lawlibrarianship/CILLPapers/Wale2011.pdf. Accessed July 29, 2012.

Webber, Desiree, and Andrew Peters. *Integrated Library Systems: Planning, Selecting, and Implementing.* Santa Barbara, CA: ABC-CLIO, 2010.

WEBSITES

CyberTools for Libraries. http://www.cybertoolsforlibraries.com.

InfoPeople. http://infopeople.org.

Library Security Primer. http://www.libraryworks.com/LW_Best%20Practices/ BP_Library_Security_Primer_0807.aspx.

Chapter 7

Software, Hardware, and Network Architecture

Advances in technologies, cloud computing, and the offerings many integrated library system (ILS) companies (proprietary and open source) are providing to libraries are shifting library applications to the cloud. In the last few years, libraries have entered "into a new phase of the history of library automation characterized by new technology underpinnings, including cloud computing, fully web-based systems, and service-oriented architecture and fresh approaches to functionality that recognize current library realities" (Breeding 2011). This chapter covers the following main topics:

- Software architecture

- Hardware architecture

- Network architecture

SOFTWARE ARCHITECTURE

In the context of this chapter, software architecture refers to the software deployment models available for libraries to host the ILS. This includes on-site hosting, cloud hosting, and remote hosting

On-Site Software Hosting

Traditionally, libraries have hosted their ILS software on-site (on premises). In this setting, a staff member with IT skills takes responsibility of installing the software and managing the operation of the network. Library personnel store, update, and manage records and patron data in the ILS. The ILS is made accessible to staff and patrons over the web.

Advantages

On-site hosting gives library staff control over the hosted software, trouble-shooting, and data security, among other things.

Disadvantages

On-site hosting incurs cost for hiring personnel with IT skills to maintain and manage the network where the ILS is stored. In addition, servers and other hardware required in support of the ILS software will be needed, thus, bringing upon additional expenses. Software updates may be monthly and are not as frequent as they are for a cloud-hosted application, which may be performed on a daily basis.

Cloud Software Hosting

Many libraries, regardless of type, are migrating from on-site hosting to cloud-based hosting solutions of the ILS. Cloud software hosting is built on a cloud computing platform. According to the National Institute of Standards and Technology (2011), "Cloud computing is a model for enabling ubiquitous, convenient, on-demand network access to a shared pool of configurable computing resources (e.g., networks, servers, storage, applications, and services) that can be rapidly provisioned and released with minimal management effort or service provider interaction" (Mell and Grance 2012). One of the models characterizing cloud computing is software-as-a-service (SaaS), which is described in the next section.

Software-as-a-Service (SaaS)

This cloud computing model provides the capability to run ILSs and other applications on a cloud infrastructure maintained by a designated service provider. The provider manages or controls this underlying infrastructure (e.g., network, servers, operating systems, storage) though there may be limited application configuration settings that the library needs to do up front to customize and gain access to the ILS (http://csrc.nist.gov/publications/nistpubs/800-145/SP800-145.pdf). As one of the service models of "true" cloud computing, SaaS takes advantage of resource pooling, meaning that the service provider's "computing resources are pooled to serve multiple consumers using a multitenant model, with different physical and virtual resources dynamically assigned and reassigned according to consumer demand" (http://csrc.nist .gov/publications/nistpubs/800-145/SP800-145.pdf). Libraries can save on the cost of IT resources, software updates, and hardware infrastructure such as servers, technical personnel salary, and software maintenance contracts, and also other computing resources needed to operate the ILS.

In choosing a SaaS provider, make sure you distinguish between multitenant and single-tenant software hosting.

Multitenant Software Hosting

A multitenant model is built on an architecture where a single instance of the ILS or application is shared by multiple tenants or libraries where each library organization is considered a tenant. Each tenant or library is provided with a limited ability to customize or configure the software (e.g., changing colors in the user interface; changing business rules), but they cannot customize the application's source code (Grant 2012).

Advantages

In this model, any updates that the provider makes to the software are propagated to all its users at once. This is because only one set of ILS application program gains access to a centralized, robust, knowledge base that is shared among the tenants or libraries (Burke 2013). This approach results in quicker updates and upgrades to the software, faster delivery of services to users, and lower cost. In addition, the ability to share global knowledge bases is an advantage of this hosting model.

Disadvantages

This hosting solution requires limited hardware infrastructure for accessing the hosted ILS and a high-speed Internet connection for efficient access through a web browser, thus incurring some cost.

Single-Tenant Software Hosting

A single-tenant software hosting is an architecture where each tenant or library has its software application hosted individually rather than shared with other libraries. A library may be given access to the application's code.

Advantages

In this model, each tenant or library has its own instance of the software stored by the service provider, thus preventing data migration from other tenants or libraries.

Disadvantages

The disadvantages of the single-tenant model overweigh the advantages. Since the provider stores an instance of the ILS software for each tenant or library individually, the provider performs software updates and upgrades to each tenant or library individually, thus incurring more overhead that translates to higher cost for each tenant or library. Another disadvantage of single tenancy is that a tenant or library may experience delay in software updates or upgrades (Grant 2012).

Overall, the SaaS model "has become one of the most desirable solutions for providing access to the ILS software and other electronic materials in libraries" (Corrado and Moulaison 2012). Note that while a service provider uses a centralized hardware platform, the service model may not be a SaaS, especially if each library's ILS is separate and needs to be upgraded individually, negating the real benefits of the new model (Burke 2013).

Remote Software Hosting

In this service model, the ILS provider hosts the ILS software on behalf of the library and runs the hosted application remotely on existing hardware. However, the provider is not responsible for maintaining the software, meaning that software upgrades and maintenance are the responsibility of the library. This solution is also called access service provider (ASP). Note that this hosting service is not a true cloud computing service delivery model.

Advantages

Libraries can save on the cost of hardware because the ILS software is run on the service provider's hardware platform. Because the software is stored in a nonshared environment, there is no potential of data migration from one library's system to another.

Disadvantages

One disadvantage of this solution resides in the library's responsibility of maintaining the ILS software. Because a library's ILS is hosted individually, it does not take advantage of sharing resources with other libraries. In addition, this hosting model is less efficient and flexible than SaaS.

HARDWARE ARCHITECTURE

In the context of this chapter, hardware architecture refers to computers, servers, and devices used to access the ILS. Today's technological environment offers different options for hosting hardware. These are described in the next section.

On-Site Hardware Hosting

The traditional model for hosting the hardware that supports the operation of the ILS software is either on-site or on library premises. This hosting has advantages and disadvantages.

Advantages

On-site hosting provides library staff with control over managing and maintaining hardware. In addition, staff will have control over data privacy, upgrades, and design option for networking the hardware pieces through which the ILS software is accessed.

Disadvantages

On-site hosting incurs a high cost of computers, servers, and networking. In addition, technical or IT personnel will be needed to manage and maintain the hardware and network. Troubleshooting hardware and network problems is time consuming and can reduce the time spent on providing new services to users.

Cloud Hardware Hosting

Cloud computing offers two hardware service models:

Platform-as-a-Service (PaaS)

According to the National Institute of Standards and Technology, PaaS is "the capability provided to the consumer is to deploy onto the cloud infrastructure consumer-created or acquired applications created using programming languages, libraries, services, and tools supported by the provider. The consumer does not manage or control the underlying cloud infrastructure including network, servers, operating systems, or storage, but has control over the deployed applications and possibly configuration settings for the application-hosting environment" (http://csrc.nist.gov/publications/nistpubs/800-145/SP800-145.pdf). In other words, PaaS is "a way to rent hardware, operating systems, storage and network capacity over the Internet. The service delivery model allows the customer [e.g., library] to rent virtualized servers and associated services for running existing applications or developing and testing new ones" (http://searchcloudcomputing.techtarget.com/definition/Platform-as-a-Service-PaaS).

Infrastructure-as-a-Service (IaaS)

According to the National Institute of Standards and Technology, IaaS is "the capability provided to the consumer [e.g., library] is to provision processing, storage, networks, and other fundamental computing resources where the consumer is able to deploy and run arbitrary software, which can include operating systems and applications. The consumer does not manage or control the underlying cloud infrastructure but has control over operating systems, storage, and deployed applications; and possibly limited control of select networking components (e.g., host firewalls)" (http://searchcloudcomputing.techtarget.com/definition/Platform-as-a-Service-PaaS).

IaaS refers to the "provision model in which an organization [e.g., a library] outsources the equipment used to support operations, including storage, hardware, servers and networking components. The hosting service provider owns the equipment and is responsible for housing, running, and maintaining it. The client (library) typically pays on a per-use basis" (http://searchcloudcomputing.techtarget.com/definition/Infrastructure-as-a-Service-IaaS).

Overall, cloud hardware and software hosting may not fit the needs of every library. Therefore, it is important that you gain knowledge of the characteristics, service models, advantages and disadvantages of cloud computing before making a decision to move applications and services into the cloud.

ADVANTAGES OF CLOUD COMPUTING

Cloud computing provides a library with a way to deal with the lack of staff with technical expertise. By outsourcing the ILS software and hardware in the cloud, the cost of computing, in many cases, may be less than the cost of on-site computing (Corrado and Moulaison 2012). Moreover, cloud computing could offer the library reliability through quicker disaster recovery and continuity in case of a system failure. The fact that the hosting service provider uses multiple web servers to host the ILS software and the fact that hardware is independent from the software, a single web server failure, for example, hardly affects services and could be unnoticeable (Wale 2011). According to Miller (2009), additional benefits of cloud computing are the following:

- Lower computer cost: low-end computers may be purchased instead of high-end with processing power or hard disk space.

- Improved performance: computers in a cloud computing system run faster than client computers over a network because multiple servers may be used to host the application program.

- Reduced software cost: the software is installed on one or more servers, and the cost is shared among subscribers, resulting in a lower software cost.

- Instant software updates: updates are available automatically and access to the latest version is usually provided, reducing the time staff takes in downloading an upgrade.

- Increased data reliability and safety: computer crashing in the cloud or local computer crashes on-site should not affect the storage of the data in the cloud.

- Compatible hardware platform: access to applications in the cloud is provided regardless of the computer used (PC or Mac).

- Universal access to applications: access to applications hosted in the cloud is available anywhere and from any computer equipped with a web browser and an Internet connection.

DISADVANTAGES OF CLOUD COMPUTING

Despite the many benefits of cloud computing, there are these disadvantages (Miller 2009):

- Constant Internet connectivity and access to high-speed Internet are required to access the hosted applications.

- Web-based applications tend to be slow at times even when high-speed Internet is available.

- Applications hosted in the cloud may not be as full-featured as the same applications hosted on the premises.

- Data security may be at risk.

- Stored data can be lost if the cloud provider fails to back up the hosted applications.

The bottom line is that a library that is moving its applications into the cloud, must have a reliable high-speed Internet connectivity that is constant because without such connectivity, "it might be a detriment" to access some cloud applications or services (Corrado and Moulaison 2012). While cloud-based hosting of the ILS software can be an option for many small libraries, a network may still be needed on-site (Webber and Peters 2010). As libraries are becoming a part of their larger institution, network management and maintenance has shifted to the IT unit, alleviating the need for technical staff on-site to manage the network. The IT unit has become responsible for contract negotiation with the cloud service provider, licensing, implementing the ILS, fee negotiation, and quality control, among other things, in many institutions. The following section provides guidelines for contract negotiation with a cloud service provider.

CONTRACT NEGOTIATION

A contract with a cloud service provider should detail the provider's responsibilities in relation to managing the daily operations of the ILS, maintaining a quality performance of the system, ensuring data security and backups, keeping up with software upgrades schedule, handling disaster situations, and managing network issues (e.g., bandwidth specifications and downtime) (Webber and Peters 2010). In addition, this document should cover service availability, rates of service, and data availability in the event the provider goes out of business or is bought by another company (Wale 2011).

Some questions to ask of the cloud computing service provider include, but is not limited to, the following:

- What rights does the library have to cloud-based patron data?

- What rights does the hosting provider have to cloud-based data and can the provider mine this data?

- If the library chooses to leave the cloud-based service, what data will be returned and in what format?

- What happens if "you" (the service provider), go out of business, leaves the business, or merges with another company?

- What happens if the library does not pay its bills on time?

- What procedures do you have in place for service downtime?

- How do you determine the cost of the service?

- What happens if some data are lost?

- What architecture do you use for hosting the software (single or multitenant?)

- What is the typical response time of the hosted application or service?

- What is the highest percent in your service uptime?

- What kind of data backup do you do, and how often is it done?

- How do you handle disaster situations?

- What procedures do you have in place for power outage?

- Is the service available 24/7?

- How do you keep up with the ILS software upgrades?

- How do you ensure your network security?

- Does the library need to have a backup of the ILS on-site and run simultaneously with the virtual application?

- Is the ILS hosted virtual application as full-featured as the physical application libraries host on-site?

- What hardware specifications should the library have to support the virtual access of the ILS software?

- What is the minimum Internet speed required to access the hosted applications?

The list of questions above was compiled by the author based on writings by Corrado and Moulaison (2012); Wale (2011); Breeding (September 2011; 2013); Webber and Peters (2010); and Miller (2009).

NETWORK ARCHITECTURE

A network architecture consists of "a set of specifications that defines every aspect of a data network's communication system, including but not limited to the types of user interfaces employed, the networking protocols used and the structure and types of network cabling that may be used" (http://www .wildpackets.com/resources/compendium/glossary_of_networking_terms#N).

Today, managing and maintaining the library's network has shifted to the larger institution's IT unit. The latter determines and maintains the network architecture. In small or special libraries, a technology expert manages and maintains the network owned by each library.

In an academic setting, David Ratledge, Head of Digital Services, for example, describes the responsibilities between the academic library technical staff and the institution's IT unit as follows:

> The library desktop support staff primarily takes care of library faculty and staff non-server computing needs. The rest of my department includes another Systems Librarian besides myself and six technical staff that take care of many of our online public services such as the physical servers we run, our library web sites, the programming/development/web serving part of our many digital collections, our inter-library loan system, media streaming, digital signage, and so on. Another Systems Librarian and her two technical staff in another library department are responsible for running the library catalog, discovery system, link resolver, proxy server, and play a big role in eResources.

Ratledge also notes that:

> Most networked computers in our public access areas are managed by staff in the IT unit. They buy and replace them with Tech Fee funds, install and configure them (hardware and software), and repair them if they break. The few areas still managed by library's desktop support staff are Map Services that use highly complex software and configurations. It is anticipated, however, that all networked computers in public access areas will eventually be managed by the campus IT unit.

The exceptions are the ones I noted above. The reason for these exceptions is that the IT unit likes to build computers all the same, while these particular cases require specialized software and configurations so we handle them ourselves. The network these computers connect to are fully managed by the IT unit. We pay them a monthly fee for each network port we have and they do the work of turning them on, installing them [where] we need them if one isn't already there, and repairing them if they break. The Unit also pays for and manages the routers and switches that are scattered in closets throughout our library buildings that all the ports connect to. The Unit pays for, installs, and maintains all the wireless access ports as well.

In a school library setting, Scot Smith, a librarian in a middle school, describes similar responsibilities between staff and the larger IT unit of the school district or administration, but at a smaller scale.

Only staff from the IT department has network access. Staff workstations are unlocked, but the IT department handles all network issues. A staff member from the IT department is the district administrator for the ILS. Each librarian has complete control over the school-level administration of the ILS. ILS updates are handled by the IT staff and no librarian has that level of access to the program/application. All student workstations are locked. To install updates or a new application, student computers must be unlocked by IT.

Although you do not need to be articulate in network architecture and technologies, it is important that you obtain a basic level of knowledge about networking concepts, standards, and protocols so that you are able to communicate with IT staff about issues or problems as they arise in your library. The next section describes various telecommunications for connecting to the Internet including broadband access.

Broadband

The Federal Communications Commission (FCC) defines broadband as a "high-speed Internet access allows users to access the Internet and Internet-related services at significantly higher speeds than those available through 'dial-up' Internet access services. Broadband speeds vary significantly depending on the particular type and level of service ordered and may range from as low as 200 kilobits per second (kbps), or 200,000 bits per second, to 30 megabits per second (Mbps), or 30,000,000 bits per second. Some recent offerings even include 50 to 100 Mbps. Broadband services for residential consumers typically provide faster downstream speeds (from the Internet to your computer) than upstream speeds (from your computer to the Internet)" (http://www.fcc.gov/guides/getting-broadband).

Different types of broadband used in libraries include: Digital subscriber line (DSL), coaxial cable, fiber-optic cable, and wireless, among others.

Digital Subscriber Line (DSL)

A DSL provides high-speed Internet connections using regular telephone lines. DSL transmits data faster over traditional copper telephone lines. It uses different frequencies that split voice and data services over the same phone line, meaning that a telephone call and an Internet connection can share the same DSL link. Access with DSL is *asymmetric*—the downstream channel has a higher transmission rate than the upstream channel. Because DSL is a dedicated service, each user has a private circuit to the central phone line. Consequently, neither the service speed nor the bandwidth is affected in using the Internet.

Coaxial Cable

A coaxial cable access provides high-speed Internet connections through use of the cable television company's infrastructure. Coaxial cable has a single core conductor surrounded by layers of insulation and shielding.

Fiber-Optic Cable

A fiber-optic cable offers significantly higher transmission rates than DSL or coaxial cable. An optical fiber is a "thin, flexible medium that conducts pulses of light, with each pulse representing a bit" (Kurose and Ross 2009, 23). The attenuation signal for a fiber-optic cable is measured as decibels per kilometer (db/km). A fiber-optic cable can carry hundreds of gigabits per second and transmits data at speeds 20 times faster than DSL or coaxial cable connections (http://www.itu.int/osg/spu/publications/birthofbroadband/faq.html). Because it uses light to transmit signals, it is not subject to electro-magnetic interference (EMI).

A fiber-optic cable can be used as the network's backbone. A coaxial cable connects to the fiber-optic cable through a fiber node. The node connects to the

Table 7.1
Categories of twisted-pair cables

Category	Data Rate (Mbps)
Cat5	100
Cat5e	125
Cat6 (unshielded)	200

head end of the coaxial cable through which data transmission is achieved. This type of connection exists in a hybrid fiber-coaxial (HFC) access network (Kurose and Ross 2009).

The two main types of fiber-optic cables are fiber-to-the-home (FTTH), where a fiber cable is run directly to a designated location or library; and fiber-to-the-node (FTTN), where a fiber cable is run to a node where there is an existing telephone line (copper) that delivers the service to a designated location or in library (Salway 2012).

Wireless

"Wireless broadband uses a radio link between the user's location and the service provider's facility" (Salway 2012). Wireless technologies have made their ways to many rural areas that did not have DSL, cable, or other broadband services due to high cost. Connection to the Internet has become a reality to these areas (Kurose and Ross 2009) and provided opportunities to libraries that have automated their catalogs to establish presence on the web. Besides the local network, a library may be a part of a larger wide area network (WAN) to share the ILS with other libraries. A WAN covers a much larger geographic area than a local building or a group of building. It can expand over a whole city, country, or boundaries, or worldwide. WAN uses varied broadband services including but not limited to fiber-optic cables, coaxial cables, and telephone lines. The Internet is an example of the largest WAN in the world (Shelly and Vermaat 2011).

NETWORK PROTOCOLS, TOPOLOGIES, AND STANDARDS

Protocols

A protocol is "a standard that outlines characteristics of two network devices communicate" (Shelly and Varmaat, 2011, 477). The primary network protocol is the Transmission Control Protocol (TCP) Internet Protocol (IP), referred to as TCP/IP, which "defines how messages (data) are routed from one end of a network to the other, ensuring data arrives correctly" (Shelly and Vermaat, 2011, 478). All operating systems (e.g., Windows, Linux, Unix, and Mac OS X) have TCP/IP capabilities (see also IPv6 section).

Internet Protocol Version 6 (IPv6)

IPv6 is the current standard of communication across networks and over the Internet. IPv6 expands on the current IP standard known as IPv4.

Compared to IPv4, IPv6 offers better addressing, security, and other features to support large worldwide networks (Mitchell 2013). Unlike IPv4 which is based on a 32-bit address system, this protocol is based on 128-bit address, and supports a very high number of Internet addresses. Many networks continue to use IPv4 because IPv6 is backwardly compatible. Use of the IPv6 protocol will allow the amalgamation of varied devices (e.g., PCs, cell phones, home appliances) to run over the Internet (Mitchell 2013). Deployment of IPv6 requires training and compatible hardware (Hilson 2012).

Topologies

A network topology refers to the physical layout of computers and devices connected in a network. The most common topology used in modern Ethernet is the "star" where all computers and devices on the network connect to a central switch forming a star. The switch replaced the hub in the early 2000s. A switch is a network device that provides a connection between two or more computers on a network with some intelligence. That is, it forwards data only to the designated port rather than to all connected ports instead of every port in the connected network like the hub does.

In modern Ethernet, the physical media may be a mixture of twisted-pair cables and fiber-optic cables and at varied transmission speeds (see the next section on modern Ethernet for additional information). Almost all networks use high-performance Ethernet switches as backbones.

Standards

"A network standard defines guidelines that specify the way computers access the medium to which they are attached, the type(s) of medium used, the speed used on different types of networks, and the type(s) of physical cable and/or the wireless technology used" (Shelly and Varmaat 2011, 477). The

Table 7.2
Ethernet type, name, data rates, and cable/fiber category

Type	Ethernet Name	Date Rate	Cable/Fiber
100BASE-T	Twisted-pair	100 Mbps	CAT5e
1000BASE-T	Gigabit twisted-pair	1 Gbps	CAT6
10GB-SR*	10GBASE-SR	10 Gbps	MMF**
10GB-LR+	10GBASE-LRM	10 Gbps	MMF

*SR = short reach; +LR = long reach; **MMF = multimode fiber.

Institute of Electrical and Electronics Engineers (IEEE) is a leading organization that develops international standards in areas such as telecommunications, information technology, power generation products, and services. Example of these standards is IEEE 802 for wireless networking (http://www.ieee.org).

Modern Ethernet

Ethernet is the most common network in use today. Modern Ethernet runs on twisted-pair cable or fiber-optic cable (OC192). High-performance Ethernet networks are used for high-volume traffic with an Internet backbone that is mostly built on T4 and faster. "An OC192 is a super large group of T1 lines that are used by large businesses and campuses as the network backbone. The OC192 provides high-speed connection and is capable of transmitting data at a whopping 9.6 gigabits per second. OC192 provides the largest bandwidth available and can handle full motion, real-time video, sound, very large databases and any number of other Internet applications over a busy network" (Theoduru 2013). (OC stands for Optical Carrier; 192 refers to the digital signal range.)

The different categories of Ethernet are as follows:

> 100BASE-T: This is considered a fast Ethernet based on IEEE 802.3u standard. It uses UTP Category 5 (Cat5) cable and can transmit data at a transfer rate up to 100 Mbps.

> 100BASE-FX: This a fast Ethernet based on the standard; it uses a baseband fiber-optic cable, requires a multimode fiber, and transmits data at 100 Mbps (Dean 2012).

> 1000BASE-T: Gigabit Ethernet that uses UTP Category 5e cable (Cat5e), or Cat6, or Cat7 can transmit data at a maximum transfer rate of 1 Gbps (Shelly and Vermaat 2011).

> 1000BASE-LX: It transmits data at 1,000 Mbps or 1 Gbps LX (i.e., long reach) because it relies on long wavelengths cable (maximum 5,000 meters).

> 1000BASE-SX: It is similar to the LX in terms of transmission throughput (i.e., 1 Gbps). The difference is that it relies on multimode fiber cable and uses short wavelengths cable from the node to the hub or switch (220 to 500 meters).

IEEE standard 802.3ae has also specified varied options of the 10-Gigabit fiber-optic Ethernet. This includes the 10GBase-SR (short reach, for use in local or building level networks) and 10GBase-SW (short reach, for use in WANs). The 10GBase transmits data at 10 Gbps. There is also a "long reach" equivalent to each of these (10GBase-LR and 10GBase-LW, respectively) (Table 7.2). Each of these has an equivalent Ethernet technology with "extended reach"

Table 7.3
Selected companies for network products and media

Name	Web Address*	Phone Number
Cisco	http://www.cisco.com	800 553 NETS (6387)
HP Networking Solutions	http://h17007.www1.hp.com/ us/en/index.aspx	(800) 334 514
Lucent Technologies Inc.	http://www.alcatel-lucent .com/wps/portal/Products	(908) 508 8080
Proxim Wireless	http://www.proxim.com	(800) 229 1630
Solectek Broadband Wireless	http://www.solectek.com	(858) 450 1220
Waters Network Systems	http://www.watersnet.com	(800) 328 2275

* URLs last accessed December 15, 2013.

(the longest fiber-optic cable) (10GBase-ER and 10GBase-EW, respectively) (Dean 2012).

The first part of the Ethernet acronym refers to the speed (e.g., 100, 1,000) and Mbps stands for megabits per second. "BASE refers to the baseband Ethernet, meaning that the physical media only carries Ethernet traffic" (Kurose and Ross 2009, 484). The final part of the acronym (e.g., T) indicates the physical media used. For example, the 1000BASE-T used twisted-pair copper wires. Much faster Ethernet are 40 GBase (40 Gbps) and 100-GBase (100 Gbps) (Shelly and Vermaat 2011).

SUMMARY

Today, libraries have different models for hosting the ILS software and hardware. These software models or architecture include on-site hosting, SaaS, and traditional remote hosting. Each model has advantages and disadvantages. SaaS is one of the three service models that characterize "true" cloud computing; it is the trend in libraries.

The other two service models of cloud computing are PaaS and IaaS. Like the SaaS model, these two hardware architecture models offer cost savings and efficiency in managing library operations and providing services to users.

Before migrating software and hardware to the cloud, you should become familiar with the advantages and disadvantages of cloud computing and understand the terminology so that you become capable enough to communicate with the IT personnel in charge of negotiating a contractual agreement with cloud service providers.

In addition to software and hardware architecture, you should develop a basic level of knowledge about networking architecture including, but not limited to broadband access, network topology, and standards. In general, broadband access is made via a DSL, coaxial cable, fiber-optic cable, or wireless, among others. The recent Internet network protocol in place is IPv6 (IP version 6).

The star topology is commonly used in today's modern Ethernet. Modern Ethernet runs on twisted-pair cable or fiber-optic cable (OC192). High-performance Ethernet networks are used for high-volume traffic with an Internet backbone that is mostly built on T4 and faster. The different categories of Ethernet vary in terms of transmission speed and cabling used. Hosting ILS applications in the cloud requires a fast Ethernet. Ethernet technologies used the IEEE 802.3 standard.

REFERENCES

Breeding, Marshall. "Automation Marketplace 2011: The New Frontier." April 2012. http://lj.libraryjournal.com/2011/03/library-services/automation-marketplace-2011-the-new-frontier/. Accessed August 1, 2013.

Breeding, Marshall. "Automation Marketplace 2013: The Rush to Innovate." April 2013. http://www.thedigitalshift.com/2013/04/ils/automation-marketplace-2013-the-rush-to-innovate. Accessed March 20, 2013.

Breeding, Marshall. "The Cloudy Forecast for Libraries." September 2011. http://www.infwaotoday.com/cilmag/sep11/Breeding.shtml. Accessed August 1, 2013.

Burke, Jane. "We Are Ready for the New Model. But Is It Ready for Us?" 2013. http://www.serialssolutions.com/en/words/detail/we-are-ready-for-the-new-model.-but-is-it-ready-for-us. Accessed March 30, 2013.

Corrado, Edward M., and Heather L. Moulaison. "The Library Cloud: Pros and Cons." *The Digital Shift*. 2012. http://www.thedigitalshift.com/2012/03/software/the-library-cloud-pros-and-cons. Accessed January 18, 2013.

Dean, Tamara. *Networks+ Guide to Networks*. 6th ed. Boston, MA: Course Technology, Cengage Learning, 2012.

Federal Communications Commission. What Is Broadband? 2012. http://www.fcc.gov/guides/getting-broadband. Accessed July 16, 2013.

Grant, Carl. The Future of Library Systems: Library Services Platforms. 2012. *Information Standards Quarterly*, 24 (4): 1–13. Available: http://www.niso.org/apps/group_public/download.php/9922/FE_Grant_Future_Library_Systems_%20isqv24no4.pdf.

Hilson, Gary. "World IPv6 Launch Day Is Here: Time for an IPv6 Deployment Strategy." 2012. http://www.networkcomputing.com/ipv6tech-center/world-ipv6-launch-day-is-here-time-for-a/240001570/. Accessed January 11, 2013.

IEEE Standards Association. IEEE 802.3: Ethernet. 2012. http://standards.ieee
.org/about/get/802/802.3.html. Accessed July 1, 2013.

Kurose, James F., and Keith W. Ross. *Computer Networks: A Top-Down Approach.*
5th ed. New York: Addison-Wesley, 2009.

Mell, Peter, and Timothy Grance. The NIST Definition of Cloud Computing:
Recommendations of the National Institute of Standards and Technology.
2012. http://csrc.nist.gov/publications/nistpubs/800-145/SP800-145.pdf.
Accessed July 16, 2013.

Miller, Michael. *Cloud Computing: Web-Based Applications That Change the Way
You Work and Collaborate Online.* Indianapolis, IN: Que Publishing, 2009.

Mitchell, Bradley. "IPv6." 2013. http://compnetworking.about.com/od/
networkprotocolsip/g/bldef_ipv6.htm. Accessed January 2, 2014.

Ratledge, David. *Dania Bilal's Interview with David Ratledge, Head of Digital Initiatives, The University of Tennessee Libraries, Knoxville, Tennessee.* May 31, 2013.

Salway, David. "Not All Broadband Is Created Equal: Different Broadband
Technologies Deliver Higher Speeds." 2012. http://broadband.about.
com/od/technologyandbandwidth/a/Not-All-Broadband-Is-Created-
Equal.htm. Accessed January 18, 2013.

Shelly, Gary, and Misty Vermaat. *Discovering Computers 2011: Living in a Digital
World.* Boston, MA: Course Technology, Cengage Learning, 2011.

Smith, Scot. *Dania Bilal's Interview with Scot Smith, Librarian Media Specialist
Robertsville Middle School, Oak Ridge, Tennessee.* May 30, 2013.

Theoduru, Van. OC192 Internet. 2013. http://www.worldnetsolutionsinc
.com/oc192-internet. Accessed July 16, 2013.

Wale, Carla P. *Cloudy with a Chance of Open Source? An Examination of Open
Source Integrated Library Systems and Cloud Computing.* 2011. https://
lib.law.washington.edu/lawlibrarianship/CILLPapers/Wale2011.pdf.
Accessed April 25, 2013.

Webber, Desiree, and Andrew Peters. *Integrated Library Systems: Planning,
Selecting, and Implementing.* Santa Barbara, CA: ABC-CLIO, 2010.

Chapter 8

System (ILS) Migration

Today's digital age poses many challenges to all libraries willing to "offer an experience that has the simplicity of Google—which users expect—while searching the library's rich digital and print collections—which users need" (Luther and Kelly 2011). Increasingly, many libraries are turning to a new generation of integrated library system (ILS) powered with search tools that allow for information discovery. A recent survey of librarians' assessments of their library-automated systems reveals that these information professionals "want their software to be intuitive, capable, and modern" (Breeding and Yelton 2011, 11). Many libraries are migrating to new ILSs, whether proprietary and open source. Although the migration from one system to another fluctuates, every library will eventually migrate to a new ILS at least once after its procurement of the original ILS. This chapter describes the process of migration and covers the following main topics:

- What is migration?
- Why migrate?
- The process of migration
  - Tasks to undertake
    - Data cleanup
    - Data extraction and testing
- Data migration through outsourcing
  - Criteria for choosing a data migration outsourcing company

◦ Questions to ask

• Successful migration

WHAT IS MIGRATION?

Migration is the process of moving ILS applications from one ILS to another that better meets the library's needs. A full migration is not in total a repeat of the LALC since the data that resulted from the Recon project the first time around need not to be converted again, thus saving time and money on record conversion. However, the ILS project team needs to look at the system requirements and functionalities with a different perspective. The rapidly increasing expectations of users and the continuously evolving way libraries are expected to meet the challenges of the digital age will necessitate new ways for evaluating ILSs (Cervone 2007). Cervone notes that in the past, library-automated systems have been evaluated along standardized lines, such as developing requirements for circulation, cataloging, acquisitions, and so forth. Today, the focus in system evaluation should take into account the continuously changing nature of services and practices and the evolving needs and expectations of users.

WHY MIGRATE?

Migration to a new ILS is a continuous trend by libraries, especially those owning legacy systems. The overarching motivation for migration to a "modern" ILS is the ability to tailor the new ILS more closely to their needs and requirements and meet today's user information needs and expectations (Boss 2008; Walls 2011). There are many specific reasons for migration. These include, but are not limited to, the following:

• The existing ILS is traditional in its interface design and features, and the library is moving toward enhancing the user's experience and information discovery while providing staff with robust modules that are customizable and responsive to their needs and requirements.

• The existing ILS is old, inefficient, and the vendor no longer supports the software.

• The recurring cost of the existing ILS is high, especially when compared to the features and functionalities it supports; the return on investment (ROI) can no longer be justified.

• The ILS's vendor performance is unsatisfactory.

• The library is joining a regional or state-wide consortium and will migrate to the system decided upon by the library consortium group.

THE PROCESS OF MIGRATION

Most of the steps involved in selecting and implementing a new ILS (see Chapters 5 and 6), apply to migration to a new ILS, including the formation of an advisory committee with a project manager to assess the needs and explore various options of migration (proprietary or open-source software (OSS) ILS). This is especially true in terms of defining and gathering user needs and requirements, evaluating existing ILSs, developing specifications (in the form of a request for proposal (RFP)), or drafting a document profiling the desired ILS. In defining needs this time around, it is important to assess the weaknesses and strengths of the existing ILS, identify unresolved system problems, and note the positive features and functionalities that the new ILS should and must have.

At the core of ILS migration is the *data* that will have to be exported from the current ILS and imported into the new ILS. Understanding the schemas and scripts (e.g., SQL) employed in the current ILS is critical for retrieving data that will be used for testing in the new ILS. Similarly, an adequate level of knowledge of the MARC 21 and associated standards employed in the system are important for understanding the structure and relationships across the components of the entire ILS. What is the relationship between bibliographic records and corresponding item records? What elements does a MARC 21 record include? (e.g., variable fields, fixed fields, tags, indicators, subfield codes, and delimiters) and what current practices are in place?. Learning about the structure of existing records in all modules of the ILS (e.g., circulation, acquisitions, and serials) should allow you to develop an understanding of the various fields in these records and how they should map into the new ILS under consideration.

Tasks to Undertake

Migrating from one system to another is a tedious process and involves tasks that you should do and tasks that the replacement vendor or firm will do. The level of work associated with your tasks will depend on whether you will fully or partially outsource the migration and the type of system to which you will be migrating. For example, if your library is migrating to an open-source ILS, you will be performing most of the work. That is, identify data to extract from various modules in the existing ILS, extract the data, install the ILS test site, load the data, test the data, and identify errors or problems in data mapping, retest the data after the problems are fixed, as applicable, and import the data into the new system upon implementation of the new ILS. If you are considering an OSS ILS, consult the OSS online community site for guidelines about the process. In addition, consult with the company or firm that supports the chosen OSS ILS about the process. Case studies of migration can be valuable for learning about the process and avoiding problems that others have committed. For example, there are case studies at both the national and international levels of libraries that have completed the migration process that can be valuable to you and other libraries that are undergoing ILS migration. At the international level, for example, Balas (2011) examines case studies of ILS migration by libraries in various developing countries that have migrated to free or OSS and especially those countries that are in partnership with the Electronic Information for Libraries (EIFL), a nonprofit organization that works with libraries worldwide to enable access to digital information in 60 developing and transition countries in Asia, Africa, Europe, and Latin America. It is based in Europe with a global network of partners (http://www.eifl .net/who-we-are#name). EIFL's project, Free Open-Source Software (FOSS), is designed to help libraries to evaluate and migrate to FOSS and OSS ILS. Projects, tools, and ILS case studies are found at http://www.eifl.net/foss-projects-tools. Other companies that offer migration services to open source is BibLibre (http://www.biblibre.com/en), which is located in Marseille, France.

At the national level, Singh (2013) describes the migration process and experiences of librarians in rural Appalachia and nearby regions, whereas Walls (2011) reports on the experience of the NYU health sciences libraries' migration from an existing proprietary ILS to an OSS ILS. Covering both national and international levels, Breeding's *Integrated Library System Turnover*, available through his *Library Technology Guide* (http://www.librarytechnology.org/ils-turnover .pl), provides a chart that identifies the name of each ILS and number of libraries that have acquired the given ILS along with the names of ILSs replaced and the number of libraries that had these products. As of May 2013, reports with charts of ILS acquisitions and replacements are available for the period from 2007 to 2013. You can limit the search to a specific year and by academic or public libraries. Breeding notes that the numbers in each report are not comprehensive as they only include libraries that are registered in *lib-web-cats*, a directory of libraries worldwide (http://www.librarytechnology.org/libwebcats). Clicking on a given ILS in the chart will direct you to the names of libraries that have acquired the software. Contacting these libraries to learn about their migration experiences should enrich your learning experience about the migration process.

Besides learning about the migration process and the existing ILS in terms of its components, data, and record structure in the modules, you will need to weed and inventory the collection and clean up the data in the current ILS. Refer to Chapter 5 for detailed information about weeding and inventorying the collection. Data cleanup is covered in the next section.

Data Cleanup

Data cleanup is highly recommended before migrating to the new ILS to save time and money in the long term. Following is a list of sample tasks to undertake in preparation for data cleanup:

- Take an inventory of your library's collection to ensure that collection titles on the shelf are in the cataloging database (i.e., MARC 21 bibliographic records) and vice versa.

- Remove bibliographic records for which you have no holdings.

- Decide on what to do with records for missing or lost items from the collection. If you want to keep them, negotiate with the ILS replacement company how the export of these items will be handled in terms of status (i.e., codes used) such as *lost*, *withdrawn*, or *missing*.

- Weed your collection and remove bibliographic records for withdrawn items from the cataloging database.

- Identify bibliographic records that have data field problems and correct them. These fields may include, but are not limited to access points (main entry, title, added entries, subject headings, and content notes); call numbers and call number prefixes; MARC tags, indicators, and subfield codes; misspellings; and abbreviations. If these corrections are not possible at the time you are migrating, flag these records to correct at a later time.

- Evaluate the circulation database (transactions, fines, overdue notices, and other patron information). Purge records of patrons who are no longer affiliated with the host institution. Make sure that all patron records with overdue items and fines are cleared. If not, discuss this matter with the replacement company representative to determine how to handle these records.

If you are considering an OSS ILS, you will need to clean up the data in the same way as already described. Seek advice from the OSS community and/ or colleagues that have undergone data migration to the same ILS you are considering. If you have a contract with a firm to manage the migration project, inquire about guidelines for data migration and required cleanup.

Regardless of the type of the replacement ILS under consideration (OSS or proprietary), you should communicate with both the ILS company or firm that supports the existing software and the company or firm of the ILS under consideration. From the former, you need to obtain information about data export from the current system, whereas from the latter, you need to learn about the process of data export, testing, and import into the new ILS, among other things. Before proceeding with data export, make sure you develop specifications for data migration, identify sample data to extract from existing modules, and develop data testing procedures.

Data Extraction and Testing

Data extraction can be a time-consuming and challenging process. At the outset, it is recommended that you familiarize yourself with the existing data schemas and scripts of the current ILS so that you are able to extract appropriate data sets from various modules that should be tested in the ILS to which you are migrating. Data testing should include all types of records (bibliographic, patron, authority, circulation transactions, etc.).

To ensure the compatibility of the existing data with the new ILS data schemas, do the following:

- Install a test version of the new ILS (or a demo site) after ensuring that the compatible hardware is in place and has been configured. This version may be supplied by the ILS replacement company/firm; it can also be developed in-house for an OSS ILS.

- Develop your own scripts (e.g., XML, SQL, and Javascript) and extract data from each module in the existing ILS for testing, including data with normal and problematic elements or features (e.g., records with long fields in the MARC 21 records; patron records with fines, overdues, and prohibited access to certain collection items). You may extract data that works well with .xls or .cvs file extensions (Cervone 2007). If writing such scripts is not possible and the library does not have the technical expertise to do so, consider hiring a consultant or outsourcing some parts of the migration process to a company that specializes in data migration.

- Run tests on extracted data sets, review results, and keep test logs. Tests should include data with long and short fields, fields with special symbols, characters, and/or codes, and content notes, among others. Examine whether records are formatted based on the MARC 21 standard and that they are correctly formatted; check whether data are described based on the Anglo-American Cataloging Rules (AACR2R) or Resource Description and Access (RDA), and that all data are in the appropriate fields.

- When tests are run on MARC 21 records, examine the accuracy of the following:

  ○ Full MARC records with fields such as 520 and 505

  ○ Brief MARC records

  ○ MARC records for multivolume items and multiple copy items

  ○ MARC records with long call numbers.

- When tests are run on circulation records, examine the accuracy of the following:

  ○ New and existing patron IDs or numbers to input

  ○ Patron status, address, and other information

  ○ Items with fines and overdues, as applicable

  ○ Item checkouts (to examine whether the status appears in bibliographic records) and item check-ins (to ensure that the status appears in bibliographic records and that no coded field is missing or incomplete).

- Run tests using the ILS and hardware peripherals (e.g., scanner, printer, and self-checkout device) to ensure proper workability. Identify problems and relay them to technical staff (as applicable) or the outsourcing company.

- Run new tests after problems are fixed and before going "live" to ensure proper transformation or mapping of data from the current to the new ILS.

- Ensure that extracted data transform or map well in the test version or demo site for each data entity, field, and across the overall database (macro-data). This is part of understanding data schemas in the current and new ILS.

See also the section on "Data Migration through Outsourcing" for questions to ask of an ILS replacement company about circulation and bibliographic data. For these questions, consider developing tasks to perform during testing.

- Allow sufficient time for data testing and problem solving of data that do not load or map well in the ILS test version of the software. It may take more than four weeks to perform data testing, and therefore, you should factor the expected time for completing data loading, testing, and correction of errors in the migration project timeline.

DATA MIGRATION THROUGH OUTSOURCING

If a proprietary ILS is being considered, or if you are hiring a firm to manage the data migration project of the OSS under consideration, you will be asked to provide sample data sets to the company or firm to test in the ILS under consideration on their system. The data sets should be extracted based on the guidelines provided by the company or firm. The data will be tested and records that fail to load and/or records that loaded properly but have errors will be identified, and strategies for solving the problems will be communicated to the library. After the problems have been corrected, another data testing should be performed by the company or firm, and once the final data tests are accepted by the library, the data should be ready for import into the ILS upon the implementation of the ILS software. Note that the ILS company or firm should be given a reasonable time to correct data loading (e.g., 30 days) and perform more than one data testing.

Criteria for Choosing a Data Migration Outsourcing Company

Libraries that are migrating to a new ILS and planning on outsourcing the data migration project should consider these criteria:

- The previous level of experience with successful data migration for all types of records (MARC 21, circulation, etc.) of the company or firm

- The performance record of the company or firm in exporting and importing ILS data

- The accuracy level of data migration provided by the company or firm to libraries like your own in the past years

- The reliability record of the migration projects or activities of the company or firm

- The number of data tests the company or firm is willing to handle

- The level of support the company or firm is willing to provide during and after the migration process. This should be determined not only by asking the company or firm, but also by communicating with colleagues and finding reviews, among other things.

Questions to Ask

If an RFP is developed to secure a new proprietary ILS, make sure data migration is covered in the proposal. For example, include how the current ILS handles circulation data, bibliographic data, and other data supported, and ask questions about how the ILS under consideration will handle such data. Sample questions about the circulation data include the following:

- How does the system handle current circulation transactions?

- How does the system handle overdues?

- How does the system handle holds?

- How does the system handle fines?

- How does the system handle fines that are pending?

- How does the system handle items with missing or lost status?

- How does the system handle reserve transactions?

- How does the system handle records created "on-the-fly?"

- What barcode symbology (if this barcode system is being considered) or radio frequency identification (RFID) tags does the system support?

Sample questions to ask about bibliographic data include the following:

- What standards do you use for data records?

- How do bibliographic records relate to item records?

- How are links to bibliographic records, item records, and other interacting records established and broken?

- What fields exist in long bibliographic records?

- What fields exist in short bibliographic records?

- What fields are copied from a bibliographic record to a linked record?

- What data fields do you support in bibliographic records?

- What is the size of each data field in each type of record?

- How do you handle the export of nonstandard and customized MARC 21 records?

- How do you handle MARC 21 records imported from the web that have missing data fields?

- How do you handle MARC 21 records that contain errors in cataloging?

- To what extent do the MARC 21 records you supply conform to the Library of Congress MARC 21 format?

- How will the new system handle volume holdings?

- How will the new system handle multiple copy holdings?

- How will you handle authority records?

- What MARC 21 field does the current system support for local holdings?

Provide a description for some of the items just listed. For example, when asking about the MARC 21 field for local holdings, mention whether your existing ILS supports field 852 or 900. Similarly, you may want to describe the most common cataloging errors, missing data fields, and so on that you have in current MARC 21 records and attach a sample of these records to the RFP. Although the current system supports the MARC 21 standard, the MARC format used by different vendors may vary. In importing data from one system into another, make sure that data elements in MARC 21 records map correctly in the ILS to which you are migrating.

SUCCESSFUL MIGRATION

Successful system migration depends on many factors, including, but not limited to, the following:

- Adequate level of understanding of the migration process

- Project planning and preparation for migration, including collection weeding and inventory, and data cleanup

- Level of specifications developed for data migration

- Level of understanding of data schemas of records in all modules in the existing ILS and how they should transform or map into the new ILS

- Type of data sets extracted from the old ILS

- Data testing strategies in place

- Staff involvement and preparation for the change to the new ILS

- Learning from those who had undergone migration and avoiding the mistakes they had made

- Effective communication among staff members, especially the ones serving on the migration project advisory committee

- Effective communication with the company or firm and other parties involved, as applicable

- Sufficient, reasonable time scheduled for data testing using a test-drive site

- Data import into the new ILS and thorough test runs during and after implementation

- Adequacy and experience of the replacement's company or firm, as applicable

- Quality of the RFP and data migration stipulations including contract terms and conditions

- Availability of technical staff to write scripts for data extraction and testing especially in the case of an OSS ILS, as applicable

If the replacement company agrees to take care of all the odds and ends, make sure you dictate everything the company promises to do in the contractual agreement.

SUMMARY

System migration can be a very time-consuming process. Having a good plan for carrying out the migration project along with a timeline for completing every aspect of it is essential. Regardless of the ILS product to which you are migrating, involve staff in the migration project because their experience and knowledge of the operations of the library can contribute positively to the migration project. Form an advisory or project committee with a project manager to oversee the migration project.

Review current literature on library automation, preview automation software packages, visit neighborhood libraries, and read published case studies on ILS migration to acquire as much knowledge as possible about the migration process. Most of the tasks involved in selecting a new ILS for the first time apply to choosing an ILS product as a replacement to the existing ILS. Developing an RFP with required and preferred specifications for the new ILS, regardless of whether the ILS is proprietary or open source is essential. Weeding and inventorying the collection, as well as data cleanup are prerequisites not only to successful migration to a new ILS but also to reduce the cost of the migration and save on personnel time in the long term.

Developing good understanding of the current ILS data structure and the relationships between records that interact during transactions is essential so that you are able to extract data and write scripts as needed. At the core of successful migration is identification of data to extract from various modules in the existing ILS to test for mapping in the new ILS. Overall, there are tasks that you should do and tasks that the replacement company or firm will do. Being well informed of data migration is pivotal to successful implementation of the new system.

Outsourcing the data migration project will also incur work on your side, including data extraction representative of various types of records in the existing ILS that will be destined for testing by the outsourcing company or firm. You should have guidelines for data migration at hand from the company or firm to guide you through the data migration process. Do not forget about the online community of the ILS under consideration as you can learn from the experiences of its members.

Library automation is a never-ending activity. After you migrate to a new ILS, you may have to change over to another one in a few years, especially if the ILS no longer meets your library needs. At the core of the migration process is a well-developed RFP and a solid plan for the data migration process.

REFERENCES

Balas, Janet I. "Online Treasures. How They Did It: ILS Migration Case Studies." *Computers in Libraries*, 31, no. 8 (2011): 37. See also, http://www.eifl.net/koha-ils-case-studies. Accessed May 21, 2013.

Boss, Richard. W. *"Open Source" Integrated Library System Software*. 2008. http://www.ala.org/pla/tools/technotes/opensourceils. Accessed February 1, 2012.

Breeding, Marshall. *Integrated Library System Turnover 2013*. 2013. http://www.librarytechnology.org/ils-turnover.pl?Year=2013. Accessed May 29, 2013.

Breeding, Marshall, and Abdromeda Yelton. "Librarians' Assessments of Automated Systems Survey Results, 2007–2010." *Library Technology Reports*, 47, no. 4 (2011): 1–32.

Cervone, Frank. "ILs Migration in the 21st Century: Some New Things to Think About This Time Around." Computers in Libraries 27, no. 7 (2007): 6–8, 60–62.

Luther, Judy, and Kelly C. Maureen. "The New Generation of Discovery." *Library Journal* March 15, 2011. http://www.libraryjournal.com/lj/home/889250-264/the_next_generation_of_discovery.html.csp. Accessed January 15, 2013.

Singh, Vandana. "Experiences of Migration to Open Source Integrated Library Systems." *Information Technology and Libraries*, 32, no. 1 (2013): 36–51.

Walls, I. "Migrating from Innovative Interfaces' Millennium to Koha: The NYU Health Sciences Libraries' Experiences." *International Digital Library Perspectives*, 27, no. 1 (2011): 51–56.

WEBSITES

BibLibre. http://www.biblibre.com/en.
EIFL. http://www.eifl.net/foss-projects-tools.
Library Technology Reports. http://www.librarytechnology.org.
Lib-Web-Cats. http://www.librarytechnology.org/libwebcats.

Chapter 9

LALC Phase 5

EVALUATING SYSTEM USE THROUGH USABILITY

Almost every library has a presence on the web. A library's web page is a gateway to finding all types of information, including print and digital resources provided through the integrated library system (ILS) online catalog interface, discovery interface, or a variety of other tools. Once in full operation, evaluation of the interface should uncover its capability in fulfilling users' information needs effectively and efficiently. For example, you will need to know whether users are able to effectively find known items or materials within a specific topic, either starting from the organizational website, the library's website, or from the online catalog interface, or the discovery interface or discovery service. Additionally, you will want to know the following: Whether users are successful in finding information on a specific topic of interest; whether they know or are able to find out how to limit search results within a specific topic (e.g., journal articles, time period, or eBooks); whether the time they take to complete a given task is within the acceptable time range you have benchmarked in advance (i.e., minimum and maximum time); and whether they abandon searching too soon in the process and if they did, you should uncover the reasons for this behavior. Such an evaluation can be performed through measuring one or more components of the library's website, online catalog interface, discovery interface, or discovery service based on usability principles and methods.

Usability addresses the relationships between a system or interface and its users. It measures the system's effectiveness in relation to the user's experience and goals rather than to the system's specifications (Nielsen 2003). Usability emerges from the human-computer interaction (HCI) field, which studies "how people work with computers and how computers can be designed to help people effectively use them" (http://www.usabilityfirst.com/glossary/hci/). However, usability should not be disconnected from information behavior (IB). The former focuses on the design aspects of an interface that cause problems in interacting with a system or interface whereas the latter examines a user's information needs, seeking, use, sharing, or avoidance of information. IB has cognitive and affective dimensions that can be employed to develop a holistic understanding of the user's experience in interacting with any interface.

While one may argue that staff in small- and medium-sized libraries may not have the time or personnel needed to perform usability assessments using the methods and techniques covered in this chapter, a "quick and dirty" usability method may be used as an alternative to typical usability to reduce the cost and time (Nielsen 2009). As Nielsen notes, "simple user testing with 5 participants, paper prototyping, and heuristic evaluation offer a cheap, fast, and early focus on usability, as well as many rounds of iterative design . . . It often gives better results than deluxe usability because its methods drive an emphasis on early and rapid iteration with frequent usability input"(http://www.useit .com/alertbox/discount-usability.html). Thus, this type of usability can provide firsthand knowledge and a feel about the user's experience of any interface.

Note that while "discount usability" can be useful, a quantitative assessment of user performance using *metrics* such as time, errors, problems, satisfaction, and so forth will require a minimum of 20 users to reconcile differences in performance across users (Nielsen 2006). Use of metrics will require involving actual users in the evaluation process rather than expert reviewers. Varied types of metrics are described in Tullis and Albert (2013).

This chapter discusses usability assessment methods for evaluating the ILS online catalog interface, discovery interface, or discovery service. Evaluating an interface in terms of credibility, reliability, and the like criteria or in relation to design elements and content is beyond the scope of this chapter. Be mindful that not all methods described in this chapter will suit all types of libraries or information centers. Therefore, you should select the usability method and technique that best suit the library's environment, goals of the evaluation, needs, time, cost, and return on investment (ROI).

This chapter provides theoretical and practical frameworks for assessing the usability of any interface, with a focus on the online catalog interface or discovery interface of the ILS or discovery services (hereafter, interface). It covers the following main topics:

- Usability dimensions
    - User characteristics or attributes

- ○ System attributes
- ○ Task attributes
- Collecting data about users
- Usability methods
  - ○ Methods with expert reviewers
  - ○ Methods involving users
- Going beyond traditional data collection methods
- Getting started

USABILITY DIMENSIONS

Different dimensions of usability make the assessment of an interface a multifaceted endeavor. Usability considers whether a system or interface is socially acceptable. For example, does the language of a library's website mesh with the culture and background of the user community it serves? Does the interface design of the system or interface mesh with the user's expectations? Will novice users be able to learn how to use an interface effectively and efficiently? How effective is the interface in helping users overcome difficulties or problems experienced during the interaction? Usability assessment does not operate in a vacuum because it requires learning about the characteristics or attributes of users targeted in the evaluation, attributes of the interface being evaluated, and attributes of the tasks that users perform to achieve their goals. These three dimensions are the pillars of any usability assessment project.

User Characteristics or Attributes

Users differ in their cognitive abilities, motor skills, experience, cultural background, and mental models, among other things. For example, younger children, aged 6–8, possess different cognitive abilities, levels of experience, and problem-solving skills from older children, aged 9–12. Similarly, young adults differ from older adults in their motivation, experience, and the way they learn. Learning about users' characteristics, goals in achieving tasks, and information-seeking behaviors could unveil errors, problems, or failures. Studies have found that "search and information architecture are large factors in task failures" (Nielsen and Loranger 2007, 133). Indeed, an interface design that does not mesh well with the expectations and experiences of its target users may not only cause failure, but also yield negative affective reactions (anxiety, frustration, sense of inferiority, or dissatisfaction) that could discourage use of the interface, if not abandoning it all together (Bilal 2007; Nahl and Bilal 2007).

Children as Users

Children are not "small adults." They are a group of users with cognitive and affective traits, as well as experiences that vary from those of adult users. Children vary among one another based on cognitive development stage. For example, younger children (ages 3–5) tend to be more attracted to visual cues, color, sound, and animation than mid-range children (ages 6–8). Similarly, older children (ages 9–12) have needs, experience, and knowledge that vary from those of the other two groups. Distinguishing between the three groups of children is important in designing and evaluating these interfaces. As Nielsen (2010) notes, "there's no such thing as 'designing for children,' defined as everybody aged 3–12 . . . each group has different behaviors and [children] get substantially more web savvy as they get older" (http://www.useit.com/alertbox/children.html).

Naturally, it is recognized that children's reading skills, reading comprehension, attention span, amount of vocabulary they possess, and memory recall vary across the stages of their cognitive developments. Jean Piaget, a cognitive theorist during the late 19th and early 20th century, believed that children have four stages of development: sensorimotor, preoperational, concrete operational, and formal operational, and that each stage lasts for specific years of age (Piaget and Inhelder 1969). Although these stages may not apply to today's "digital natives," they provide a foundation for understanding child development.

It is also recognized that children's affective traits and, subsequently, their affective IB vary throughout the developmental stages (from infancy to childhood, juvenility, adolescence, and to adulthood) (Spink 2010), and that these traits interact with cognitive thoughts and actions (Bilal 2007). In his theory of socio-emotional child development, Erikson (1963, 1968) reflected on eight stages of emotional development that begin with trust versus mistrust during infancy and end with ego integrity versus despair in older adulthood years. Overall, Erikson advised that technology "must reach meaningfully into [a child's] life, supporting in every child a feeling of competence—that is, the free exercise of dexterity and intelligence in the completion of serious tasks unimpaired by an infantile sense of inferiority" (1968, 126). Though written in 1968, Erikson's stages of emotional development and his conception of technology remain relevant in today's digital information environment, especially in relation to designing interfaces that support the affective traits of target users.

Adults as Users

Adults differ among one another and as a group and learn differently from children and teenagers. Malcolm Knowles (1968), a pioneer in adult education, popularized the concept, "andragogy," meaning "the art and science of helping adults learn." He contrasted it with the concept, "pedagogy," or "the art and science of helping children learn." He notes that adults are self-directed and reflective with a rich experience repertoire and are problem solvers as well as motivated internally to learn a subject matter that they can put to use immediately (Knowles 1980).

Adults possess a higher level of cognitive abilities, memory recall, problem solving, and reasoning skills than children and teens. Children's reading and comprehension, decision making, and language communication skills differ from those of adults. Therefore, the design and evaluation of interfaces targeted toward these groups should account for these skills and abilities. In addition, adults are able to recover from problems experienced during the interaction much faster than children (Bilal and Kirby 2002).

Older Adults as Users

Another group of users to learn about is older adults. This group varies from adult users in that their cognitive, physical, and perceptual abilities may be on the decline due to aging (Shneiderman and Plaisant 2009). Therefore, you should employ usability methods and strategies that support these abilities. For example, observing or interviewing older adults in naturalistic environments may be more effective than using web-based surveys to gauge their experience with the interface. In addition, mediating the information need, allocating extra time to perform tasks, and providing affective support throughout the evaluation process are essential in working with older adults.

Users with Special Needs

Users with special needs or disabilities have unique needs that differ by disability (e.g., cognitive, physical). The U.S. Department of Justice published its revised regulations for Titles II and III of the Americans with Disabilities Act (ADA) of 1990 in the *Federal Register* on September 15, 2010, which include the 2010 ADA Standards for Accessible Design (http://www.ada .gov/2010ADAstandards_index.htm) that cover website design.

Standards for web accessibility were established in the Web Accessibility Initiative (W3C) (http://www.w3.org), which also covers a spectrum of guidelines, resources, training, authoring tools, and website navigation features, among other things. The standards for designing web applications for people with disabilities are located at (http://www.w3.org/WAI/intro/people-use-web/principles). Some basic functions for accessibility include enlargement capabilities for reading text, sensitive speakers, voice input components, keypad or joystick components, dual design option (i.e., graphical user interface (GUI) and text alternatives).

System Attributes

System attributes focus on the design and quality of a system's performance. Nielsen (2003) describes four major attributes of a "usable" system or interface.

Learnability

The ease of use of the system to accomplish basic tasks the first time a user interfaces with it and the speed at which the user can perform a given task once the user is acquainted with the system. One should keep in mind the learning curve it takes a user to learn how to use a new system.

Memorability

The degree a user remembers the design and functions embedded in the system after a period of not using it.

Errors

The type of errors a user makes, the severity of these errors, and the causes of these errors. The system should prevent errors to occur, but once they are made, the system should allow a user to recover from these by giving constructive feedback. Errors that are simple in nature and do not interfere with the user's productivity or completion of a given task are considered minor whereas those that do affect the productivity or completion of a task are major and should be fixed as quickly as possible by interface designers.

Satisfaction

The likeability of the system by its users and the level of satisfaction felt in completing their task goals. Users may be satisfied with the design of the interface, but may be unsatisfied with the results it retrieved for their search queries (see also "Usability," "Heuristics," and "Principles").

Norman (1998) identified six essential *design attributes* of a system or interface to learn about the user's experience. These include consistency, aesthetics, ease of navigation, affordance, visual cues, and functionality. These attributes are reflected in the usability heuristics, rules, and principles described under "Usability Methods."

Task Attributes

A task reflects an information need or knowledge gap with a goal to be achieved. Tasks vary by type (open-ended versus closed), nature (complex versus simple), and administration (fully assigned, semi-assigned, and fully self-generated) (Bilal 2002). Open-ended tasks do not have a target answer; these tasks require gathering relevant information from a variety of sources to establish meaning and understanding and have multiple components or facets. These types of tasks are more complex than closed tasks because they are ill-defined. In contrast, closed tasks tend to be well-defined and can be much simpler than open-ended tasks, in that they include one or two facets instead of multiple facets (Bilal 2002). Tasks should be clear and well formulated, and the user should understand the task and its requirements before interacting with an interface. Tasks should be relevant to the design elements and functionality (or priority elements and components) of the interface. Pilot-test the assigned tasks before you administer them to users to perform.

Other types of tasks are those that are generated by the user based on interest in a specific topic or specific information need. These tasks are more naturalistic and tend to yield more successful results than the assigned tasks (Bilal 2002). However, self-generated tasks could result in a large amount of data collection, coding, and analysis because they are not known to the observer (you) in advance of the interaction. In addition, the outcomes of these tasks may be more complex to measure using one single metric. Moreover, these tasks may require mediation to assist users in clarifying their information needs.

COLLECTING DATA ABOUT USERS

Understanding users and their interaction in the interface requires collection of demographic data (e.g., age, gender, prior experience, education level, cultural background, and economic status) and data on psychological factors (e.g., attitude, motivation, and individual differences), as applicable to the goals of the evaluation. Constraints (e.g., time, space, and context) are also important factors to consider in learning about users. Specific theories in HCI and IB can be used to establish a basis for understanding users' cognitive (thoughts), affective (emotions), and psychomotor (actions) behaviors in interacting with the interface.

Donald Norman, a cognitive scientist and an engineer, in his work *The Design of Everyday Things* (1998), introduced seven stages of action that a user goes through in interacting with varied interfaces. To understand these stages, the author of this book provided a *practical meaning* of each stage.

Stage 1—Forming the goal: User formulates the goal of the interaction. Practical *meaning*: User recognizes the information need.

Stage 2—Forming the intention: The user defines the intention. Practical *meaning*: The user conceptualizes the information need and thinks about appropriate interface(s) to use.

Stage 3—Specifying the action: The user defines the search. Practical *meaning*: The user constructs or formulates the syntax of the search in the selected interface.

Stage 4—Executing the action: The user executes the action specified in the earlier step. Practical *meaning*: The user clicks on or pushes a button to send the formulated search statement for execution by the interface.

Stage 5—Perceiving the system state: The user views the status of the search being executed. Practical *meaning*: The user waits for the results to be retrieved and notices the system status.

Stage 6—Interpreting the system state: The user processes the results retrieved. Practical *meaning*: The user scans or examines the results retrieved by the system to identify information of interest.

Stage 7—Evaluating the outcome: The user determines whether the actions supplied the appropriate output to fulfill the goal. Practical *meaning*: The user judges relevance of retrieved results and takes further action. If retrieved results meet the user's need, the user stops the interaction; otherwise, the user may go back to earlier stages as applicable, use another interface, or abandon the interface altogether. These stages are iterative, reflecting the dynamic nature of user interaction with an interface.

In the library and information science field, many models of user information-seeking behavior in both traditional and digital environments are available (see Wilson 2013; Case 2012; Hearst 2009; Fisher, Erdelez, and Mckechnie 2005). However, the information-seeking model that is in line with Norman's stages of actions is that by Marchionini and White (2008), which consists of the following:

(1) Recognizing a need for information

(2) Accepting the challenge to take action to fulfill the need

(3) Formulating the problem

(4) Expressing the information need in a search system

(5) Examination of the results

(6) Reformulation of the problem and its expression

(7) Use of the results

The model from Marchionini and White and Norman's model represent the processes or actions a user performs to solve a general, simple task and are iterative in nature, contrary to their sequential presentation.

While these two models are cognitive in nature, Kuhlthau's model of the Information Search Process (1991, 2004) describes common patterns of searching and emotional experiences that students in varied settings (e.g., college, high school) exhibited over a period of time in finding information in resources and tools for assigned, complex tasks. Kuhlthau's model divides the search process into six stages:

(1) Task initiation: User recognizes the need for finding information. Common affective responses include uncertainty, apprehension, and confusion.

(2) Topic selection: User needs to select a general topic. Common affective responses include feelings of uncertainty after the selection is made.

(3) Topic exploration: The user investigates the general topic to find a focused perspective. Negative affective responses include feelings of confusion, uncertainty, doubt, and frustration.

(4) Topic formulation: The user finds a focused perspective on the selected topic, resulting in optimism and decrease in uncertainty. This is a turning point in the process. Note that 50 percent of the students were unable to reach a focused perspective throughout the process.

(5) Collection of information: The user collects information in support of the focused topic and makes more accurate relevance judgments of the gathered information. Positive feelings include increased self-confidence.

(6) Presentation: The gathered information is completed. Affective responses vary from including feelings of relief and satisfaction, if the search was successful, or disappointment and dissatisfaction if the search failed.

The resources the students used in Kuhlthau's study were traditional and less interactive in nature than today's search tools such as web search engines, online databases, and discovery interfaces or services. However, recent studies have shown that some of the stages in this model persisted in using digital tools to locate information on assigned tasks.

USABILITY METHODS

There are several methods to consider in assessing the user's experience in the ILS interface. The method you choose should be based on factors, including, but not limited to, the library's environment, the goals of the evaluation, time, cost, personnel resources, access to actual users, and also ROI.

Usability methods fall into two main categories: (1) methods that employ expert reviewers (also known as system inspection) and (2) methods that involve actual users. A mix of methods may be used to enrich your understanding of the user's experience.

Methods with Expert Reviewers

This method involves hiring usability experts to evaluate an interface in cases where recruiting actual users is difficult due to cost, time, legal and ethical concerns, or in cases where you need to determine to what extent the design of the interface meets or violates usability guidelines. In this situation, a team of expert reviewers who possess adequate knowledge of the target users of the interface (e.g., characteristics, IB) are hired or identified within the organization to inspect the interface. The reviewers use a set of heuristics, rules, or principles in the evaluation, or may decide to employ the cognitive walkthrough method to that end, or use both methods. The depth and breadth of the evaluation should be based on the goals of the evaluation. The more complex the design and content of the interface is, the more time consuming and costly the evaluation will be.

Usability Heuristics

Usability heuristics are a set of rules or heuristics that describe the common properties of usable interfaces (Nielsen 1994). In this method, a team of expert evaluators go through the elements or features of an interface and evaluate them against predefined heuristics. An observer or a team leader coordinates the logistics of this evaluation with the evaluators. Each evaluator goes through each designated feature or element of an interface, evaluates it against the heuristics (see Nielsen's 10 heuristics (http://www.useit.com/papers/heuristic/heuristic_evaluation.html), and rates its severity on a scale such as the one suggested by Nielsen, whose scale ranges from 0 to 4, where

> "**0** = I don't agree that this is a usability problem at all
> **1** = Cosmetic problem only that does not need to be fixed immediately but should be fixed as time is available
> **2** = Minor usability problem: fixing this should be given a low priority
> **3** = Major usability problem: important to fix, and should be given high priority
> **4** = Usability catastrophe: imperative to fix this problem before the product can be released" (http://www.useit.com/papers/heuristic/severityrating.html)

Each evaluator keeps notes during the evaluation process and compiles a report of the findings to submit to the observer or team leader. The latter combines all reports, holds a debriefing session with the reviewers to discuss the findings, and issues a final usability report.

Identification of Design Elements to Evaluate

One may use a website's analytics to identify the elements or components of a website or interface to evaluate. Many ILSs have an analytics tool to track users' interaction and provide detailed reporting that once analyzed and interpreted should result in a user profile. In the absence of analytics, the landing page (i.e., default page) of the discovery interface, for example, is normally used the most and can be the subject of this evaluation. Because the default interface has fewer elements or components than the advanced interface, the evaluation of the former should take less time to complete than the latter.

Evaluators may identify these elements or the team leader may suggest priority elements to consider for the evaluation.

Each evaluator goes through the interface and focuses on the specific elements or components that are the subject of the evaluation. Problems found may be communicated verbally to the team leader. However, it is recommended that written reports be issued to maintain records of this activity. After each leader compiles the notes and reports generated by the reviewers, she holds a debriefing session to discuss the findings, reach a consensus about the problems found and their severity, and generates the final usability report.

Jakob Nielsen's Heuristics

Jakob Nielsen's heuristics (1994) are widely used for evaluating the quality of most interfaces (http://www.useit.com/papers/heuristic/heuristic_evaluation.html). These heuristics are described in the following section. Each heuristic is followed by a practical meaning or an example of how to use it during the evaluation.

Visibility of System Status

The interface should always keep users informed about what is going on through appropriate feedback within reasonable time. Practical *meaning* or *example*: if the website or discovery interface is processing a request that may take time to complete, it should inform the user about the status of the request (e.g., "retrieving information," "loading information," or "please wait").

Match between System and the Real World

The interface should speak the users' language, with words, phrases, and concepts familiar to the user, rather than system-oriented terms. Follow real-world conventions, making information appear in a natural and logical order. Practical *meaning* or *example*: What does "anywhere in the record" or "contain my query words" mean to a user? To a novice user, this terminology or "system" language may be difficult to understand. In contrast, it may be easy for an experienced user or a professional.

User Control and Freedom

Users often choose interface functions by mistake and will need a clearly marked "emergency exit" to leave the unwanted state without having to go through an extended dialogue. Support *undo* and *redo*. Practical *meaning* or *example*: if a user types the name of a book title in the search box of a discovery interface and realizes that he has made an error or decided on another title, the user should be able to correct the error or title easily and fast by using a function to "undo" the request such as clicking on a reverse arrow icon or a start-over icon.

Consistency and Standards

Users should not have to wonder whether different words, situations, or actions mean the same thing. Follow platform conventions. Practical *meaning* or *example*: the design of the results page side bar should be consistent across the layout of the retrieval page of the discovery interface.

Norman (1998) outlined four types of consistency in interface design to evaluate the following:

> *Aesthetic*: Aesthetic consistency communicates membership, sets the tone, and enhances familiarity. The user may make associations to system quality and reliability.
>
> *Functional*: Functional consistency sets the expectations for action, creates a platform for scaffolding learning through repetition and expansion, and requires that signage have the same meaning and occur in the same places throughout the system.
>
> *Internal*: Internal consistency forms a cohesive unit within the system, which cultivates a sense of trust and allows for regular planning to take place.
>
> *External*: External consistency includes environmental consistency, not only in system (e.g. stop is always red octagon), but also deals with the harder issues of transfer between systems due to individual design standards and requirements.

Error Prevention

Even better than a good error message is a careful design, which prevents a problem from occurring in the first place. Either eliminate error-prone conditions or check for them and present users with a confirmation option before they commit to the action. Practical *meaning* or *example*: A library's website or discovery interface should provide instructions on how to enter a search request in the search box. If a user is performing an author search, for example, directions or an example showing the proper entry of the author's name should be provided to prevent the user from making an error.

Recognition Rather than Recall

Minimize the user's memory load by making objects, actions, and options visible. The user should not have to remember information from one part of the dialogue to another. Instructions for use of the system should be visible or easily retrievable whenever appropriate. Practical *meaning or example*: The interface should assist the user in choosing terms or phrases to support recognition and reduce recall from memory. The "autofill" or "autocomplete" provided in many of today's interfaces meet this design criterion.

Flexibility and Efficiency of Use

Accelerators—unseen by the novice user—may often speed up the inter-action for the expert user such that the system can cater to both inexperienced and experienced users. Allow users to tailor frequent actions. Practical *meaning or example*: the design of an interface should support novice users by providing a simple or default interface with simple features and support an advanced search feature to accommodate experienced users.

Aesthetic and Minimalist Design

Dialogues should not contain information that is irrelevant or rarely needed. Every extra unit of information in a dialogue competes with the relevant units of information and diminishes their relative visibility. Practical *meaning* or *example*: Simplicity in design (Google like) has proved to be more acceptable by today's users than a cluttered interface. The interface should show features that are most frequently accessed by users and should hide (e.g., in a menu) those that are less frequently used.

Help Users Recognize, Diagnose, and Recover from Errors

Error messages should be expressed in plain language (no codes); they should precisely indicate the problem and constructively suggest a solution. Practical *meaning* or *example*: If a user commits an error, the user should be informed of the error made, and the interface should provide a user with suggestions for correcting the error—thus, a recovery. A broken link, for example, that displays the 404 error is meaningless for the user. Suggestions for correcting misspelling or automatic correction of it should help users recover from the error quickly.

Help and Documentation

Even though it is better if the interface can be used without documentation, it may be necessary to provide help and documentation. Any such information should be easy to search, focus on the user's task, list concrete steps to be carried out, and not be too large. Practical *meaning* and *example*: the "Help" feature in an interface should be visible and easy to find so that a user can access it quickly and find information easily as needed.

Eight Golden Rules for Usability

Another set of principles to consider in evaluating the interface is Ben Shneiderman's "Eight Golden Rules for Usability." These rules are consistent with most of Nielsen's heuristics and include the following: *Strive for consistency, cater to universal usability, offer informative feedback, design dialogs to yield closure, prevent errors, permit easy reversal of actions, support internal locus of control,* and *reduce short-term memory load.* It is clear that most of these rules conform to Nielsen's heuristics. The exception is *catering for universal usability* and *design dialogs to yield closure.*

Catering for universal usability means that signs, symbols, and colors may have ubiquitous connotations. There are logical flows to specific processes. The system should be built to meet the needs of diverse users—novice to experienced users, with differences in ages and disabilities. An example of universal design is a website that besides being a GUI-compatible provides a text alternative to accommodate visually impaired users (see also the section "Users with Special Needs"). Designing for universal usability can be challenging to designers as one interface may not meet the needs of all users, of all cultures, and age ranges.

The rule, *design dialogs to yield closure* means that the sequences of actions should have a clear beginning, middle, and end. Once a user completes an action by logging out, for example, the interface should end the user's task with a confirmation about logging out from the system. Interface information and instruction should be clearly visible as needed throughout so that important processing information does not have to be remembered while focusing on the task at hand. This rule conforms to Nielsen's heuristic, "Recognition rather than Recall."

Donald Norman's Seven Principles for Usability Assessment

Donald Norman (1998) developed seven principles for usability assessment of an interface:

(1) Use knowledge in the world and in the brain

(2) Visibility—can I see it?

(3) Feedback—what is it doing now?

(4) Design for error recognition and recovery

(5) Affordance—how do I use it?

(6) Mapping—where am I and where can I go?

(7) Constraint—why can't I do that?

Norman considered the environment or context in which the user interacts with an interface, visibility of frequently performed actions, and hiding of infrequent ones (e.g., under a menu) until requested by the user so that the interface is simpler in design Simplification of interface design elements, achieving user orientation through directional visual cues (e.g., meaningful labeling of functions), avoiding visual cues or signs that do not support one another, and using standard conventions and vocabulary will create familiarity with the interface and, thus enhance the user's ability to learn how to use it.

The heuristics, rules, and principles can be consolidated into a list of "unique" criteria for evaluating the online catalog interface or discovery interface. Note that this evaluation method alone does not provide a full understanding of the user's experience since proxies (i.e., expert reviewers) are evaluating the interface. However, this method informs webmasters or developers of the design problems that violate the heuristics, rules, or principles and that should be resolved by designers.

Cognitive Walkthrough

The cognitive walkthrough is a system inspection method used to uncover issues and problems users may experience in using an interface. Expert evaluators walkthrough an interface, put themselves in the users' shoes, and evaluate designated elements and features in the interface vis-à-vis the target users' goals in completing them. Lewis and Reiman (1994) note that this method requires four things: (1) a description or a prototype of the interface, (2) a task description, (3) a complete, written list of the actions needed to complete the task with the interface, and (4) an idea of who the users will be and what kind of prior experience they possess. The latter should have been acquired through user analysis. This method is more complex than the previous one. However, it predicts problems that actual users may experience in using the interface.

This method consists of two main phases: a preparatory phase and an analysis phase (Wharton, Reiman, Lewis, and Polson 1994).

Preparatory Phase

In this phase, an experimenter or observer (e.g., you) chooses the expert reviewers and coordinates the evaluation. In addition, the observer does the following:

- Plans the walkthrough project.

- Meets with expert evaluators prior to data collection to decide on parts of the system interface to evaluate and discuss the broad scope of the tasks to be performed.

- Prepares specific tasks to be performed in an interface.

- Develops usability materials (e.g., checklist, instructions, and written tasks).

- Schedules a debriefing session with evaluators before data collection to introduce the walkthrough project.

- Decides on the time and location of data collection.

- Develops benchmarks to evaluate success in each task performed by each evaluator.

- Observes and take notes of each evaluator's interaction with the interface.

- Interviews each expert individually upon completion of the tasks to learn about her experience with the interface and gain additional insights about the walkthrough. The experimenter may schedule a debriefing session with the experts as a group to do this activity. More than one meeting may be needed if the experimenter and the experts decide to analyze, synthesize, and write the usability report together.

- Schedules a debriefing session with experts after data collection to discuss the findings.

- Reviews data collection report compiled by each evaluator.

- Analyzes collected data by evaluators.

- Prepares a draft of the usability report.

- Meets with evaluators to discuss the usability report.

- Finalizes the usability report.

Analysis Phase

Each evaluator walks through the interface to complete each given task, analyzes the actions or sequences entailed for completing it by stepping through the user's actions and decisions at every stage of the process. In addition, each expert does the following:

- Performs each of the assigned tasks independently

- Records problems that the actual user may experience in performing each task and describes reasons for these problems

- Asks himself questions as he performs each task vis-à-vis the characteristics of the typical novice user in mind (cognitive ability, thoughts, etc.)

Examples of questions the evaluators ask during the walkthrough about the online catalog interface or discovery interface:

- How easy is it for the novice user to recognize that *Book Plus* (for example) is the library's online catalog or discovery interface?

- How easy is it for the novice user to search the basic interface of the online catalog or discovery interface by keyword?

- What cognitive processes are required to find a known book item in the online catalog or discovery interface successfully?

- What learning is required in order for the novice user to perform the given task successfully?

- How much time should the user take to complete a given task successfully? To what extent does the time taken by the user meet or exceed the acceptable time for completing the task?

- Is the action sequence for each step taken appropriate (or intuitive or logical) for the novice user to follow to complete the given tasks?

- Is it possible that the novice user will be able to perform each step successfully? If not, what problems may the user experience?

- Does the interface provide enough cues as to what actions should be performed?

- To what degree does the interface help the novice user recognize, diagnose, and recover from errors?

- Is there a match between the interface and the novice user's cognitive processes (i.e., does the system speak the user's language?).

The evaluators also do the following:

- Construct success and/or failure stories if found.

- Provide suggestions for solving the problems found.

- Discuss with the experimenter the problems found in each task during the interaction.

- Rate the severity of each problem found using an agreed upon severity rating scale. Note that not all walkthrough methods involve severity rating of problems.

Scenarios, Success, and Failure Stories

Each evaluator provides examples of one or more credible success and failure stories based on a scenario she develops about the target user who will be using specific components or elements in the interface. The evaluator gives a *defense of credibility* of each success story by listing *common features/criteria for success*. Three or four success stories may be provided.

Failure stories are discussed in relation to target users and the difficulty they may experience in finding a task or function difficult to achieve without additional knowledge because the system's interface does not speak the user's language. In this case, criteria are used, and questions are asked for each criterion. A question may be: Will the user know that the correct action is available? Using this criterion allows the evaluator to determine the cause of failure.

A successful evaluation of the interface using the cognitive walkthrough method depends on critical factors, including:

- Appropriate selection of the tasks. Tasks should vary by type (closed and open-ended) and complexity (simple and complex).

- Concrete and realistic benchmarking of the actions for completing a given task by the experimenter or observer.

- Knowledge of the characteristics of target users and their prior experience or knowledge level.

- Elements and features covered in the evaluation of a given interface.

- Experience and knowledge of the evaluators.

- Experience and knowledge of the observer or team leader of the project.

Results from the cognitive walkthrough method could lead to further inspection of the interface using "actual" users (e.g., observation) to confirm the problems found so that design improvements are made accordingly. For additional information about this method, see Mahatody, Sager, and Kolski, 2010; Hollingsed and Novick, 2007.

METHODS INVOLVING USERS

User involvement in assessing the usability of the interface is a more user-centered approach than the methods requiring expert reviewers. The most commonly used methods include surveys, interviews, observation, and focus groups.

Surveys

Surveys are the most common way to collect data about broad issues from many users. Questions in survey instruments may be closed, yielding Yes/No answers, or open-ended, generating ideas and opinions that may result in qualitative data. Surveys are based on questionnaire instruments developed to obtain information about users' information needs, the use of the interface, issues, problems, perceptions, and satisfaction, among other things. Instruments should be pretested before their distribution to ensure validity of the questions. Regardless of the purpose of the data collection, a questionnaire should have a space for users to provide comments or suggestions. A totally closed questionnaire may not allow you to interpret certain responses. Surveys that rely on Yes/No questions do not provide sufficient understanding of the user's tasks, context, actions performed, or IB and, therefore, may not yield data that can be used to design a new design or improve the existing design of an existing interface. Surveys are adequate for exploring broad issues, directions, or preferences. Their value in testing the usability of the interface depends on the type of questions asked (closed versus open-ended), how these questions are stated, internal validity of the survey instrument, and user response rate.

Consider adapting standardized, pretested questionnaire instruments for gathering data from users. In the HCI field, a commonly used instrument is the *Questionnaire for User Interaction Satisfaction* (QUIS) (http://hcibib.org/ perlman/question.cgi?form=QUIS). Note that permission is needed to use or adapt this instrument. In the academic library setting, the *LibQual* (http:// www.libqual.org/about/about_lq/general_info) questionnaire instrument is employed to assess the quality of library services and use of the library. However, this instrument does not elicit detail about a user's interaction or experience with the ILS interface.

Survey instruments require time to develop, test, and refine so that they are valuable for collecting data from users. Low response rate and subjectivity in responses make surveys less reliable than observation or interview methods.

Interviews

An interview can be described as a "conversation with a purpose." Just as a reporter interviews a person to gain insight into a story, the interviewer directs the conversation to gain information from the interviewee. Interviews can be one-on-one or with a group of users. One-on-one seeks to obtain deeper into the experience of a user whereas a group interview seeks to obtain a broader understanding of the experience of users. Thus, the conversation between the interviewer and the interviewee differs depending on the goals of the interview. Interviews vary by design, that is, structured, unstructured, and semistructured (Rogers, Sharp, and Preece 2011).

Structured Interviews

Structured interviews use predetermined questions in a predetermined order and a script or interview guide to use during the interview. This type of communication is particularly useful when the information one hopes to gain is very specific. Interview questions need to be developed carefully, pilot-tested, refined, and used during the interview. The structured interview can be an in-person meeting or one with the use of communication technology (e.g., phone, video link, Skype, etc.). Structured interviews may result in qualitative data such as expressions, ideas, and stories told by the interviewee, but only if open-ended questions are asked. These interviews may also generate data that can be analyzed quantitatively using descriptive statistics (mean, median, mode, and percentage). Depending on the goals of the interview and its design, inferential statistics may be used to find correlation or relationships between predefined variables (dependent and independent variables).

Unstructured Interviews

Unstructured interviews are also known as open-ended interviews. They differ somewhat from structured in that the questions are often open-ended, and the format of the question and the answers are not predetermined. The interviewer may have a plan of topics that he or she wants to include, but both the interviewer and the interviewee can steer the interview. The interviewer should be prepared in this instance to follow new lines of inquiry that move the discussion forward, but it is imperative that he or she also knows when and how to lead the conversation back on topic when it has drifted off course (Rogers, Sharp, and Preece 2011). In using this type of interview, be friendly and sympathetic, but remember your role as the interviewer. Having an outline for the interview is recommended so that one ensures that the intended topics have been covered. Data generated from unstructured interviews will be more qualitative than quantitative. However, the data may be richer and deeper than the data generated from structured interviews.

Semistructured Interviews

Semistructured interviews allow for a balance between the two types of interviews described earlier. In this case, the interviewer uses both closed and open-ended questions and also references an interview guide or a script as needed. The interviewee may be asked to fill out an instrument with closed questions, and the interviewer may ask the interviewee the open-ended questions. Responses to questions are either recorded using a digital audio recorder or are written by the interviewer on the instrument used. The interviewer uses prompts to encourage the interviewee to continue the conversation as appropriate. Asking "why" and "can you explain?" are examples of prompts to use for open-ended questions. Semistructured interviews generate both qualitative and quantitative data that if analyzed properly could yield rich information about the user experience.

Questions to develop for structured and semistructured interviews vary based on the goals of the data collection. Turner (2010) provided guidelines for designing interview questions that can be used by novice researchers. In addition, the *Research Methods Knowledge Base: Interviews*, located at (http://www .socialresearchmethods.net/kb/intrview.php) has a description of interview procedures and questions.

Regardless of type, interview instruments should elicit user demographic data, education level, and prior experience, among other things. They should also generate data about the user's experience with the website or interface, including but not limited to, satisfaction, attitudes, motivation, affect, and perceived success. Users should have the opportunity to provide comments and suggestions about improving the interface. For additional information about interviews, see Chapter 3.

Observation

Observation is another method that is rooted in field research. A user is observed while performing given tasks in a given website or interface to obtain necessary data about the user's IB and interaction with the interface, information needs, success, and failure, among other things. There are two main types of observation: direct and indirect.

Direct Observation

Direct observation occurs in naturalistic or seminaturalistic contexts or environments such as a user's workplace, home, or other environment that meets the goals of the observation. In a naturalistic environment, the observer is observing a user's interaction with the site or interface and taking notes during the observation. Tasks are not assigned; rather, the user may be asked to recall tasks they had recently performed to find information in the site or interface and repeat how the user had approached the tasks. The observer takes notes during the observation and/or uses a digital camera to video capture the user's interaction. The user may also be asked to verbalize or think aloud his or her actions and decision making during the interaction. If you decide to use this technique, prepare a checklist to guide you and others during data collection.

Observing users is seminaturalistic in cases where tasks are assigned by the observer rather than selected by the user.

Indirect Observation

Unlike the direct observation, indirect observation occurs in a laboratory or other environment where software is used to capture the user's interaction with the interface (searching, clicking, sites visited, scrolling, etc.). The software can also be configured to capture the user's verbalization or think-aloud and facial expressions. In this case, a microphone and camera, respectively, should be used. Upon completion of the tasks, the user's interaction session is saved on the computer used and then exported to a flash drive or other type of media for coding and analysis. Morae (http://www.techsmith.com) is an example of such usability software tool; it has three components: observer (to observe the user from one's remote computer while interacting with the interface); recorder (to capture the user's interaction activities); and manager (to import recorded activities for data coding, analysis, and management).

Eye tracking software tools can be used to examine the user's interaction with the interface based on eye movements and gazing. These tools record, calculate, and generate visualizations of eye movements and gazing during the interaction. Tobii Studio is an example of such tools (http://www.tobii.com/en/eye-tracking-research/global/products/software/). Tobii integrates with Morae, allowing the combination of recorded or logged interaction activities and eye gaze trails. The latest development in eye tracking movement is the eye tracking glasses (http://www.tobii.com/en/eye-tracking-research/global/products/hardware/tobii-glasses-eye-tracker). These are mobile eye trackers to use in real-world environments (instead of laboratories) unobtrusively. Using these tools can be challenging as they require a sufficient level of training, especially in relation to data analysis and interpretation. In addition, they may not be suitable for all usability projects.

One of the main advantages of indirect observation is the amount of data that can be collected in a short amount of time using usability software. Another advantage is that the observer has more control over the context in which the observation occurs. The main disadvantage of indirect observation is that the user's interaction and behavior may be influenced by the presence of the observer or anyone coordinating data collection on-site.

Focus Groups

A focus group is a qualitative research method that uses groups with a purpose. Krueger and Casey (2009) developed guidelines for using a focus group for data collection from users. Focus groups are defined by certain characteristics. The members express opinions and do not perform any function such as interacting with an interface. The method is not an easy or cheap evaluation procedure, and it is a time-consuming process. An important factor to take into consideration is choosing a proper and a well-trained facilitator for the group. Cost and time aside, focus groups are an excellent method for facilitating the generation of ideas by a group of users. In addition, they can provide insight on user concerns and issues, satisfaction, as well as give suggestions for improving design and training, among other things. Focus groups as a research method has many issues, including, but not limited to, the possibility of intellectualizing the participants. Also, participants can make up answers, and dominant participants can influence collected data (Krueger and Casey 2009). To minimize these problems, focus groups should be used with other research methods such as interviews, observations, or surveys.

Going beyond Traditional Data Collection Methods

Advanced data gathering methods include contextual inquiry, task analysis, and experimental testing.

Contextual Inquiry

Contextual inquiry is a technique used in contextual design that was developed specifically to elicit detailed data to use in customer-centered product design (Holtzblatt 2002). "The core premise of contextual inquiry is very simple: go where the customer works, observe the customer as he or she works, and talk to the customer about the work. Do that, and you can't help but gain a better understanding of your customer" (Beyer and Holtzblatt 1998). Contextual inquiry is a method of field study that includes direct observation with simultaneous interviewing of the user during the interaction. What differs this method from other methods is that it elicits more detailed "work practice data," meaning that it does not leave out any actions or individual steps that a user performs, thus providing detailed understanding of the "nuances" of the user's IB (Holtzblatt 2002) in context. Contextual inquiry allows understanding of each of the actions, decisions, and behaviors demonstrated by the user, exhibits and provides an answer to the "why" question.

Task Analysis

Task analysis is a method used to investigate how a user accomplishes a given task. It focuses on the user's cognitive and physical processes in performing the task and asks: *What is the user trying to achieve (goal)? What knowledge and skill level did the user have to perform the task? To what extent did the user's background knowledge or experience influence how he performed the task (cognitively and physically)? How did the user perform the task? Why did the user follow certain sequences or actions? What prior skills level is needed to successfully perform the task?* These are examples of questions to ask in conducting a task analysis. Task analysis provides understanding of the user's mental and physical activities in performing a task, thus allowing webmasters and system designers to reference this analysis against the actual design of the functions and features embedded in the interface (http://www.usabilitynet.org/tools/taskanalysis.htm). Task analysis begins with decomposing a task into subtasks and operations. This decomposition is best represented in a hierarchical format using hierarchical task analysis (HTA), which begins with the user's goal and captures the user's physical and observable actions in achieving the goal. The captured actions will establish the baseline of the user's execution of a task, thus enabling webmasters and designers to envision the goals, tasks and subtasks, plans, and operations to design or improve in the interface.

Note that HTA requires extensive hierarchy construction for complex activities. Therefore, it can be time consuming and costly. In addition, it requires adequate understanding of the task domain itself, training, and knowledge of how to represent the task hierarchy in verbal and graphical formats. Crystal and Ellington (2004) recommend integrating this method with other usability methods to maximize its effectiveness and efficiency.

Experimental Testing

Experimental testing is a type of empirical research that emerges from the scientific method and is used in evaluating the usability of any interface in a controlled environment. The goal of an experiment is to test hypotheses that have been formulated based on assumptions. A hypothesis predicts a relationship or lack thereof between two variables known as independent and dependent variables. A hypothesis is tested by manipulating one or more variables, known as independent variables. These are called "independent" because the researcher created them independently before the experiment started (Rogers, Sharp, and Preece 2011) to test their influence or effect on the dependent variables. The variable the researcher manipulates is the independent variable. A dependent variable is what the researcher measures in the experiment. It is called "dependent" because what is affected in the results of the experiment depends on the independent variable. Both independent and dependent variables must exist to conduct experimental testing. In the example, "anxiety will influence children's research process in the discovery interface" will be tested by manipulating the *independent variable* "anxiety." The "research process" is the *dependent variable* because the "research process" depends on the way "anxiety" is manipulated by the experimenter.

The design of the experiment varies based on variables and conditions (e.g., with one independent variable and one dependent variable, or two or more independent variables) and with assigning participants to conditions. There are three main approaches for assigning participants to conditions: different participants for all conditions, the same participants for all conditions, and matched pairs of participants (Rogers, Sharp, and Preece 2011). Experimental testing requires adequate knowledge of the scientific experimentation and inferential statistics. The latter is used to test formulated hypotheses, which results in refuting or accepting the hypotheses.

Note that there are additional methods that one can use in combination with other methods to conduct usability assessment. These include card sorting, persona development, and use cases. For information about these methods, visit these two websites as a starting point: http://www.usability.gov/how-to-and-tools/methods/index.html and http://www.uie.com/browse/personas/.

GETTING STARTED

There are many methods to use for evaluating the usability of the ILS interface. Choosing the method(s) to use for a particular evaluation may be challenging for novice librarians or information professionals. Therefore, additional learning about the user experience and usability is needed.

As you implement the ILS, you may assume that since it is based on new Web 2.0 or beyond and is user-centered, the interface is simple, and users should not experience problems finding information. Reality may prove otherwise as you begin to observe how users interact with the interface to seek information, or as you informally learn from others, or through user online feedback that users are experiencing problems finding information or understanding the meaning of certain features. Now it is the time to plan the evaluation project. The next step is to figure out who should do the evaluation and how. For example, will library staff conduct a heuristic evaluation of the online catalog interface or discovery interface? Will users be recruited to participate in a full or discount usability assessment of the interface?

Keep in mind what your goal is by asking these questions: *What are the goals of the evaluation? What do I need to know and why? What data should I collect? How much time do I have? Are personnel resources available to assist with the evaluation? What usability method(s) should I consider? Are financial resources available for planning the evaluation, collecting the data, analyzing the data, and interpreting the results? Who will be the users or participants in data collection? How many users or participants do I need? How will I recruit these users or participants? What ethical and legal concerns should I be aware of? What organizational procedures should I follow?* Answering these questions should guide you in planning the evaluation of the interface based on usability principles or methods.

Consider using templates and tools in planning the evaluation project. These are available at http:/www.usability.gov. This site also includes guidelines, project management tips, and a visual representation of the whole evaluation process. To understand how to measure the user's experience, consult the book *Measuring the User Experience: Collecting, Analyzing, and Presenting Usability Metrics* by Tullis and Albert (2013). This book describes how to design a usability study, use appropriate metrics or measures, and code and also analyze collected data; it also contains case studies of the user's experience in various settings. Basic learning about social research methods is also necessary for the whole evaluation project. Consider using this website as a start (http://www.socialresearch.net), and read introductory books on the topic or attend workshops.

Evaluating the ILS interface through usability is an ongoing process. Therefore, keep up to date on the topic by subscribing to Jakob Nielsen's Alertbox (http://www.useit.com/alertbox/quantitative_testing.html) and articles on website design available at (http://www.nngroup.com/articles/subscribe/). Note that Nielsen's website has recently changed from http://www.useit.com to http://www.nngroup.com.

SUMMARY

The last phase of the Library Automation life cycle (LALC) is evaluating user effectiveness and satisfaction in using the ILS interface through usability principles and methods. Conducting such an evaluation requires that you learn about user characteristics, attributes of the interface, and attributes of the tasks the user performs to achieve a specific goal. Measuring the user experience in the interface should uncover design problems, causes of these problems, and whether they are indeed associated with the design of the interface or the user's inadequate level of knowledge of the search process or other aspects.

While design problems can be resolved through improving the design of the interface, problems associated with the user's knowledge should be remedied through effective user instruction.

Evaluating the ILS interface through usability assessment, as described in this chapter, covers theoretical frameworks that should inform practice. Usability methods are divided into two categories: one that involves expert reviewers (also known as system inspection) and one that includes actual users. The former category covers heuristics, rules, and principles, as well as cognitive walkthrough. The latter includes different methods, including, but not limited to, surveys, interviews, observation, and focus groups. Advanced methods embrace contextual inquiry, experimental testing, and task analysis. Case studies of usability assessment and metrics are provided in Tullis and Albert (2013).

Selecting a specific evaluation method should be based on your library's environment, the goals of the evaluation, time, cost, personnel resources, access to users or participants, and ROI.

Although you may not have total control over the design of the interface and its functionality, design problems found through the evaluation of the interface over a period of time should be shared with system vendors or firms so that they may make design improvements that support the user's experience.

REFERENCES

Beyer, Hugh, and Karen Holtzblatt. *Contextual Design: Defining Customer-Centered Systems.* San Francisco, CA: Morgan Kaufmann Publishers Inc., 1998.

Bilal, Dania. "Children's Use of the Yahooligans! Web Search Engine. III. Cognitive and Physical Behaviors on Fully Self-Generated Tasks." *Journal of the American Society for Information Science & Technology*, vol. 53, 13 (2002): 1170–83.

Bilal, Dania. "Grounding Children's Information Behavior and System Design in Child Development Theories." In *Information and Emotion: The Emergent Affective Paradigm in Information Behavior Research and Theory*, eds. Diane Nahl and Dania Bilal. Medford, NJ: Information Today, 2007.

Bilal, Dania, and Joe Kirby. "Differences and Similarities in Information Seeking: Children and Adults as Web Users." *Information Processing & Management*, vol. 38, 5 (2002): 649–70.

Case, Donald O. *Looking for Information: A Survey of Research on Information Seeking, Needs and Behavior.* 3rd ed. Bingley, UK: Emerald Book Publishing, 2012.

Crystal, Abe, and Beth Ellington. "Task Analysis and Human-Computer Interaction: Approaches, Techniques, and Levels of Analysis." *Proceedings of the*

Tenth Americas Conference on Information Systems, New York, August 2004. http://www.ils.unc.edu/~acrystal/AMCIS04_crystal_ellington_final .pdf. Accessed February 25, 2013.

Erikson, E. H. *Youth: Change and Challenge*. New York: Basic Books, 1963.

Erikson, E. H. *Identity: Youth and Crisis*. New York: WW Norton and Company, 1968.

Fisher, Karen E., Sanda Erdelez, and Lynne Mckechnie (eds.). *Theories of Information Behavior*. Medford, NJ: Information Today Inc., 2005.

Hearst, Marti. *Search User Interfaces*. Cambridge, MA: Cambridge University Press, 2009.

Hollingsed, Tasha, and David G. Novick. "Usability Inspection Methods after 15 Years of Research and Practice." 2007. http://mcom.cit.ie/staff/ Computing/prothwell/HCI/papers/UI%20Inspection%20Hollingsed. pdf. Accessed December 29, 2013.

Holtzblatt, Karen. "Why Contextual Inquiry vs. Other Marketing Techniques." *InContext Customer Centered Design*, November 8, 2002. http://incontext design.com/articles/why-contextual-inquiry-vs-other-marketing-techniques. Accessed February 25, 2013.

Knowles, Malcolm S. "Andragogy, not Pedagogy." *Adult Leadership*, vol. 16, 10 (1968): 350–52, 386.

Knowles, Malcolm S. *The Modern Practice of Adult Education: from Pedagogy to Andragogy*. New York: The Adult Education Company, 1980.

Krueger, Richard A., and Mary Anne Casey. *Focus Groups: A Practical Guide for Applied Research*. Thousand Oaks, CA: Sage Publications Inc., 2009.

Kuhlthau, Carol C. "Inside the Search Process: Information Seeking from the User's Perspective." *Journal of the American Society for Information Science*, vol. 42, 5 (1991): 361–71.

Kuhlthau, Carol C. *Seeking Meaning: A Process Approach to Library and Information Services*. 2nd ed. Westport, CT: Libraries Unlimited, 2004.

Lewis, Clayton, and John Rieman. *Task-Centered User Interface Design: A Practical Introduction*. 1994. http://hcibib.org/tcuid/chap-4.html. Accessed February 20, 2013.

Mahatody Thomas, Mouldi Sagar, and Christophe Kolski. "State of the Art on the Cognitive Walkthrough Method, Its Variants and Evolutions." *International Journal of Human-Computer Interaction* vol. 26, 8 (2010): 741–85.

Marchionini, Gary, and Ryen W. White. "Find What You Need, Understand What You Find." *Journal of Human-Computer Interaction*, vol. 23, 3 (2008): 205–37.

Nahl, Diane, and Dania Bilal (eds.). *Information and Emotion: The Emergent Affective Paradigm in Information Behavior Research and Theory*. Medford, NJ: Information Today, 2007.

Nielsen, Jakob. "Discount Usability: 20 Years." September 14, 2009. http://www .useit.com/alertbox/discount-usability.html. Accessed February 6, 2013.

Nielsen, Jakob. "How to Conduct a Heuristic Evaluation." 1994. http://www .useit.com/papers/heuristic/heuristic_evaluation.html. Accessed March 6, 2013.

Nielsen, Jakob. "Quantitative Studies: How Many Users to Test." June 26, 2006. http://www.useit.com/alertbox/quantitative_testing.html. Accessed February 25, 2013.

Nielsen, Jakob. "Usability 101: Introduction to Usability." 2003. http://www.useit.com/alertbox/20030825.html. Accessed February 6, 2013.

Nielsen, Jakob, and Hoa Loranger. *Prioritizing Web Usability*. Berkeley, CA: New Riders Press, 2007.

Norman, Donald. *The Design of Everyday Things*. Cambridge, MA: MIT Press, 1998.

Piaget, Jean, and Bärbel Inhelder. *The Psychology of the Child*. New York: Basic Books, 1969.

Research Methods Knowledge Base: "Interviews." http://www.socialresearchmethods.net/kb/intrview.php. Accessed March 19, 2013.

Rogers, Yvonne, Helen Sharp, and Jenny Preece. *Interaction Design: Beyond Human-Computer Interaction*. 3rd ed. New York: John Wiley & Sons, 2011.

Shneiderman, Ben, and Catherine Plaisant. *Designing the User Interface: Strategies for Effective Human-Computer Interaction*. 5th edition. Boston, MA: Addison-Wesley, 2009.

Spink, Amanda. *Information Behavior: An Evolutionary Instinct*. Berlin: Springer-Verlag, 2010.

Tullis, Tom, and Bill Albert. *Measuring the User Experience: Collecting, Analyzing, and Presenting Usability Metrics*. Boston: Elsevier, 2013.

Turner, Daniel W., III. "Qualitative Interview Design: A Practical Guide for Novice Investigators." *The Qualitative Report,* 15 no. 3 (2010): 754–60. http://www.nova.edu/ssss/QR/QR15-3/qid.pdf. Accessed February 20, 2013.

Wharton, Cathleen, John Reiman, Clayton Lewis, and Peter Polson. *The Cognitive Walkthrough Method: A Practitioner's Guide*. 1994. In Nielsen, J., and Mack, R. L. (Eds.), *Usability Inspection Methods*. New York: John Wiley & Sons, pp. 105–40.

Wilson, T. D. (Ed.). *Theory in Information Behaviour Research*. 2013. https://itunes.apple.com/us/book/theory-in-information-behaviour/id662992330?ls=1. Accessed August 10, 2013.

WEBSITES

Jakob Nielsen's Alertbox. http://www.useit.com/alertbox/quantitative_testing.html.

LibQual+. http://www.libqual.org/home.

Morae Usability Software. http://www.techsmith.com.

Questionnaire for User Interaction Satisfaction. http://hcibib.org/perlman/question.cgi?form=QUIS.

Research Methods. http://www.socialresearchmethods.net.

Research Methods Knowledgebase, Interviews. http://www.socialresearch methods.net/kb/intrview.php.

Standards for Accessible Design. http://www.ada.gov/2010ADAstandards_ index.htm.

Task Analysis. http://www.usabilitynet.org/tools/taskanalysis.htm.

Tobii Eye Tracking Products.http://www.tobii.com/en/eye-tracking-research/ global/products/software/.

Usability.gov. http:/www.usability.gov.

Usability.gov. Methods. http://www.usability.gov/how-to-and-tools/methods/ index.html.

User Interface Engineering (UIE). https://www.uie.com/.

User Interface Engineering (UIE). Personas. http://www.uie.com/browse/ personas/.

Chapter 10

Library Automation "On the Move"

Library automation has been "on the move" or "in motion" for the past few years. Some of the facets of this dynamic that drive technology strategies in libraries include:

- The changing nature of library collections to include increasing proportions of electronic content and digitized materials

- The rise of library services platforms (LSPs) as next-generation automation systems

- Continued advancements in computer technologies, such as cloud computing, open platforms offering application programming interface (API) and based on the service-oriented architecture (SOA)

- Migrations among automation platforms, including moving from one proprietary integrated library system (ILS) to another one or to an open-source equivalent, and from open source to proprietary

- The requirement to deliver library services on smartphones and mobile devices

This chapter describes these developments and speculates on the future of the ILS.

Many enhancements in the functionality of traditional ILSs, including both proprietary and open-source alternatives, have recently taken place. The discovery services arena has also been an area of intense interest. Based on indexes representing licensed scholarly publications combined with locally held content, discovery services support one search box, which is able to search all types of resources and retrieve results that include journal articles from a library's subscription databases, and display results using relevance ranking (Luther and Kelly 2011) These index-based discovery services stream-line searching across different resource types and formats and save time in finding information. These products will continue to be attractive to libraries.

Many libraries, especially those in the research and academic arenas have embraced various forms of digital collections that require innovative automation solutions which can efficiently accommodate the management of print, electronic, and digital collections. These libraries are finding that traditional ILSs are deficient in integrating and managing these collections efficiently (Grant 2012). In recent years, new generation ILSs that focus on content management and support the entire lifecycle of a resource (from selection of resources, to acquisitions, to cataloging and metadata management, information discovery, and fulfillment) have been developed by a number of proprietary system vendors. Breeding coined the term for these systems as library services platforms (LSPs). LSPs are built on the "open system" concept, SOA, and web-based interfaces, including next-generation discovery services that are designed for deployment as software-as-a-service (SaaS) (Breeding 2013). In addition, LSPs are designed to offer more flexibility in managing different kinds of library materials and "to bring new services and capabilities to end users" (Grant 2012, 4). As of August 2013, the three LSPs in the marketplace were the Online Computer Library Center (OCLC) WorldShare Management Services (WMS) (http://www.oclc.org/worldshare-management-services.en.html), Ex Libris' Alma (http://www.exlibrisgroup.com/category/AlmaOverview), and Innovative Interfaces' Sierra (http://sierra.iii.com). Two LSPs currently in development include Serials Solutions' Intota (http://www.serialssolutions.com/en/services/intota) and VTLS Open Skies (http://www.vtls.com/node/132). Intota's release is expected sometime in 2014. The first Open Skies component, MozGo Mobile App, is currently available. The implementation of other functions (online catalog, circulation, and digital asset management) is expected by the end of 2013. In the open-source software arena, Kuali OLE (http://www.kuali.org/ole) is the only LSP (as of August 2013) developed as open-source software. Kuali OLE is being developed by a community of college and research libraries for higher education institutions. The success of Kuali OLE in the academic arena could serve as a model for other types of libraries interested in designing their own open-source platforms. Similarly, the success of proprietary LSPs "depends on easier access to the data held in their knowledge bases, which are their greatest asset, and in the flexibility to generate and process the growing diversity of data and metadata models" (Breeding 2012). All these platforms support next-generation discovery interfaces. WMS, Alma, and Intota are "paired" with next-generation discovery services (World-Cat Local (http://www.oclc.org/worldcat-local/about.en.html), Primo Central Index (Vaughn, 2011), and Summon Discovery (http://www.serialssolutions.com/en/services/summon), respectively and offered by the same providers, resulting in matching existing back-end systems with front-end discovery services. Open Skies from VTLS (http://www.vtls.com/node/155), which is in development, will be paired with Chamo Discovery interface (http://

www.vtls.com/products/chamo). Breeding (2011) notes that this paring is "an on-going trend that is expected to dominate in the near future" by companies that design platforms for research and academic environments. Libraries in other environments, such as small ones, may benefit from using these LSPs provided that they are a part of a larger consortium that uses these platforms.

While LSPs may become the choice for large libraries, smaller libraries including those in schools can still gain access to these sophisticated platforms by joining a consortium. By doing so, these libraries will gain access to a consolidated online catalog of member libraries, share resources, benefit from centralized or distributed acquisitions and processing of library materials, and save on the cost of the ILS. Participation in consortia is on the rise in the library arena, and pursuing this option should preserve the identity of individual libraries, meet their automation specifications, as well as allow them to configure the shared ILS based on their own individual needs and requirements.

Small libraries with small collections that are not part of a consortium and desire to automate their collections and establish a web presence should be on the lookout for the OCLC's Small Libraries Project that was implemented on February 14, 2012 as a beta service (http://www.oclc.org/en-US/news/releases/2012/201211.html) to support any small library wishing to create to provide basic web-based automation services to its users. Libraries with collections of 20,000 items or less will be able to set up users, check materials in and out, place holds, and provide contact information, events, and other basic information about the library and its services. As of August 2013, OCLC has not provided further information about this project.

Increased demand for eBooks in libraries has stimulated demand to provide simplified discovery, delivery, and access. Selected system vendors have developed new solutions to provide users with unified access to all types of resources including eBooks, eJournals, and print items using one single discovery interface. Taking advantage of the APIs made available by library-oriented eBook services, such as OverDrive, 3M Cloud Library, and Baker & Taylor Axis 360, several developers of online catalog and discovery interfaces have fully integrated the ability for library users to discover, view, or download eBook titles without having to interact directly with external eBook lending platforms. In addition, some next-generation electronic resource management (ERM) solutions are offered as cloud-based, enabling libraries to save on the cost of downloading eBooks, licensing, and metadata creation, among other things. These solutions will be "on the move" as more vendors partner with eBook providers to provide a seamless information discovery experience to users, while offering cost-effective content management of e-resources. ILSs with discovery interfaces that foster these types of innovations and allow libraries to customize interfaces based on their own needs will continue to be attractive in the near future.

Advances in cloud computing and the offerings provided by proprietary system vendors and open-source firms have shifted many library applications and services to the cloud. As described in Chapter 7, there are three service models that characterize "true" cloud computing. In relation to software, SaaS is the service model for hosting software in the cloud. This model is based on a multitenant hosting service that delivers efficiency, quick updates, and faster delivery of library services to users. Libraries, especially in the academic arena, continue to invest in products deployed as SaaS. In terms of hardware, the two hosting services are platform-as-a-service (PaaS) and infrastructure-as-a-Service (IaaS). Both services deliver cost savings on hardware needed to run the software and on hiring IT personnel to manage the network. SaaS, PaaS, and IaaS are expected to increase as service providers continue to provide innovative solutions that meet the needs of libraries. SaaS will most likely become the norm for accessing the ILS or LSP and using other library applications.

Migration has been "on the move" in all types of libraries. In the academic arena, migration from traditional ILSs to LSPs has begun, though at a slow pace. For example, in 2012, Ex Libris signed 17 contracts for Alma; Innovative Interfaces had 117 contracts for Sierra; and OCLC had 87 contracts for WMS. As Breeding (2013) notes, "early successes in the short term can amplify long-term prospects" of these platforms. On all fronts, migration from proprietary to another proprietary ILS, proprietary to open source, one open-source ILS firm to another, and from open-source to proprietary ILS has continued in the past few years. In a report about ILS turnover in 2013, Breeding (http://www.librarytechnology.org/ils-turnover-reverse.pl?Year=2013) identified the ILS products that libraries registered in *lib-web-cats* (http://www.library technology.org/libwebcats) and the new ILSs or LSPs they have selected. For example, of the 404 libraries that had the Millennium ILS from Innovative Interfaces (http://www.iii.com/products/millennium_ils.shtml), one library replaced this ILS with Alma platform, one with EOS.Web (http://www .eosintl.com/eos-web/academic/), 11 with Koha (ByWater Solutions), one with Polaris (http://www.polarislibrary.com/polaris-products/polaris-integrated-library-system/), 383 with Sierra platform, three with Symphony, and three with OCLC WMS. Similarly, of the 70 libraries (as of September 7, 2013) that had Liblime Koha, two migrated to Apollo from Biblionix (http://www.bib lionix.com/products/apollo), 64 to Koha by ByWater Solutions, two to Sierra, and two to WMS. As to libraries with ILSs designed for small libraries, of the nine libraries that had Destiny from Follett Software Company (http://www .follettsoftware.com/library-automation-software), for example, five replaced it with Apollo, two migrated to Koha (ByWater Solutions), and two turned over to Koha (LibLime). Note that Breeding's 2013 report is based only on information registered in *lib-web-cats* from August to September 7, 2013. These numbers may change as transitions from one system to another get recorded in the *lib-web-cats* database. Additional information about this report and previous system turnover counts is provided at http://www.librarytechnol ogy.org/ils-turnover-reverse.pl. Though Breeding's system turnover list is not comprehensive, it provides an overview about the status and nature of system migration in libraries. ILS migration will be "on the move" as the nature of library collections, library operations, and user needs and expectations continue to change.

The interfaces through which libraries deliver their services to users are impacted by evolving technologies. Increased use of smartphones, tablets, and other mobile devices will influence how libraries will accommodate user needs. Mobile apps to support users' remote access of the ILS are being offered by system vendors. Use of these devices inside the library to access the ILS discovery interface and other library applications will require access through a wireless connection. As demand on the network's bandwidth increases, the network's bandwidth should be upgraded to accommodate high traffic. Though this will increase expenses, libraries may still save on the cost of public access computers.

Small libraries with limited budgets have unique opportunities to establish web presence to serve their user communities. Options include joining consortia such as Open-Source Automated Library System (OPALS) managed by Media Flex Inc. to share the ILS and becoming members of the Social OPAC (SOPAC) open-source platform to share bibliographic data. The OCLC Small Library Project, now called Website for Small Libraries (WSSL), which was announced in February 2012 to help small libraries create a website that provides basic automation functionality, is available as a beta service. A demo and free trial are located at http://beta.worldcat.org/lib/-/-/public/home. WSSL may be an easy, inexpensive option for libraries with collections of 20,000 items or less.

Overall, the developments described in this chapter will be on the rise. As envisioned by Breeding (2012; 2013), the future of ILSs will be shaped by increase in cloud-based software hosting, rise in migration to LSPs, growth in discovery products designed for academic libraries, delivery of services on mobile devices, and continued investment in technology products, especially by research and academic libraries. Increase in ILS capabilities that allow the integration of all types of e-resources, including eBooks, in a single discovery interface, and increase in collaboration among libraries through consortia are likely to remain "on the move."

ILSs that will survive in the near future are those that are user-centered, offer innovative solutions based on the needs of library users and staff, can effectively and efficiently accommodate the management of all types of resources in all formats, and streamline library operations, while taking advantage of advanced and innovative technologies including cloud computing.

REFERENCES

Breeding, Marshall. "Automation Marketplace 2011: The New Frontier." *Library Journal*. 2011. http://www.libraryjournal.com/lj/home/889533–264/auto mation_marketplace_2011_the_new.html.csp. Accessed March 3, 2013.

Breeding, Marshall. "Automation Marketplace 2012: Agents of Change." *Library Journal.* 2012. http://www.thedigitalshift.com/2012/03/ils/automation-marketplace-2012-agents-of-change. Accessed June 29, 2013.

Breeding, Marshall. "Automation Marketplace 2013: The Rush to Innovate." 2013. http://www.thedigitalshift.com/2013/04/ils/automation-marketplace-2013-the-rush-to-innovate. Accessed July 3, 2013.

Breeding, Marshall. "Integrated Library System Turnover in 2013." 2013. http://www.librarytechnology.org/ils-turnover-reverse.pl?Year=2013. Accessed August 4, 2013.

Breeding, Marshall. "Library Technology Forecast for 2014 and Beyond." *Computers in Libraries*, vol. 33, 10 (2013). http://www.infotoday.com/cilmag/dec13/Breeding--Library-Technology-Forecast%20-for-2014-and-Beyond.shtml. Accessed December 27, 2013.

Grant, Carl. "The Future of Library Systems: Library Services Platforms." *Information Standards Quarterly*, vol. 24, 4 (2012): 1–13.

Luther, Judy, and Maureen C. Kelly. "The Next Generation of Discovery." *Library Journal.* 2011. http://www.libraryjournal.com/lj/home/889250-264/the_next_generation_of_discovery.html.csp. Accessed March 10, 2012.

Mell, Peter, and Timothy Grance. The NIST Definition of Cloud Computing: Recommendations of the National Institute of Standards and Technology. 2011. http://csrc.nist.gov/publications/nistpubs/800-145/SP800-145.pdf. Accessed July 16, 2013.

Miller, Michael. *Cloud Computing: Web-Based Applications that Change the Way You Work and Collaborate Online.* Indianapolis, IN: Que Publishing, 2009.

Vaughn, Jason. "Ex Libris Primo Central." *Library Technology Reports*, 47, 1 (2011): 39-47.

WEBSITES

Biblionix. Apollo. http://www.biblionix.com/products/apollo/.

ByWater Solutions. Koha. http://bywatersolutions.com/what-is-koha.

Ex Libris Group. Alma. http://www.exlibrisgroup.com/category/Alma Overview.

Ex Libris Group. Primo Central. http://www.exlibrisgroup.com/category/PrimoCentral.

Follett Software Company. Destiny. http://www.follettsoftware.com/library-automation-software.

Innovative Interfaces Inc. Millennium. http://www.iii.com/products/millennium_ils.shtml.

Innovative Interfaces Inc. Sierra. http://sierra.iii.com.

Kuali OLE. http://www.kuali.org/ole.

Liblime Koha. http://www.koha.org.

Lib-web-cats. http://www.librarytechnology.org/libwebcats/.

Media Flex. OPALS. http://www.mediaflex.net/showcase.jsp?record_id=52.

OCLC. Website for Small Libraries (WSSL). http://beta.worldcat.org/lib/-/-/
public/home.

OCLC. WorldCat Local. http://www.oclc.org/worldcat-local/about.en.html.

OCLC. WorldShare Management Services. http://www.oclc.org/worldshare-
management-services.en.html.

OPALS. See Media Flex.

Polaris Library. http://www.polarislibrary.com/polaris-products/polaris-inte
grated-library-system/.

Serial Solutions. Intota. http://www.serialssolutions.com/en/services/intota.

Serials Solutions. Summon Discovery. http://www.serialssolutions.com/en/
services/summon.

VTLS. Chamo Discovery. http://www.vtls.com/products/chamo.

VTLS. Open Skies. http://www.vtls.com/node/132.

Appendix: Sample Request for Proposal by the Brentwood Library, Brentwood, TN

Brentwood Library ILS RFP authored by Mary Barksdale, Missy Dillingham, Susan Earl, Kenny Hartman, Heather Lanier, Maria Sochor, Sue Szostak, and Robin Walden. Reprinted with permission.

THE BRENTWOOD LIBRARY

A CENTER FOR FINE ARTS

REQUEST FOR PROPOSALS
INTEGRATED LIBRARY SYSTEM
Issued August 18, 2011

- PROPOSALS DUE NO LATER THAN 2:00 P.M. CST, SEPTEMBER 15, 2011. LATE PROPOSALS WILL NOT BE CONSIDERED.

- ONE DIGITAL COPY AND FOUR PRINT COPIES MUST BE SUBMITTED.

Submit proposals to: Susan Earl, Library Director
                        Brentwood Municipal Center
                        5211 Maryland Way
                        Brentwood, TN 37027

Refer questions to: Maria Sochor, Librarian
                        sochorm@brentwood-tn.org

Legal Notice

Request for Proposals
for Purchase of an Integrated
Library System

The City of Brentwood is seeking proposals for a complete
Integrated Library System, including fully operational circulation,
cataloging, serials, acquisitions (with fund accounting), electronic ordering,
and reporting modules in addition to a public access catalog.

Request for Proposals documents may be obtained at the Brentwood
Library, 8109 Concord Road, Brentwood, Tennessee, 37027, Monday
through Friday, 9:00 a.m. to 5:00 p.m. or downloaded from the City website
at http://brentwood-tn.org.

Responding firms shall submit their proposals to the Brentwood
Municipal Building at 5211 Maryland Way in Brentwood, Tennessee,
37027 in the format specified in the Request for Proposals. All proposals
are due on September 15, 2011 at 2:00 p.m. CST.

Questions concerning the Request for Proposals should be addressed
to Maria Sochor at sochorm@brentwood-tn.org.

Verbal or faxed quotations will not be accepted. The City of Brentwood
reserves the right to reject any and/or all proposals, to waive any irregulari-
ties or informalities in a proposal, and to accept any proposal, which, in its
opinion, may be in the best interest of the City.

Williamson A.M.
Submitted for publication on August 18, 2011.

The Brentwood Library
Request for Proposals
Integrated Library System

Including Fully Operational Circulation, Cataloging, Serials, Acquisitions (with Fund Accounting), Electronic Ordering, and Reporting Modules in Addition to a Public Access Catalog

TABLE OF CONTENTS

I. OVERVIEW

1.1. Introduction

Brentwood Library is seeking proposals for a new turnkey Integrated Library System (ILS), complete with automated and customer-friendly end services; this system must be capable of supporting an online public access catalog, circulation, acquisitions, serials, interlibrary loan, inventory, reporting, cataloging, authority control, federated searching, and administrative modules.

All costs incurred by the proposer in preparation of a response to this RFP shall be the full responsibility of the proposer.

1.2. Mandatory Requirement

The ILS shall run on the Windows 2008 platform using the 2008 MS SQL Server database. No other operating systems or databases will be acceptable. Proposers must be licensed sellers and certified in Microsoft systems.

1.3. Background Information on Library

The Brentwood Library is a main library in the City of Brentwood, located in northeastern Williamson County, directly south of Nashville, Tennessee. Williamson County is the fastest growing county in Tennessee. Brentwood is the 17th largest city in Tennessee.

The City of Brentwood is progressive with traditional values, and is known for great customer service from all of its city departments. The Brentwood Library is considered to be one of the crown jewels of the community and is often featured in local newspapers and city publications. Partnered with all other City services, the library helps to make Brentwood attractive to potential businesses and residents.

Additionally, this library is touted for its exemplary customer service within the state's library community. This customer-centered service coupled with an attractive, Craftsman-style building draws many librarians and other visitors for tours and meetings.

The Brentwood Library has 40 employees in 26 FTE positions serving a population of 37,000 with over 20,000 registered users. The Library has approximately 162,000 item records. Over 1,100 patrons visit the library each day with an annual circulation exceeding 625,000 items. The library is open 66 hours per week, across seven days per week. Hours of operation are 9:00 a.m. to 8:00 p.m. Monday through Thursday, 9:00 a.m. to 6:00 p.m. Friday, 10:00 a.m. to 6:00 p.m. Saturday, and 1:00 p.m. to 6:00 p.m. Sunday.

The current integrated library system is SirsiDynix Symphony, version 3.3.102652.12. It is a hosted system with 30 workstations. The library runs on a fiber network at 1000 mbps speed.

The City of Brentwood's internet providers are Comcast and Time Warner (2 lines; 1 cable and 1 fiber optic). The library uses EnvisionWare Time Management, Print Management, and RFID systems. The library went live with a RFID (Radio Frequency Identification) system in July 2010. There are 6 self check-out stations. Barcode wands are Honeywell. Brentwood uses 18 receipt printers (Star TSP 650 and TSP 600).

The library's network is managed by the City of Brentwood IT department with one staff member assigned to the library. This technician is on call as needed and the City operates a 24 hour help desk.

1.3.1. Library Mission and Goal

Our mission is to serve patrons with materials that will help them:

- Be productive
- Contribute to our society

204

- Elevate their economic stature
- Enhance their humanity
- Enjoy life every day

Our goal is to provide service with:

- Competence
- Professionalism
- Courtesy

1.3.2. Current Statistics and Five Year Estimates

Category	Current	Projected 5 Years
Number of member libraries and branches	1	1
Number of item records	162,201	224,784
Number of patrons	20,672	21,499
Number of annual circulation transactions	625,000	812,500
Number of staff workstations	30	35
Annual materials budget	$308,353	$314,520

1.3.3. Library's Timetable

The library reserves the right to delay or otherwise alter any portion of this timetable if the library deems that change to be in its best interests.

Event	Date
Proposals due	2:00 p.m., September 15, 2011
Vendor selection	Late Oct. 2011
Soft launch deadline	Feb. 14, 2012
Full launch deadline	March 27, 2012

2. PROPOSAL SUBMISSION AND EVALUATION REQUIREMENTS

2.1. Selection Criteria

The Brentwood Library will review all valid, complete proposals and evaluate the extent to which each meets the desired specifications given in section 3. The cost of each proposed set of services and products will then be considered, given the determined effectiveness of each proposal in meeting the library's needs.

The Brentwood Library is not bound to accept the lowest priced proposal. The Brentwood Library reserves the right to reject any or all responses to this RFP if the library deems that action to be in its best interests. The Brentwood Library reserves the right to request clarification on any item in a proposal or to request additional information when necessary to perform a complete proposal evaluation. The Brentwood Library reserves the right to contact any of the library references given in a proposal in order to request clarification or to seek additional information. The Brentwood Library reserves the right to postpone selection or contract award for any reason.

2.2. Minimum Requirements

Failure to meet any of the following requirements will result in rejection of a proposal:

- Proposals must be received in a complete state, including every item listed in section 2.5 (*Proposal Response Format*).
- Proposers must be legal entities which are legally authorized to do business in the State of Tennessee.
- Proposers must comply with all City of Brentwood contracting requirements as well as all applicable local, state, and federal laws.
- Proposed systems must comply with relevant ADA requirements.
- Proposers must be able to provide a soft launch of the ILS with the following functionality no later than February 14, 2012:
  - Complete datasets migrated from SirsiDynix so the library staff and new ILS vendor staff can make a comprehensive evaluation of the migration results
  - Complete functionality of all staff client modules and related services so the library staff and new ILS vendor staff can configure toolbars, access levels, and other critical staff client administration elements; library staff must be able to interact fully with the staff client for testing and configuration purposes without causing undesirable effects to patron accounts, item records, or other elements of the existing SirsiDynix-held datasets or ILS
  - Complete PAC functionality delivered via a private, library-configurable access model so library staff and other selected stakeholders can access the PAC while normal patron PAC traffic still routes to the existing SirsiDynix PAC
  - Complete training materials and training services for all library staff using the library's own datasets and soft launch ILS workstation configurations as the basis for training
- Proposers must be able to provide a full launch of the ILS with the following functionality no later than March 27, 2012:
  - Complete ILS package must be running at 100% full functionality, 99.9% uptime, and 100% complete configuration to meet library policies, workflows, and other library-defined setup schema
  - Complete datasets migrated from SirsiDynix, with all additional work completed to the library's satisfaction as needed to correct any and all data corruption or undesirable data alteration, including but not limited to issues related to the migration of data from one field schema to a different and/or noncompatible field schema as well as issues related to workflows or policy implementation in the new ILS that differ from the existing ILS in such a manner that inhibits efficient or proper workflows, as defined by the library
  - Complete functionality of all staff client modules and related services (including self check-out stations) with 100% completed configuration to meet the library's needs for efficient and policy-adherent data processing
  - Complete PAC functionality delivered via the library website and all other existing PAC access portals or links

2.3. Nondiscrimination

The Brentwood Library shall not discriminate based on race, color, sex, creed, religion, ancestry, disability, familial status, sexual orientation, or national origin in selecting the vendor for the Integrated Library System. The successful vendor agrees that it shall not discriminate in its performance of the contract based on race, color, sex, creed, religion, ancestry, disability, familial status, or national origin.

2.4. Open Records

Brentwood Library, as a department of the City of Brentwood, is subject to the Open Records Laws of the State of Tennessee, including but not limited to T.C.A. 10–7–701. Materials submitted in response to this RFP may be subject to public inspection. Each proposer, by submitting a proposal, agrees to hold the City of Brentwood harmless for its good faith efforts to comply with the Open Records Laws.

2.5. Proposal Response Format

Proposals must be sealed. Proposal envelopes/packages must be clearly marked on the outside as follows:

Proposal for Integrated Library System
Do not open until September 15, 2011, 2:00 p.m.

A proposal must include all of the following items in order to be considered complete, and thus eligible for consideration:

- Cover letter on proposer's letterhead, signed and dated by a duly authorized representative of the proposer
- Vendor profile (Background, Product Line, Financial Information, Staff Information)
  - Provide a statement as to whether there is current pending litigation against the proposer; if so, attach opinion of counsel as to whether that pending litigation will impact the proposer's ability to provide goods and services under this RFP.
  - Provide a statement as to whether the proposer has filed or has had filed against it any bankruptcy or insolvency proceeding, whether voluntary or involuntary, or undergone the appointment of a receiver, trustee, or assignee for the benefit of creditors (provide a summary of relevant details if so).
- Complete responses to all items in section 3 (*ILS Requirements*) Complete responses to all items in section 4 (*Cost Proposal*)
- Complete responses to all items in section 5 (*Contract and Statement of Non-Discrimination*)
- Complete responses to all items in section 6 (*Disaster Recovery Plan*) Complete responses to all items in section 7 (*Customer References*)
- Complete responses to all items in section 8 (*Server and IT Support Requirements*) Complete responses to all items in section 9 (*Workstation Requirements*)
- Statement of acceptance of the General Terms and Conditions of this RFP (see section 10)
- Product demo information with sample dataset and library site access for evaluation purposes

2.6. Protests and Disputes

Proposers who wish to dispute a disqualification of proposal or award of contract must follow the City of Brentwood's Bid Protest Policy, accessible at http://brentwood-tn.org.

3. ILS REQUIREMENTS

3.1. Overview of ILS Requirements

Proposals must include complete responses to every requirement contained in the requirements section of this RFP using the following criteria, except where a narrative response is indicated. Responses must be in the same order in which questions appear in this RFP, and must use the same numbering scheme used in this RFP.

O	Operational	In use by at least 90% of customers, and available to 100% of customers
A	Available	In use by less than 90% of customers, and available to 100% of customers

D	In development	Testing and release planned within two years from the due date of this RFP
P	Planned	Capability is planned; no development is underway and/or release planned for a date more than two years from the due date of this RFP
N	Not available	Not planned, and no development underway

For any specifications for which a response is given other than O (Operational) or A (Available), an explanation must be given below the question with the following components:

- For features, functions, products, or services being planned or developed, indicate the date of general release and operation in the system proposed to the library.
- Indicate whether the library will incur any added cost for the feature, function, product, or service once it becomes available, either as a direct cost of the feature, function, product, or service, or because the feature, function, product, or service will require replacement of or addition to hardware or software originally proposed for initial installation.
- If the feature, function, product, or service is not available, in development, or planned, provide an explanation of how the specification might otherwise be met using alternative features, functions, products, or services available from the vendor or a third-party partner, including availability dates for any such alternative and any added costs, either direct or indirect.

Any such exception taken to any specification must be stated in the cost proposal with deviation noted and any associated cost stated. Vendors are advised that the library is interested in receiving proposals from vendors who can offer an integrated library system already in use by an installed customer base, and that proposals for systems in an alpha or beta phase of development will not be considered. The library reserves the right to evaluate all proposals solely on the basis of currently existing features, functions, products, or services meeting the specifications as stated.

3.2. System Requirements

3.2.1.   The ILS must comply fully with the Z39.50 version 3 standard on both the client and the server sides.
_____O = Operational   A = Available   D = Development   P = Planned   N = Not Available

Explain:

3.2.2.   The ILS must include its own SMTP email server for sending out email notices to patrons.
_____O = Operational   A = Available   D = Development   P = Planned   N = Not Available

Explain:

3.2.3.   At a minimum, the ILS must include the following as the core product:

3.2.3.1.   Circulation, including inventory and offline functionality
_____O = Operational   A = Available   D = Development   P = Planned   N = Not Available

3.2.3.2.   Cataloging with authority control
_____O = Operational   A = Available   D = Development   P = Planned   N = Not Available

3.2.3.3.   Bibliographic import
_____O = Operational   A = Available   D = Development   P = Planned   N = Not Available

3.2.3.4.   Acquisitions with fund accounting

_____*O = Operational*   *A = Available*   *D = Development*   *P = Planned*   *N = Not Available*

3.2.3.5.   Electronic ordering (EDI)

_____*O = Operational*   *A = Available*   *D = Development*   *P = Planned*   *N = Not Available*

3.2.3.6.   Selection list import via 9XX

_____*O = Operational*   *A = Available*   *D = Development*   *P = Planned*   *N = Not Available*

3.2.3.7.   Serials control

_____*O = Operational*   *A = Available*   *D = Development*   *P = Planned*   *N = Not Available*

3.2.3.8.   Interlibrary loan

_____*O = Operational*   *A = Available*   *D = Development*   *P = Planned*   *N = Not Available*

3.2.3.9.   System administration

_____*O = Operational*   *A = Available*   *D = Development*   *P = Planned*   *N = Not Available*

3.2.3.10. Public access catalog, including remote patron authentication

_____*O = Operational*   *A = Available*   *D = Development*   *P = Planned*   *N = Not Available*

3.2.3.11. eCommerce for patrons

_____*O = Operational*   *A = Available*   *D = Development*   *P = Planned*   *N = Not Available*

3.2.3.12. RSS feeds

_____*O = Operational*   *A = Available*   *D = Development*   *P = Planned*   *N = Not Available*

3.2.3.13. Z39.50 interface

_____*O = Operational*   *A = Available*   *D = Development*   *P = Planned*   *N = Not Available*

3.2.3.14. Web-based reporting

_____*O = Operational*   *A = Available*   *D = Development*   *P = Planned*   *N = Not Available*

Explain: (refer to item by number)

3.2.4.   The following must be available at library's option:

3.2.4.1.   Email (to and from patron)

_____*O = Operational*   *A = Available*   *D = Development*   *P = Planned*   *N = Not Available*

3.2.4.2.   Text messaging (to and from patron)

_____*O = Operational*   *A = Available*   *D = Development*   *P = Planned*   *N = Not Available*

3.2.4.3.   eCommerce for staff

_____*O = Operational*   *A = Available*   *D = Development*   *P = Planned*   *N = Not Available*

3.2.4.4.   Self-check (SIP2 or NCIP) interface

_____*O = Operational*   *A = Available*   *D = Development*   *P = Planned*   *N = Not Available*

3.2.4.5.   Debt collection interface

_____*O = Operational*   *A = Available*   *D = Development*   *P = Planned*   *N = Not Available*

3.2.4.6.   Outreach services (homebound)

_____*O = Operational*   *A = Available*   *D = Development*   *P = Planned*   *N = Not Available*

3.2.4.7.   Inventory manager

_____*O = Operational*   *A = Available*   *D = Development*   *P = Planned*   *N = Not Available*

3.2.4.8.   Mobile PAC

_____*O = Operational*   *A = Available*   *D = Development*   *P = Planned*   *N = Not Available*

3.2.4.9.   Smartphone app

_____*O = Operational*   *A = Available*   *D = Development*   *P = Planned*   *N = Not Available*

3.2.4.10. Social media
_____O = Operational   A = Available   D = Development   P = Planned   N = Not Available

3.2.4.11. Children's PAC
_____O = Operational   A = Available   D = Development   P = Planned   N = Not Available

3.2.4.12. Digital collection management integration (CONTENTdm)
_____O = Operational   A = Available   D = Development   P = Planned   N = Not Available

3.2.4.13. Program and room reservation management
_____O = Operational   A = Available   D = Development   P = Planned   N = Not Available

Explain: (refer to item by number)

3.2.5. Subscription services must include the following. List third-party vendors in explanation below.

3.2.5.1. Enhanced data content for PAC
_____O = Operational   A = Available   D = Development   P = Planned   N = Not Available

3.2.5.2. Cataloging record source (bibliographic, authority, and audio/visual)
_____O = Operational   A = Available   D = Development   P = Planned   N = Not Available

3.2.5.3. Real-time authority header update service
_____O = Operational   A = Available   D = Development   P = Planned   N = Not Available

3.2.5.4. Authority header update service subscription (i.e., yearly, 6-month, quarterly, bimonthly, monthly, weekly; explain options)
_____O = Operational   A = Available   D = Development   P = Planned   N = Not Available

Explain: (refer to item by number)

3.2.6. The ILS must enable operators to access any and all system functions for which they are authorized from any screen on any workstation, limited only by the library's choice.
_____O = Operational   A = Available   D = Development   P = Planned   N = Not Available

Explain:

3.2.7. The ILS must not require a separate login to access different subsystems. The initial login must set all privileges for all subsystems. If moving across subsystems or working in multiple modules simultaneously, the vendor must state if this increases the tally of simultaneous users.
_____O = Operational   A = Available   D = Development   P = Planned   N = Not Available

Explain:

3.2.8. The ILS must provide a user-friendly search tool that is uniform across all subsystems.
_____O = Operational   A = Available   D = Development   P = Planned   N = Not Available

Explain:

3.2.9. The system must provide on-screen contextual help functionality.
_____O = Operational   A = Available   D = Development   P = Planned   N = Not Available

Explain:

3.2.10. The system must provide on-screen error alert messages as interactive dialog boxes.
_____O = Operational   A = Available   D = Development   P = Planned   N = Not Available

Explain:

3.2.11. The search tool must allow truncation or wild card capability.
_____O = Operational   A = Available   D = Development   P = Planned   N = Not Available

Explain:

3.2.12. The library must have the option to set the search tool to use an auto-suggest feature for keyword and phrase searches for patron, item, bibliographic and authority records.
_____*O = Operational   A = Available   D = Development   P = Planned   N = Not Available*

Explain:

3.2.13. The search tool must provide *search by*, *limit by*, and *sort by* options.
_____*O = Operational   A = Available   D = Development   P = Planned   N = Not Available*

Explain:

3.2.14. The ILS must allow users to perform certain tasks on records listed in search results without having to open the records either globally or individually.
_____*O = Operational   A = Available   D = Development   P = Planned   N = Not Available*

Explain:

3.2.15. The ILS must allow users to create record sets directly from the search results without having to open the records.
_____*O = Operational   A = Available   D = Development   P = Planned   N = Not Available*

Explain:

3.2.16. The ILS must include the following products and services to the full extent required for successful system implementation and operation:

3.2.16.1. Data migration services
_____*O = Operational   A = Available   D = Development   P = Planned   N = Not Available*

3.2.16.2. Software (operating system, database and application)
_____*O = Operational   A = Available   D = Development   P = Planned   N = Not Available*

3.2.16.3. Server hardware and any additional hardware components or peripherals specific to the proposed system
_____*O = Operational   A = Available   D = Development   P = Planned   N = Not Available*

3.2.16.4. Policy profiling/generation
_____*O = Operational   A = Available   D = Development   P = Planned   N = Not Available*

3.2.16.5. Installation and database loading
_____*O = Operational   A = Available   D = Development   P = Planned   N = Not Available*

3.2.16.6. Training on all subsystems
_____*O = Operational   A = Available   D = Development   P = Planned   N = Not Available*

3.2.16.7. Documentation
_____*O = Operational   A = Available   D = Development   P = Planned   N = Not Available*

3.2.16.8. Hardware and software maintenance
_____*O = Operational   A = Available   D = Development   P = Planned   N = Not Available*

Explain: (refer to item by number)

3.2.17. The vendor must offer a subscription option to enhance the content of the library's catalog records and PAC through automatic web links to:

3.2.17.1. Book reviews, summaries, book jacket images, cover art, digital images, etc.
_____*O = Operational   A = Available   D = Development   P = Planned   N = Not Available*

3.2.17.2. Moderated, patron-generated reviews
_____*O = Operational   A = Available   D = Development   P = Planned   N = Not Available*

3.2.17.3. Author biographies and tables of content
_____O = Operational   A = Available   D = Development   P = Planned   N = Not Available

3.2.17.4. Bestseller lists
_____O = Operational   A = Available   D = Development   P = Planned   N = Not Available

3.2.17.5. Most popular titles, subjects, and authors, based on automatic analysis of the library's recent circulation statistics
_____O = Operational   A = Available   D = Development   P = Planned   N = Not Available

3.2.17.6. Third-party databases such as NoveList or Books and Authors
_____O = Operational   A = Available   D = Development   P = Planned   N = Not Available

Explain: (refer to item by number)

3.2.18. The system must enable control of staff permissions without the need to log off workstations between users with different permissions levels.
_____O = Operational   A = Available   D = Development   P = Planned   N = Not Available

Explain:

3.2.19. The system must provide full API access at no cost beyond the standard annual maintenance fees quoted in the cost proposal.
_____O = Operational   A = Available   D = Development   P = Planned   N = Not Available

Explain:

3.2.20. The ILS must allow staff to have multiple modules open simultaneously.
_____O = Operational   A = Available   D = Development   P = Planned   N = Not Available

Explain:

3.2.21. Licenses must be governed in such a manner that permits unlimited access to all modules for which a user has access permission without utilizing more than a single license. The user must be able to perform workflows that utilize multiple modules without encumbering more than a single license.
_____O = Operational   A = Available   D = Development   P = Planned   N = Not Available

Explain:

3.2.22. The staff client must enable easy customization and sharing of toolbars.
_____O = Operational   A = Available   D = Development   P = Planned   N = Not Available

Explain:

3.2.23. A test server must be provided for use in training staff during the implementation process and for testing during future upgrades.
_____O = Operational   A = Available   D = Development   P = Planned   N = Not Available

Explain:

3.2.24. The ILS must support named stations/named logins so that library administrators can easily determine who performed a specific action or transaction, and for statistical reporting.
_____O = Operational   A = Available   D = Development   P = Planned   N = Not Available

Explain:

3.2.25. The ILS must include an optional programs and room reservation management module, at no additional cost beyond the itemized costs and annual maintenance fees listed in the cost proposal.
_____O = Operational   A = Available   D = Development   P = Planned   N = Not Available

Explain:

3.2.26. The programs and room reservation module must include:

3.2.26.1. A Web-based calendar with both self-registration and staff-mediated registration for programs

_____O = *Operational*   A = *Available*   D = *Development*   P = *Planned*   N = *Not Available*

3.2.26.2. Email alerts for registrants

_____O = *Operational*   A = *Available*   D = *Development*   P = *Planned*   N = *Not Available*

3.2.26.3. A mechanism for accepting and managing payments for program fees based on funds on deposit on a patron's library account or online payment, at the patron's option

_____O = *Operational*   A = *Available*   D = *Development*   P = *Planned*   N = *Not Available*

3.2.26.4. Automated wait list management

_____O = *Operational*   A = *Available*   D = *Development*   P = *Planned*   N = *Not Available*

3.2.26.5. Automated inclusion of relevant calendar items in PAC search results

_____O = *Operational*   A = *Available*   D = *Development*   P = *Planned*   N = *Not Available*

3.2.26.6. No-conflict room booking for large meeting rooms and associated optional equipment and small study rooms, including application of library-defined policies governing booking limits and a staff-mediated reservation acceptance mechanism for large meeting rooms only

_____O = *Operational*   A = *Available*   D = *Development*   P = *Planned*   N = *Not Available*

3.2.26.7. Repeat session management

_____O = *Operational*   A = *Available*   D = *Development*   P = *Planned*   N = No t Available

3.2.26.8. Low and high demand alerts for staff based on event registration tallies

_____O = *Operational*   A = *Available*   D = *Development*   P = *Planned*   N = *Not Available*

Explain: (refer to item by number)

3.2.27. The ILS must allow the library to choose which social media-related options that act within or via the PAC or any other component of the ILS are activated. These activation options must be governed through a graphical user interface.

_____O = *Operational*   A = *Available*   D = *Development*   P = *Planned*   N = *Not Available*

Explain:

3.2.28. The ILS must provide itemized fine support that is compatible with EnvisionWare eCommerce Services. The ILS must provide itemized fine and fee support using the established AV SIP messages currently provided by the existing SirsiDynix ILS.

_____O = *Operational*   A = *Available*   D = *Development*   P = *Planned*   N = *Not Available*

Explain:

3.2.29. The ILS must support a declining balance deposit account that can be accessed externally via SIP and which is compatible with EnvisionWare's protocol for deposit account payment for printing, fines and fees, copies, and other services.

_____O = *Operational*   A = *Available*   D = *Development*   P = *Planned*   N = *Not Available*

Explain:

3.2.30. The ILS must provide patron type and related categories that are compatible with PC Reservation. Describe patron type support and how it is passed to EnvisionWare via a SIP message.

_____O = *Operational*   A = *Available*   D = *Development*   P = *Planned*   N = *Not Available*

Explain:

3.2.31. The ILS must support interactive voice response (IVR). Specify all options available.
_____*O = Operational*   *A = Available*   *D = Development*   *P = Planned*   *N = Not Available*

Explain:

3.2.32. The ILS must integrate with OCLC/WorldCat in order to download bibliographic and authority records, perform interlibrary loan functions, and related tasks.
_____*O = Operational*   *A = Available*   *D = Development*   *P = Planned*   *N = Not Available*

Explain:

3.2.33. Highlight system strengths:

3.3. Circulation Requirements

The library considers that all ILS vendors provide basic and advanced circulation functionality. The following is a list of specific features desired by the library.

3.3.1.   Data and Records Management

3.3.1.1.   The ILS must support an unlimited number of patron types without vendor intervention.
_____*O = Operational*   *A = Available*   *D = Development*   *P = Planned*   *N = Not Available*

Explain:

3.3.1.2.   The ILS must support permissions that can be set by staff member or workstation to restrict viewing and/or modifying of patron records.
_____*O = Operational*   *A = Available*   *D = Development*   *P = Planned*   *N = Not Available*

Explain:

3.3.1.3.   The ILS must support manual creation of patron records.
_____*O = Operational*   *A = Available*   *D = Development*   *P = Planned*   *N = Not Available*

Explain:

3.3.1.4.   The ILS must support the ability to merge duplicate patron records. All fines, fees, notes, and circulation history must move from the record to be deleted to the surviving record.
_____*O = Operational*   *A = Available*   *D = Development*   *P = Planned*   *N = Not Available*

Explain:

3.3.1.5.   It must be possible to remove patron identification data from circulation transaction records and item histories.
_____*O = Operational*   *A = Available*   *D = Development*   *P = Planned*   *N = Not Available*

Explain:

3.3.1.6.   The ILS must allow default values to be set when creating new patron records.
_____*O = Operational*   *A = Available*   *D = Development*   *P = Planned*   *N = Not Available*

Explain:

3.3.1.7.   The ILS must provide library-modifiable patron record templates or allow the library to create its own patron record templates.
_____*O = Operational*   *A = Available*   *D = Development*   *P = Planned*   *N = Not Available*

Explain:

3.3.1.8. The ILS must allow the library to define the following fields as required: address, birth date, password, statistical class, and patron message preference (text, email, etc.).

_____*O = Operational*   *A = Available*   *D = Development*   *P = Planned*   N = Not Avai lable

Explain:

3.3.1.9. The ILS must support the ability to display patron photos in the patron registration and check-out screens.

_____*O = Operational*   *A = Available*   *D = Development*   *P = Planned*   *N = Not Available*

Explain:

3.3.1.10. It must be possible to capture patron photos from a Webcam, a digital camera, or to load images from an existing file. Loading a patron photo from any of these input options must be easy and quick enough to be done as part of a new account registration process or simple account modification, with the image loaded directly from that workstation.

_____*O = Operational*   *A = Available*   *D = Development*   *P = Planned*   *N = Not Available*

Explain:

3.3.1.11. The ILS must provide a mechanism for automatically checking for duplicate patron accounts during the new account registration process, based on library-specified fields such as name, address, or driver's license (with or without a 0 prefix).

_____*O = Operational*   *A = Available*   *D = Development*   *P = Planned*   *N = Not Available*

Explain:

3.3.1.12. The ILS must offer an option for patron self-registration from the PAC.

_____*O = Operational*   *A = Available*   *D = Development*   *P = Planned*   *N = Not Available*

Explain:

3.3.1.13. The ILS must offer a self-registered patron immediate but limited privileges as determined by the library.

_____*O = Operational*   *A = Available*   *D = Development*   *P = Planned*   *N = Not Available*

Explain:

3.3.1.14. The patron record must accommodate multiple patron addresses.

_____*O = Operational*   *A = Available*   *D = Development*   *P = Planned*   *N = Not Available*

Explain:

3.3.1.15. The ILS must allow the library to define certain fields in the patron record for its own use (user-defined fields).

_____*O = Operational*   *A = Available*   *D = Development*   *P = Planned*   *N = Not Available*

Explain:

3.3.1.16. User-defined fields must be able to be defined as free-text fields or drop-menu fields with selectable options.

_____*O = Operational*   *A = Available*   *D = Development*   *P = Planned*   *N = Not Available*

Explain:

3.3.1.17. The ILS must display a patron's last activity date and time. The date should be incremented for online activity as well as in-house transactions.

_____*O = Operational*   *A = Available*   *D = Development*   *P = Planned*   *N = Not Available*

Explain:

3.3.1.18. It must be possible within the staff client to retrieve the last patron account that had been displayed with one click.

_____*O = Operational   A = Available   D = Development   P = Planned   N = Not Available*

Explain:

3.3.1.19. The ILS must support searching patron records by, but not limited to, the following access points:

3.3.1.19.1. Barcode

_____*O = Operational   A = Available   D = Development   P = Planned   N = Not Available*

3.3.1.19.2. Former barcode (for accounts that have had a new card issued)

_____*O = Operational   A = Available   D = Development   P = Planned   N = Not Available*

3.3.1.19.3. Last name, First name

_____*O = Operational   A = Available   D = Development   P = Planned   N = Not Available*

3.3.1.19.4. First name, Last name

_____*O = Operational   A = Available   D = Development   P = Planned   N = Not Av ailable*

3.3.1.19.5. Phone

_____*O = Operational   A = Available   D = Development   P = Planned   N = Not Available*

3.3.1.19.6. Email

_____*O = Operational   A = Available   D = Development   P = Planned   N = Not Available*

3.3.1.19.7. Fields defined by the library (user-defined fields)

_____*O = Operational   A = Available   D = Development   P = Planned   N = Not Available*

3.3.1.19.8. Expiration date

_____*O = Operational   A = Available   D = Development   P = Planned   N = Not Available*

3.3.1.19.9. Registration date

_____*O = Operational   A = Available   D = Development   P = Planned   N = Not Available*

3.3.1.19.10. Last activity date

_____*O = Operational   A = Available   D = Development   P = Planned   N = Not Available*

3.3.1.19.11. Zip code

_____*O = Operational   A = Available   D = Development   P = Planned   N = Not Available*

3.3.1.19.12. Notes

_____*O = Operational   A = Available   D = Development   P = Planned   N = No t Available*

3.3.1.19.13. Blocks

_____*O = Operational   A = Available   D = Development   P = Planned   N = Not Available*

Explain: (Refer to item by number)

3.3.1.20. The ILS must support the ability to enter only the significant digits of the patron barcode for ease of use in the staff client and PAC with the capability to use truncation and wild card searching.

_____*O = Operational   A = Available   D = Development   P = Planned   N = Not Available*

Explain:

3.3.1.21. The patron record must offer private notes for staff use and "blocking" notes that will alert the staff member during check-out.

_____*O = Operational   A = Available   D = Development   P = Planned   N = Not Available*

Explain:

3.3.1.22. The ILS must natively integrate with the EnvisionWare RFID System using Envision-Ware's RFIDLink API (or bidders must have provided an API that EnvisionWare has used) in order to provide seamless, native RFID and barcode operation with the ILS circulation client. Provide a letter of certification from EnvisionWare that indicates successful implementation and testing for compliance with version 2.3 of the EnvisionWare RFIDLink API or an alternative approach that EnvisionWare has tested and certified.

_____*O = Operational   A = Available   D = Development   P = Planned   N = Not Available*

Explain:

3.3.1.23. Two specific RFID-to-ILS interaction configurations must be available for the library to test and implement at its discretion. In the first setup, the RFID pad must be activated and deactivated automatically based on workflow, without the need for staff to manually activate or deactivate the pad. In the second setup, the pad would remain deactivated until staff manually activated it at the appropriate point in a transaction and then manually deactivated the pad when it was no longer necessary to read items. The library must be able to test both options during the soft launch phase and choose which setup will be used going forward. The library must be able to change this setup back and forth if needed over time at no additional cost.

_____*O = Operational   A = Available   D = Development   P = Planned   N = Not Available*

Explain:

3.3.1.24. Describe the step-by-step workflow for a staff check-out and a staff check-in using EnvisionWare RFID, using barcodes, and using barcodes and EnvisionWare RFID. Indicate whether items are processed one at a time or in a batch.

_____*O = Operational   A = Available   D = Development   P = Planned   N = Not Available*

Explain:

3.3.1.25. The ILS must provide an efficient, easy to use service within the staff client for logging and otherwise processing "claims returned" and "claims never checked out" items.

_____*O = Operational   A = Available   D = Development   P = Planned   N = Not Available*

Explain:

3.3.1.26. The ILS must automatically convert child accounts into adult accounts based on library-customizable parameters based on the birth year stored in user accounts. Specify whether this would be done by an automatically scheduled routine report or some other method. Specify how the ILS would perform this operation without necessitating any manual staff action to reformat the account-based data on which the parameters for making these changes to existing accounts would be made.

_____*O = Operational   A = Available   D = Development   P = Planned   N = Not Available*

Explain:

3.3.1.27. The ILS must support an opt-in patron reading history that patrons must choose to enable. Patrons must be able to enable this feature via the PAC, with no staff intervention needed. It must also be possible to easily enable this feature via the staff client. This feature must include a privacy statement, customizable by the library, that patrons must accept before a reading history is stored.

_____*O = Operational   A = Available   D = Development   P = Planned   N = Not Available*

Explain:

3.3.1.28. The ILS must support the ability to sort the reading history by check-out date, title, and author. It must also be possible for patrons to easily print or export their reading history as an automated email, downloadable PDF, or other readily accessible document format.

_____*O = Operational*   *A = Available*   *D = Development*   *P = Planned*   *N = Not Available*

Explain:

3.3.1.29. The ILS must support linked or associated borrowers (family links) that do not require borrowers within a group or family to share a last name.

_____*O = Operational*   *A = Available*   *D = Development*   *P = Planned*   *N = Not Available*

Explain:

3.3.1.30. The ILS must support automatic barring with linked or associated borrowers based on library-set parameters such as a defined fine threshold. The ILS must also support automatic unbarring of those accounts when the parameters are no longer triggered (i.e., when fines are paid).

_____*O = Operational*   *A = Available*   *D = Development*   *P = Planned*   *N = Not Available*

Explain:

3.3.1.31. The ILS must support policy-based permissions for "authorized users," persons other than the card holder who are named as authorized to perform a list of library-specified transactions using the card holder's account. This feature must include a privacy statement, customizable by the library, that patrons must accept before an authorized user can be added to their account. This feature must be enabled via both the staff client and PAC.

_____*O = Operational*   *A = Available*   *D = Development*   *P = Planned*   *N = Not Available*

Explain:

3.3.1.32. The ILS must support the ability to perform global "search and replace" operations on a selected group of patron records (record set functions).

_____*O = Operational*   *A = Available*   *D = Development*   *P = Planned*   N = Not Availab le

Explain:

3.3.1.33. The ILS must allow staff with sufficient privilege to delete patron records individually.

_____*O = Operational*   *A = Available*   *D = Development*   *P = Planned*   *N = Not Available*

Explain:

3.3.1.34. The ILS must support the automatic deletion of patron records based on a library-defined period of inactivity.

_____*O = Operational*   *A = Available*   *D = Development*   *P = Planned*   *N = Not Available*

Explain:

3.3.1.35. It must be possible to stop the automatic deletion based on certain criteria:
3.3.1.35.1. Amount of money owed

_____*O = Operational*   *A = Available*   *D = Development*   *P = Planned*   *N = Not Available*

3.3.1.35.2. Any charge incurred within x days

_____*O = Operational*   *A = Available*   *D = Development*   *P = Planned*   *N = Not Available*

3.3.1.35.3. Items out

_____*O = Operational*   *A = Available*   *D = Development*   *P = Planned*   *N = Not Available*

3.3.1.35.4. Items on hold

_____*O = Operational*   *A = Available*   *D = Development*   *P = Planned*   *N = Not Available*

3.3.1.35.5. Items on order

_____*O = Operational*   *A = Available*   *D = Development*   *P = Planned*   *N = Not Available*

Explain (refer to item by number):

3.3.1.36. The ILS must be able to properly apply the library's internet permission policy based on the existing account data setup parameters, with no additional effort from staff.
_____*O = Operational   A = Available   D = Development   P = Planned   N = Not Available*

Explain:

3.3.2.   Check-Out

3.3.2.1.   The ILS must support an unlimited number of item types.
_____*O = Operational   A = Available   D = Development   P = Planned   N = Not Available*

Explain:

3.3.2.2.   The ILS must support umbrella policies governing check-out limits by item type, so that multiple item types can contribute towards a shared total limit (i.e., limit of 4 DVDs could include a total of 4 titles from any of the various DVD item types such as DVD CHILD, DVD R, etc.).
_____*O = Operational   A = Available   D = Development   P = Planned   N = Not Available*

Explain:

3.3.2.3.   The ILS must calculate loan periods and due dates according to the type of borrower and type of material.
_____*O = Operational   A = Available   D = Development   P = Planned   N = Not Available*

Explain:

3.3.2.4.   The ILS must support the assignment of specific due dates based on an exact date or a selected number of days, hours or minutes (special loan periods).
_____*O = Operational   A = Available   D = Development   P = Planned   N = Not Available*

Explain:

3.3.2.5.   The ILS must support the ability to apply a special loan period to one item during a check-out, to all items checked out to an individual patron in one transaction, or to all items checked out to all patrons during the entire check-out session.
_____*O = Operational   A = Available   D = Development   P = Planned   N = Not Available*

Explain:

3.3.2.6.   The ILS must support the ability for the library to specify which types of materials may be borrowed by which types of patrons.
_____*O = Operational   A = Available   D = Development   P = Planned   N = Not Available*

Explain:

3.3.2.7.   The ILS must support the ability for the library to specify a limit on the total number of items any patron may have at one time. The limit must be configurable by the library for each patron type.
_____*O = Operational   A = Available   D = Development   P = Planned   N = Not Available*

Explain:

3.3.2.8.   The ILS must support the ability for the library to specify a limit on the number of items of any particular type a patron may have at one time. The limit may be set by the library for each patron type.
_____*O = Operational   A = Available   D = Development   P = Planned   N = Not Available*

Explain:

3.3.2.9. The ILS must support the ability for the library to specify a limit on the number of overdue items a patron may have at one time. The limit may be set by the library for each patron type.
_____*O = Operational   A = Available   D = Development   P = Planned   N = Not Available*

Explain:

3.3.2.10. The ILS must support the ability to specify a limit on amount of money owed by patron. The limit may be set by the library for each patron type.
_____*O = Operational   A = Available   D = Development   P = Planned   N = Not Available*

Explain:

3.3.2.11. The ILS must support the ability for the library to specify a limit on the number of lost items a patron may have at one time. The limit may be set by the library for each patron type.
_____*O = Operational   A = Available   D = Development   P = Planned   N = Not Available*

Explain:

3.3.2.12. The ILS must support the ability for the library to specify a limit on the total number of hold requests any patron may have at one time. The limit may be set by the library for each patron type.
_____*O = Operational   A = Available   D = Development   P = Planned   N = Not Available*

Explain:

3.3.2.13. The ILS must support the ability for brief item and bibliographic records to be created "on the fly" to allow uncataloged items to circulate.
_____*O = Operational   A = Available   D = Development   P = Planned   N = Not Available*

Explain:

3.3.2.14. Item records added "on the fly" must be added to the bibliographic database immediately.
_____*O = Operational   A = Available   D = Development   P = Planned   N = Not Available*

Explain:

3.3.2.15. The ILS must provide an option to configure what patron data displays during check-out.
_____*O = Operational   A = Available   D = Development   P = Planned   N = Not Available*

Explain:

3.3.2.16. The ILS must provide a direct link to the complete patron record from check-out.
_____*O = Operational   A = Available   D = Development   P = Planned   N = Not Available*

Explain:

3.3.2.17. The information displayed in the patron record must include, but not be limited to:
3.3.2.17.1. All patron registration information
_____*O = Operational   A = Available   D = Development   P = Planned   N = Not Available*

3.3.2.17.2. A summary list of the patron's current standing, showing all blocks, number of items out, number of items overdue, total amount owed, number of claimed and lost items, number of items on hold, and notes
_____*O = Operational   A = Available   D = Development   P = Planned   N = Not Available*

3.3.2.17.3. A complete list of all items currently checked out to the patron, showing barcode, author, title, due date, material type, number of renewals allowed, and number of renewals taken
_____*O = Operational   A = Available   D = Development   P = Planned   N = Not Available*

3.3.2.17.4. An indication of any item that is overdue
_____*O = Operational   A = Available   D = Development   P = Planned   N = Not Available*

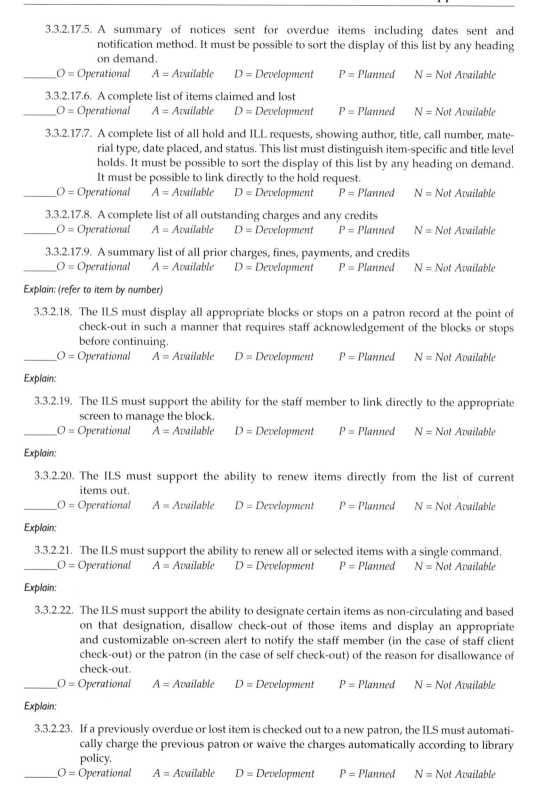

3.3.2.17.5. A summary of notices sent for overdue items including dates sent and notification method. It must be possible to sort the display of this list by any heading on demand.

_____*O = Operational   A = Available   D = Development   P = Planned   N = Not Available*

3.3.2.17.6. A complete list of items claimed and lost

_____*O = Operational   A = Available   D = Development   P = Planned   N = Not Available*

3.3.2.17.7. A complete list of all hold and ILL requests, showing author, title, call number, material type, date placed, and status. This list must distinguish item-specific and title level holds. It must be possible to sort the display of this list by any heading on demand. It must be possible to link directly to the hold request.

_____*O = Operational   A = Available   D = Development   P = Planned   N = Not Available*

3.3.2.17.8. A complete list of all outstanding charges and any credits

_____*O = Operational   A = Available   D = Development   P = Planned   N = Not Available*

3.3.2.17.9. A summary list of all prior charges, fines, payments, and credits

_____*O = Operational   A = Available   D = Development   P = Planned   N = Not Available*

Explain: (refer to item by number)

3.3.2.18. The ILS must display all appropriate blocks or stops on a patron record at the point of check-out in such a manner that requires staff acknowledgement of the blocks or stops before continuing.

_____*O = Operational   A = Available   D = Development   P = Planned   N = Not Available*

Explain:

3.3.2.19. The ILS must support the ability for the staff member to link directly to the appropriate screen to manage the block.

_____*O = Operational   A = Available   D = Development   P = Planned   N = Not Available*

Explain:

3.3.2.20. The ILS must support the ability to renew items directly from the list of current items out.

_____*O = Operational   A = Available   D = Development   P = Planned   N = Not Available*

Explain:

3.3.2.21. The ILS must support the ability to renew all or selected items with a single command.

_____*O = Operational   A = Available   D = Development   P = Planned   N = Not Available*

Explain:

3.3.2.22. The ILS must support the ability to designate certain items as non-circulating and based on that designation, disallow check-out of those items and display an appropriate and customizable on-screen alert to notify the staff member (in the case of staff client check-out) or the patron (in the case of self check-out) of the reason for disallowance of check-out.

_____*O = Operational   A = Available   D = Development   P = Planned   N = Not Available*

Explain:

3.3.2.23. If a previously overdue or lost item is checked out to a new patron, the ILS must automatically charge the previous patron or waive the charges automatically according to library policy.

_____*O = Operational   A = Available   D = Development   P = Planned   N = Not Available*

Explain:

3.3.2.24. The ILS must support the ability for the library to configure the contents of check-out receipts and to automatically email receipts to patrons as desired, either in addition to the printed receipt or instead of the printed receipt based on patron preference.

_____O = Operational   A = Available   D = Development   P = Planned   N = Not Available

Explain:

3.3.2.25. The ILS must support the ability for a custom note to be added to check-out receipts, including an automatically generated message at the bottom of checkout receipts that indicates the dollar value of the transaction based on library-set standard item format prices (i.e., "Your library membership saved you $114.00 today" for a transaction in which six children's hardcovers, valued at $15.00 each, and two music CDs, valued at $12.00 each, were checked out).

_____O = Operational   A = Available   D = Development   P = Planned   N = Not Available

Explain:

3.3.2.26. The ILS must support the ability to link to item records from the patron payment record.

_____O = Operational   A = Available   D = Development   P = Planned   N = Not Available

Explain:

3.3.2.27. All alerts and on-screen messages must be accompanied by a customizable audible alert that the library can choose to activate or deactivate as a setting based on user login. The alert sound must be configurable at the message level.

_____O = Operational   A = Available   D = Development   P = Planned   N = Not Available

Explain:

3.3.3.   Offline Function

3.3.3.1. The ILS must provide an offline function to charge and discharge materials on a circulation workstation or on a portable device, and to load these transactions into the on-line circulation system at a later time. Specify what types of portable devices are compatible.

_____O = Operational   A = Available   D = Development   P = Planned   N = Not Available

Explain:

3.3.3.2. The offline upload function should be integrated with the circulation interface, without requiring the staff member to leave the program in order to upload the files.

_____O = Operational   A = Available   D = Development   P = Planned   N = Not Available

Explain:

3.3.3.3. The ILS must produce a report of uploaded files showing any exceptional conditions, such as items to fill hold requests.

_____O = Operational   A = Available   D = Development   P = Planned   N = Not Available

Explain:

3.3.3.4. The ILS must allow the ability to register patrons offline.

_____O = Operational   A = Available   D = Development   P = Planned   N = Not Available

Explain:

3.3.3.5. The ILS must enable compensation for unexpected closed days when offline files are uploaded to prevent patrons from being charged unfairly for overdues.

_____O = Operational   A = Available   D = Development   P = Planned   N = Not Available

Explain:

3.3.4.   Check-In

3.3.4.1.   The ILS must support "book drop" or bulk check-in to allow rapid check-in with minimal staff involvement and to compensate for unexpected closed days to prevent patrons from being charged unfairly for overdues.

_____*O = Operational   A = Available   D = Development   P = Planned   N = Not Available*

Explain:

3.3.4.2.   The ILS must support RFID check-in.

_____*O = Operational   A = Available   D = Development   P = Planned   N = Not Available*

Explain:

3.3.4.3.   The ILS must support third-party check-in sorting systems.

_____*O = Operational   A = Available   D = Development   P = Planned   N = Not Available*

Explain:

3.3.4.4.   The ILS must support a "shelving status;" a temporary status assigned to items just checked in but not yet on the shelf.

_____*O = Operational   A = Available   D = Development   P = Planned   N = Not Available*

Explain:

3.3.4.5.   It must be possible for the status text to be displayed for shelving status to be customized by the library.

_____*O = Operational   A = Available   D = Development   P = Planned   N = Not Available*

Explain:

3.3.4.6.   It must be possible for the time to display the shelving status to be set differently by material type.

_____*O = Operational   A = Available   D = Development   P = Planned   N = Not Available*

Explain:

3.3.4.7.   The ILS must retain a link to the previous borrower after an item is checked in.

_____*O = Operational   A = Available   D = Development   P = Planned   N = Not Available*

Explain:

3.3.4.8.   The ability to retain a link to the previous borrower must be optional.

_____*O = Operational   A = Available   D = Development   P = Planned   N = Not Available*

Explain:

3.3.4.9.   After an item is checked in, it must be possible to determine:

3.3.4.9.1.   What date and time the item was checked in

_____*O = Operational   A = Available   D = Development   P = Planned   N = Not Available*

3.3.4.9.2.   On what workstation the item was checked in

_____*O = Operational   A = Available   D = Development   P = Planned   N = Not Available*

3.3.4.9.3.   What date and time the item was last checked out

_____*O = Operational   A = Available   D = Development   P = Planned   N = Not Available*

3.3.4.9.4.   On what workstation the item was checked out

_____*O = Operational   A = Available   D = Development   P = Planned   N = Not Available*

Explain: (refer to item by number)

3.3.4.10. The ILS must alert the user to overdues on an item when checking the item in.

_____*O = Operational   A = Available   D = Development   P = Planned   N = Not Available*

Explain:

3.3.4.11. The ILS must also alert the user to any pre-existing charges and allow the user to manage all charges at once.

_____*O = Operational   A = Available   D = Development   P = Planned   N = Not Available*

Explain:

3.3.4.12. The ILS must support customizable check-in receipts.

_____*O = Operational   A = Available   D = Development   P = Planned   N = Not Available*

Explain:

3.3.5.   Holds

3.3.5.1. The ILS must alert the staff member to items that should be trapped for a hold request.

_____*O = Operational   A = Available   D = Development   P = Planned   N = Not Available*

Explain:

3.3.5.2. The ILS must allow item trapping at check-in.

_____*O = Operational   A = Available   D = Development   P = Planned   N = Not Available*

Explain:

3.3.5.3. When trapping, the staff member must have the ability to not trap the item.

_____*O = Operational   A = Available   D = Development   P = Planned   N = Not Available*

Explain:

3.3.5.4. The staff client must allow staff to easily view expired, cancelled, and filled holds along with available holds for a given patron account.

_____*O = Operational   A = Available   D = Development   P = Planned   N = Not Available*

Explain:

3.3.5.5. The ILS must support automatically emailing or texting a customizable message to patrons, based on account settings that can be set via the staff client or the PAC, when a hold is available for check-out.

_____*O = Operational   A = Available   D = Development   P = Planned   N = Not Available*

Explain:

3.3.5.6. If the staff member does not permit the item to be held, the ILS must provide a prompt with links to keep or cancel the hold request.

_____*O = Operational   A = Available   D = Development   P = Planned   N = Not Available*

Explain:

3.3.6.   Borrow by Mail

3.3.6.1. The ILS must support a borrow by mail feature.

_____*O = Operational   A = Available   D = Development   P = Planned   N = Not Available*

Explain:

3.3.6.2. It must be possible to restrict borrow by mail options by patron type.

_____*O = Operational   A = Available   D = Development   P = Planned   N = Not Available*

Explain:

3.3.6.3.   It must be possible to charge a fee for borrow by mail service by patron type.
_____*O = Operational*   *A = Available*   *D = Development*   *P = Planned*   *N = Not Available*

Explain:

3.3.6.4.   It must be possible to exempt homebound patrons, or other specific patron types, from being charged a fee for the service.
_____*O = Operational*   *A = Available*   *D = Development*   *P = Planned*   *N = Not Available*

Explain:

3.3.7.   Overdue Fines and Accounting

3.3.7.1.   The ILS must have a configurable option to alert the staff member of overdue fines on incoming items and allow him/her to pay, waive, or charge the patron account.
_____*O = Operational*   *A = Available*   *D = Development*   *P = Planned*   *N = Not Available*

Explain:

3.3.7.2.   The staff member must have an appropriate privilege level to pay or waive fines.
_____*O = Operational*   *A = Available*   *D = Development*   *P = Planned*   *N = Not Available*

Explain:

3.3.7.3.   The ILS must support "distributed waives," the ability to waive a partial amount from several fines simultaneously.
_____*O = Operational*   *A = Available*   *D = Development*   *P = Planned*   *N = Not Available*

Explain:

3.3.7.4.   The ILS must support the ability for a staff member with sufficient privilege to access a patron account directly from check-in or check-out to manage charges if desired.
_____*O = Operational*   *A = Available*   *D = Development*   *P = Planned*   *N = Not Available*

Explain:

3.3.7.5.   The ILS must support the ability for calculation of the fine amount to include a grace period.
_____*O = Operational*   *A = Available*   *D = Development*   *P = Planned*   *N = Not Available*

Explain:

3.3.7.6.   The grace period must be configurable by material type.
_____*O = Operational*   *A = Available*   *D = Development*   *P = Planned*   *N = Not Available*

Explain:

3.3.7.7.   The ILS must support the ability to manually add a charge to a patron record.
_____*O = Operational*   *A = Available*   *D = Development*   *P = Planned*   *N = Not Available*

Explain:

3.3.7.8.   The ILS must support fine payment by credit card. Credit card payments will be supported:
3.3.7.8.1.   In the staff client
_____*O = Operational*   *A = Available*   *D = Development*   *P = Planned*   *N = Not Available*

3.3.7.8.2.   By patrons from the PAC
_____*O = Operational*   *A = Available*   *D = Development*   *P = Planned*   *N = Not Available*

3.3.7.8.3.   From the self-check unit
_____*O = Operational*   *A = Available*   *D = Development*   *P = Planned*   *N = Not Available*

Explain: (refer to item by number)

3.3.7.9.   If eCommerce is an add-on, indicate any additional costs below and add these costs as a line item cost and yearly maintenance charge on the cost proposal given in section 4.

3.3.7.10.   List accounting-related third-party vendors used. If third party vendors have user fees or add-on fees for the end-user, provide a list of those fees.

3.3.7.11.   The ILS must keep all completed account transactions in a patron account history for a library-determined length of time (but no CVV, CID, CVC2, or security code data is ever retained for any reason).

_____*O = Operational*   *A = Available*   *D = Development*   *P = Planned*   *N = Not Available*

Explain:

3.3.7.12.   The ILS must support the ability to retain item data in the patron financial history (charges/payments) even if the item is deleted. It must be possible to delete an item that has unpaid fines or fees associated with it, without the need to remove the fine or fee.

_____*O = Operational*   *A = Available*   *D = Development*   *P = Planned*   *N = Not Available*

Explain:

3.3.7.13.   The ILS must support the ability for fine receipts to be printed from any point in the program where fines can be paid (check-in, check-out, patron account), both at the time of fine payment and at any other time.

_____*O = Operational*   *A = Available*   *D = Development*   *P = Planned*   *N = Not Available*

Explain:

3.3.7.14.   The ILS must support the option of automatic emailing of payment receipts in lieu of a printed receipt and the option of producing neither an emailed receipt nor a printed receipt, as the patron prefers, via both the staff client and the self check-out stations.

_____*O = Operational*   *A = Available*   *D = Development*   *P = Planned*   *N = Not Available*

Explain:

3.3.7.15.   The ILS must support the ability for the content of fine receipts to be configurable.

_____*O = Operational*   *A = Available*   *D = Development*   *P = Planned*   *N = Not Available*

Explain:

3.3.7.16.   The ILS must automatically set items long overdue to lost when billed.

_____*O = Operational*   *A = Available*   *D = Development*   *P = Planned*   *N = Not Available*

Explain:

3.3.7.17.   The ILS must support the ability to set different policies for replacement, processing, and overdue charges by patron type.

_____*O = Operational*   *A = Available*   *D = Development*   *P = Planned*   *N = Not Available*

Explain:

3.3.8.   Notices

3.3.8.1.   The ILS must support each of the following notice types:

3.3.8.1.1.   Courtesy or "soon to be overdue"

_____*O = Operational*   *A = Available*   *D = Development*   *P = Planned*   *N = Not Available*

3.3.8.1.2.   Overdue

_____*O = Operational*   *A = Available*   *D = Development*   *P = Planned*   *N = Not Available*

3.3.8.1.3.   Fine

_____*O = Operational*   *A = Available*   *D = Development*   *P = Planned*   *N = Not Available*

3.3.8.1.4. Bill
_____O = Operational   A = Available   D = Development   P = Planned   N = Not Available

3.3.8.1.5. Statement of all charges
_____O = Operational   A = Available   D = Development   P = Planned   N = Not Available

3.3.8.1.6. Collection agency
_____O = Operational   A = Available   D = Development   P = Planned   N = Not Available

3.3.8.1.7. Hold pickup
_____O = Operational   A = Available   D = Development   P = Planned   N = Not Available

3.3.8.1.8. Hold cancellation
_____O = Operational   A = Available   D = Development   P = Planned   N = Not Available

3.3.8.1.9. Registration about to expire
_____O = Operational   A = Available   D = Development   P = Planned   N = Not Available

3.3.8.1.10. Patron has not used the library in a library-defined period of time
_____O = Operational   A = Available   D = Development   P = Planned   N = Not Available

3.3.8.1.11. Library information announcements to patrons
_____O = Operational   A = Available   D = Development   P = Planned   N = Not Available

Explain: (Refer to item by number)

3.3.8.2.   The ILS must support the ability to send notices by print, email, text message, or phone. Specify exactly how these options are elected for an individual patron, such as an account-based option, including whether the preferred notice format setting can be chosen or modified via both the staff client and the PAC.
_____O = Operational   A = Available   D = Development   P = Planned   N = Not Available

Explain:

3.3.8.3.   The ILS must support automatic distribution of notices on children's accounts to the child's named parent or guardian as an option based on account settings, with the default set to send notices addressed to the parent or guardian.
_____O = Operational   A = Available   D = Development   P = Planned   N = Not Available

Explain:

3.3.8.4.   The library must have the ability to post predefined and free-text messages to specific patron accounts.
_____O = Operational   A = Available   D = Development   P = Planned   N = Not Available

Explain:

3.3.8.5.   The library must be able to specify which staff members are permitted to post messages to patron accounts.
_____O = Operational   A = Available   D = Development   P = Planned   N = Not Available

Explain:

3.3.8.6.   Patrons must be allowed to read and manage these messages from their PAC account.
_____O = Operational   A = Available   D = Development   P = Planned   N = Not Available

Explain:

3.3.8.7.   When the patron marks the message as read, the read status must be noted in the patron account in the staff client.
_____O = Operational   A = Available   D = Development   P = Planned   N = Not Available

Explain:

3.3.8.8.   The ILS must provide the ability to delete patron messages manually or automatically according to a library-defined time limit.

_____*O = Operational   A = Available   D = Development   P = Planned   N = Not Available*

Explain:

3.3.8.9.   The ILS must support the ability for the library to determine the method for sending each individual notice, including each separate overdue notice (for example, 1st overdue by email, 2nd by print, etc.). When notices are sent by email, this must take place automatically.

_____*O = Operational   A = Available   D = Development   P = Planned   N = Not Available*

Explain:

3.3.8.10.   The ILS must support the ability for a staff member to determine the entire text of all notices and easily modify the text as necessary. Attach a sample overdue notice containing a library name and address header that has received no manual or macro-based formatting after the notice was generated (i.e., show the direct output of that notice from the ILS).

_____*O = Operational   A = Available   D = Development   P = Planned   N = Not Available*

Explain:

3.3.8.11.   The ILS must store and display a history of overdue notices and bills sent to the patron for all items currently overdue or billed.

_____*O = Operational   A = Available   D = Development   P = Planned   N = Not Available*

Explain:

3.3.8.12.   The notice history must be kept until the items are returned.

_____*O = Operational   A = Available   D = Development   P = Planned   N = Not Available*

Explain:

3.3.8.13.   The notice history must include item title, date sent, and method (print, email, text message, or phone call).

_____*O = Operational   A = Available   D = Development   P = Planned   N = Not Available*

Explain:

3.3.8.14.   The ILS must provide notification statistics reports.

_____*O = Operational   A = Available   D = Development   P = Planned   N = Not Available*

Explain:

3.3.8.15.   The ILS must support the ability for the staff member to produce, on demand, a summary statement of all charges owed.

_____*O = Operational   A = Available   D = Development   P = Planned   N = Not Available*

Explain:

3.3.8.16.   The statement may be produced for any individual patron or group of patrons.

_____*O = Operational   A = Available   D = Development   P = Planned   N = Not Available*

Explain:

3.3.9.   Holds

3.3.9.1.   The ILS must support the ability to place requests for any copy of a title (title level hold), a specific item (item level), or the first available copy of an item in a serial or multi-part set (such as the first available copy of season 1 of a TV series).

_____*O = Operational   A = Available   D = Development   P = Planned   N = Not Available*

Explain:

> 3.3.9.2.   The ILS must support the ability to place multiple requests for a single patron in one operation, without placing multiple individual requests.
> _____O = *Operational*   A = *Available*   D = *Development*   P = *Planned*   N = *Not Available*

Explain:

> 3.3.9.3.   The ILS must support the ability to place requests for a single title for multiple patrons in one operation, without placing multiple individual requests.
> _____O = *Operational*   A = *Available*   D = *Development*   P = *Planned*   N = *Not Available*

Explain:

> 3.3.9.4.   The ILS must support the ability to group multiple requests for an individual patron in such a way that when any one is filled, the others in the group are cancelled (For example, to get the first available copy of any of several Shakespeare plays.)
> _____O = *Operational*   A = *Available*   D = *Development*   P = *Planned*   N = *Not Available*

Explain:

> 3.3.9.5.   The ILS must support the ability for patrons to place requests from the PAC.
> _____O = *Operational*   A = *Available*   D = *Development*   P = *Planned*   N = *Not Available*

Explain:

> 3.3.9.6.   The ILS must support the ability for patrons to enter a note along with a request.
> _____O = *Operational*   A = *Available*   D = *Development*   P = *Planned*   N = *Not Available*

Explain:

> 3.3.9.7.   The ability for patrons to add notes to a request from the PAC must be optional and determined by the library.
> _____O = *Operational*   A = *Available*   D = *Development*   P = *Planned*   N = *Not Available*

Explain:

> 3.3.9.8.   The ILS must support the ability to designate an expiration or "not needed after" date when placing a request.
> _____O = *Operational*   A = *Available*   D = *Development*   P = *Planned*   N = *Not Available*

Explain:

> 3.3.9.9.   The ILS must support the ability to distinguish requests placed from the PAC, both visually and for reporting purposes.
> _____O = *Operational*   A = *Available*   D = *Development*   P = *Planned*   N = *Not Available*

Explain:

> 3.3.9.10. The display of titles in the PAC must include a count of all open requests.

Explain:

> 3.3.9.11. When a hold is placed via the staff client or PAC, the item format of each entry on a search results list must be clear without the need to click on a link or open a new window. Patrons or staff attempting to place a hold on a title for which the library owns copies in multiple item formats must be able to easily identify and select the desired format.
> _____O = *Operational*   A = *Available*   D = *Development*   P = *Planned*   N = *Not Available*

Explain:

> 3.3.9.12. The ILS must display a message in the PAC to inform the patron if other requests are open for the title, and how many requests are open.
> _____O = *Operational*   A = *Available*   D = *Development*   P = *Planned*   N = *Not Available*

Explain:

3.3.9.13.   The ILS must support the ability to suppress this message according to library policy.
_____*O = Operational   A = Available   D = Development   P = Planned   N = Not Available*

Explain:

3.3.9.14.   The ILS must support the ability for patrons or staff to set a blackout date range for a request at the time it is placed or after it is placed so that the hold will not come available during a period of time in which the patron does not wish to have that item. This feature must be accessible via the staff client and the PAC.
_____*O = Operational   A = Available   D = Development   P = Planned   N = Not Available*

Explain:

3.3.9.15.   The ILS must support the ability for a request that a patron has associated with a blackout period to maintain its position in the queue or to be placed at the end of the queue when the blackout period ends, according to library policy.
_____*O = Operational   A = Available   D = Development   P = Planned   N = Not Available*

Explain:

3.3.9.16.   The ILS must support the ability for staff to add notes to a request from the staff client.

Explain:

3.3.9.17.   The ILS must support the ability to add a note to the request that will print on the hold slip when the request is filled.
_____*O = Operational   A = Available   D = Development   P = Planned   N = Not Available*

Explain:

3.3.9.18.   The ILS must support the ability to set a charge for hold requests.
_____*O = Operational   A = Available   D = Development   P = Planned   N = Not Available*

Explain:

3.3.9.19.   If there is a charge for hold requests, it must be possible to display a library-customizable message advising the patron of the cost.
_____*O = Operational   A = Available   D = Development   P = Planned   N = Not Available*

Explain:

3.3.9.20.   The ILS must support the ability to set a different policy for the PAC and staff client with regard to placing requests.
_____*O = Operational   A = Available   D = Development   P = Planned   N = Not Available*

Explain:

3.3.9.21.   The ILS must support the ability to automatically change the due date of circulated items if the number of hold requests exceeds the number of available copies by a library-determined amount.
_____*O = Operational   A = Available   D = Development   P = Planned   N = Not Available*

Explain:

3.3.9.22.   The ILS must support the ability to either permit or not permit check-out if the item will fill a hold for another patron.
_____*O = Operational   A = Available   D = Development   P = Planned   N = Not Available*

Explain:

3.3.9.23. The ILS must support the ability for a staff member with sufficient privilege to adjust the order of requests in a queue at any time.

_____*O = Operational*   *A = Available*   *D = Development*   *P = Planned*   *N = Not Available*

Explain:

3.3.9.24. The ILS must support the ability for staff with sufficient permission to manually fill a request at any time with an item in hand that is appropriate to the request, rather than wait for the system to identify and hold an item.

_____*O = Operational*   *A = Available*   *D = Development*   *P = Planned*   *N = Not Available*

Explain:

3.3.9.25. The ILS must support the ability to restrict specific items or material types from filling hold requests.

_____*O = Operational*   *A = Available*   *D = Development*   *P = Planned*   *N = Not A vailable*

Explain:

3.3.9.26. The ILS must support the ability to prevent items with certain statuses (such as lost or withdrawn) from filling holds.

_____*O = Operational*   *A = Available*   *D = Development*   *P = Planned*   *N = Not Available*

Explain:

3.3.9.27. The ILS must produce a pick list of requests to be filled. This list must be formatted according to library-configurable settings (including the option to not display private patron data), must be able to be generated easily on demand, must be able to be scheduled and automatically emailed to selected staff members if the library so chooses, and must be able to be printed or displayed on mobile devices including the Apple iPad, based on the library's preference.

_____*O = Operational*   *A = Available*   *D = Development*   *P = Planned*   *N = Not Available*

Explain:

3.3.9.28. The ILS must support the ability to change the sort order of the displayed or printed pick list to suit the library's needs.

_____*O = Operational*   *A = Available*   *D = Development*   *P = Planned*   *N = Not Available*

Explain:

3.3.9.29. The ILS must automatically email, text, or call patrons when a held item is ready to be checked out, based on patron preference for notification format.

_____*O = Operational*   *A = Available*   *D = Development*   *P = Planned*   *N = Not Available*

Explain:

3.3.9.30. The ILS must generate a notice to the patron if a request is cancelled or cannot be filled.

_____*O = Operational*   *A = Available*   *D = Development*   *P = Planned*   *N = Not Available*

Explain:

3.3.9.31. The ILS must print a slip when an item is trapped for a request.

_____*O = Operational*   *A = Available*   *D = Development*   *P = Planned*   *N = Not Available*

Explain:

3.3.9.32. The ILS must support the ability to customize the content of a hold slip.

_____*O = Operational*   *A = Available*   *D = Development*   *P = Planned*   *N = Not Available*

Explain:

3.3.9.33. The ILS must support the ability to print a flexible and customizable pick-up slip with extra large print for libraries that set held items out for patron self-pickup.

_____*O = Operational*   *A = Available*   *D = Development*   *P = Planned*   *N = Not Available*

Explain:

3.3.9.34. The pick-up slip must preserve patron privacy.

_____*O = Operational*   *A = Available*   *D = Development*   *P = Planned*   *N = Not Available*

Explain:

3.3.9.35. The pick-up slip must be printable as a slip to be inserted in the item or a wrapper for the outside.

_____*O = Operational*   *A = Available*   *D = Development*   *P = Planned*   *N = Not Available*

Explain:

3.3.9.36. The ILS must display and print a list of items not picked up, to be returned to circulation (unclaimed requests).

_____*O = Operational*   *A = Available*   *D = Development*   *P = Planned*   *N = Not Available*

Explain:

3.3.9.37. The ILS must support the ability to change the sorting of the displayed and printed list of unclaimed items.

_____*O = Operational*   *A = Available*   *D = Development*   *P = Planned*   *N = Not Available*

Explain:

3.3.9.38. The ILS must support the ability to automatically delete all cancelled, unfilled, or expired requests after a library-specified period of time.

_____*O = Operational*   *A = Available*   *D = Development*   *P = Planned*   *N = Not Available*

Explain:

3.3.9.39. The ILS must support the ability to search for hold requests by:

3.3.9.39.1. Author

_____*O = Operational*   *A = Available*   *D = Development*   *P = Planned*   *N = Not Available*

3.3.9.39.2. Title

_____*O = Operational*   *A = Available*   *D = Development*   *P = Planned*   *N = Not Available*

3.3.9.39.3. Call Number

_____*O = Operational*   *A = Available*   *D = Development*   *P = Planned*   *N = Not Available*

3.3.9.39.4. ISBN

_____*O = Operational*   *A = Available*   *D = Development*   *P = Planned*   *N = Not Available*

3.3.9.39.5. Requestor (patron)

_____*O = Operational*   *A = Available*   *D = Development*   *P = Planned*   *N = Not Available*

3.3.9.39.6. Patron type

_____*O = Operational*   *A = Available*   *D = Development*   *P = Planned*   *N = Not Available*

3.3.9.39.7. Format

_____*O = Operational*   *A = Available*   *D = Development*   *P = Planned*   *N = Not Available*

3.3.9.39.8. Date placed

_____*O = Operational*   *A = Available*   *D = Development*   *P = Planned*   *N = Not Available*

3.3.9.39.9.   Pickup date (unclaim date)

_____O = Operational   A = Available   D = Development   P = Planned   N = Not Available

3.3.9.39.10. Expiration date

_____O = Operational   A = Available   D = Development   P = Planned   N = Not Available

3.3.9.39.11. Request status

_____O = Operational   A = Available   D = Development   P = Planned   N = Not Available

Explain: (refer to item by number)

3.3.9.40. The ILS must support the ability to link to all records associated with a hold request in one step (patron record, bibliographic record, or item record).

_____O = Operational   A = Available   D = Development   P = Planned   N = Not Avai lable

Explain:

3.3.9.41. The ILS must support the ability to link from any bibliographic, item, or patron record back to the hold in one step.

_____O = Operational   A = Available   D = Development   P = Planned   N = Not Available

Explain:

3.3.9.42. The ILS must support the ability to view all active hold requests attached to a bibliographic record at any time.

_____O = Operational   A = Available   D = Development   P = Planned   N = Not Available

Explain:

3.3.9.43. The ILS must support the ability to view all active hold requests for a patron at any time.

_____O = Operational   A = Available   D = Development   P = Planned   N = Not Available

Explain:

3.3.9.44. The ILS must offer a report that shows how many days it took to fill hold requests from the date the request was placed to the date the item was placed on the hold shelf.

_____O = Operational   A = Available   D = Development   P = Planned   N = Not Available

Explain:

3.3.10. Self-Check

3.3.10.1. The ILS must be able to interface with the library's existing multiple EnvisionWare OneStop self check-out machines that allow borrowers to check out their own materials and perform other self-service account-based transactions including renewals and fine payments. List supported systems and supported transactions. Describe hardware requirements.

_____O = Operational   A = Available   D = Development   P = Planned   N = Not Available

Explain:

3.3.10.2. The ILS must support item-not-present renewals via the self-check system.

_____O = Operational   A = Available   D = Development   P = Planned   N = Not Available

Explain:

3.3.10.3. The ILS must support alerts on the self-check system to notify patrons when a hold is available on the account that is being used to perform a self-check transaction.

_____O = Operational   A = Available   D = Development   P = Planned   N = Not Available

Explain:

    3.3.10.4. The ILS must support cash payments in addition to credit and debit cards via the self-check system.

_____*O = Operational   A = Available   D = Development   P = Planned   N = Not Available*

Explain:

    3.3.10.5. The ILS must provide a customizable self-check interface that is fully compatible with EnvisionWare's RFID system in addition to fully supporting the use of EnvisionWare's OneStop self-check software so the library can choose which interface it feels will best suit patron needs. Provide screen images of the ILS-provided self-check interface.

_____*O = Operational   A = Available   D = Development   P = Planned   N = Not Available*

Explain:

    3.3.11. Highlight circulation strengths:

3.4. Cataloging Requirements

The library considers that all ILS vendors provide full MARC 21 support, authority control and import/export functionality. The following is a list of specific cataloging features desired by the library.

    3.4.1. General

    3.4.1.1. The ILS must incorporate MARC21 validation tables to verify high quality, consistent cataloging input. These tables must be applied to both imported and manually created records.

_____*O = Operational   A = Available   D = Development   P = Planned   N = Not Available*

Explain:

    3.4.1.2. The cataloger must have the ability to indicate that a bibliographic and/or item record is not available for retrieval in the PAC.

_____*O = Operational   A = Available   D = Development   P = Planned   N = Not Available*

Explain:

    3.4.1.3. The ILS must support easy, efficient merging of bibliographic records including the automatic merging of any associated holds lists.

_____*O = Operational   A = Available   D = Development   P = Planned   N = Not Available*

Explain:

    3.4.1.4. The ILS must support easy assignment of a temporary home location/status to items on an individual or batch basis. Describe how this functionality is used.

_____*O = Operational   A = Available   D = Development   P = Planned   N = Not Available*

Explain:

    3.4.1.5. The ILS must allow cut, copy, and paste commands for MARC record editing.

_____*O = Operational   A = Available   D = Development   P = Planned   N = Not Available*

Explain:

    3.4.1.6. The ILS must support varieties of import template capabilities, including item level information mappings.

_____*O = Operational   A = Available   D = Development   P = Planned   N = Not Available*

Explain:

3.4.1.7. The ILS must support easy editing of 005 and 007 fields.

_____*O = Operational   A = Available   D = Development   P = Planned   N = Not Available*

Explain:

3.4.1.8. The ILS must combine and overlay records from bibliographic utilities, using library-defined match points.

_____*O = Operational   A = Available   D = Development   P = Planned   N = Not Available*

Explain:

3.4.1.9. During the duplicate detection process, the ILS must offer the ability to overlay some or all of the duplicates with the open bibliographic record.

_____*O = Operational   A = Available   D = Development   P = Planned   N = Not Available*

Explain:

3.4.1.10. The ILS must supply templates containing required and recommended bibliographic fields. These templates must be modifiable by library staff.

_____*O = Operational   A = Available   D = Development   P = Planned   N = Not Available*

Explain:

3.4.1.11. The ILS must support the ability to set a default shelving scheme for new item records.

_____*O = Operational   A = Available   D = Development   P = Planned   N = Not Available*

Explain:

3.4.1.12. The ILS must support the ability to make global or user-defined changes to user-defined sets of bibliographic and/or item records.

_____*O = Operational   A = Available   D = Development   P = Planned   N = Not Available*

Explain:

3.4.1.13. The ILS must support both the 10-digit and 13-digit ISBN standard for searching for bibliographic records and in the duplicate detection process.

_____*O = Operational   A = Available   D = Development   P = Planned   N = Not Available*

Explain:

3.4.1.14. The ILS must provide the ability to create macros for repetitive data entry tasks.

_____*O = Operational   A = Available   D = Development   P = Planned   N = Not Available*

Explain:

3.4.1.15. The ILS must include ALA/MARC21/RDA character set fonts.

_____*O = Operational   A = Available   D = Development   P = Planned   N = Not Available*

Explain:

3.4.1.16. The ILS must support UNICODE.

_____*O = Operational   A = Available   D = Development   P = Planned   N = Not Available*

Explain:

3.4.1.17. The ILS must support eBook access and the input of scripted 850 fields using EZproxy.

_____*O = Operational   A = Available   D = Development   P = Planned   N = Not Available*

Explain:

3.4.1.18. The ILS must support CONTENTdm and metadata.

_____*O = Operational   A = Available   D = Development   P = Planned   N = Not Available*

Explain:

3.4.1.19.   The ILS must support searching by commonly used bibliographic fields:
   3.4.1.19.1. Author
   _____*O = Operational*   *A = Available*   *D = Development*   *P = Planned*   *N = Not Available*

   3.4.1.19.2. Title
   _____*O = Operational*   *A = Available*   *D = Development*   *P = Planned*   *N = Not Available*

   3.4.1.19.3. Subject
   _____*O = Operational*   *A = Available*   *D = Development*   *P = Planned*   *N = Not Available*

   3.4.1.19.4. Call number
   _____*O = Operational*   *A = Available*   *D = Development*   *P = Planned*   *N = Not Available*

   3.4.1.19.5. Keyword
   _____*O = Operational*   *A = Available*   *D = Development*   *P = Planned*   *N = Not Available*

   3.4.1.19.6. ISBN
   _____*O = Operational*   *A = Available*   *D = Development*   *P = Planned*   *N = Not Available*

   3.4.1.19.7. ISSN
   _____*O = Operational*   *A = Available*   *D = Development*   *P = Planned*   *N = Not Available*

   3.4.1.19.8. LC control number
   _____*O = Operational*   *A = Available*   *D = Development*   *P = Planned*   *N = Not Available*

   3.4.1.19.9. OCLC number
   _____*O = Operational*   *A = Available*   *D = Development*   *P = Planned*   *N = Not Available*

   3.4.1.19.10. Bibliographic record number
   _____*O = Operational*   *A = Available*   *D = Development*   *P = Planned*   *N = Not Available*

   3.4.1.19.11. Item record number
   _____*O = Operational*   *A = Available*   *D = Development*   *P = Planned*   *N = Not Available*

   3.4.1.19.12. Series
   _____*O = Operational*   *A = Available*   *D = Development*   *P = Planned*   *N = Not Available*

Explain: (refer to item by number)

3.4.1.20.   Multiple record views must be available for bibliographic records.
_____*O = Operational*   *A = Available*   *D = Development*   *P = Planned*   *N = Not Available*

Explain:

3.4.1.21.   The ILS must accept, store, retrieve, print, and display diacritical marks.
_____*O = Operational*   *A = Available*   *D = Development*   *P = Planned*   *N = Not Available*

Explain:

3.4.1.22.   The ILS must support the ability for library staff to export all or part of the bibliographic
   database in full MARC21 format without vendor intervention.
_____*O = Operational*   *A = Available*   *D = Development*   *P = Planned*   *N = Not Available*

Explain:

3.4.1.23.   The ILS must support retention of deleted records (authority, bibliographic, and item) at
   the library's discretion.
_____*O = Operational*   *A = Available*   *D = Development*   *P = Planned*   *N = Not Available*

Explain:

3.4.1.24. The ILS must show statistical usage details on bibliographic and item records.

_____*O = Operational   A = Available   D = Development   P = Planned   N = Not Available*

Explain:

3.4.1.25. The ILS must show a preview version of the bibliographic record as it will appear in the PAC, including active URLs.

_____*O = Operational   A = Available   D = Development   P = Planned   N = Not Available*

Explain:

3.4.1.26. The ILS must provide a URL checking utility.

_____*O = Operational   A = Available   D = Development   P = Planned   N = Not Available*

Explain:

3.4.2.   Z39.50

3.4.2.1.   The ILS must include a Z39.50 version 3 compliant catalog without additional charge.

_____*O = Operational   A = Available   D = Development   P = Planned   N = Not Available*

Explain:

3.4.2.2.   The ILS must support the ability to search a remote Z39.50 database from the staff client, edit the record as required, and save it to the database without invoking a separate record import function.

_____*O = Operational   A = Available   D = Development   P = Planned   N = Not Available*

Explain:

3.4.2.3.   The ILS must allow Z39.50 version 3 searches of multiple databases simultaneously for a single search.

_____*O = Operational   A = Available   D = Development   P = Planned   N = Not Available*

Explain:

3.4.3.   Authority Control

3.4.3.1.   The ILS must support the ability for authorized staff to copy existing authority records from selected Z39.50 sites directly into the system.

_____*O = Operational   A = Available   D = Development   P = Planned   N = Not Available*

Explain:

3.4.3.2.   The ILS must support an import process that performs authority control on imported bibliographic records and has the ability to automatically link to a remote subscription authority database if no matching heading is found in the local database.

_____*O = Operational   A = Available   D = Development   P = Planned   N = Not Available*

Explain:

3.4.3.3.   The ILS must accommodate:

3.4.3.3.1.   Personal, corporate, and topical name headings in a name authority file

_____*O = Operational   A = Available   D = Development   P = Planned   N = Not Available*

3.4.3.3.2.   Title, uniform title, and series entries in a title index

_____*O = Operational   A = Available   D = Development   P = Planned   N = Not Available*

3.4.3.3.3.   Subject headings in a subject authority file

_____*O = Operational   A = Available   D = Development   P = Planned   N = Not Available*

Explain: (refer to item by number)

3.4.4.   Bibliographic Record Downloads and Creation

3.4.4.1.   The ILS must support the ability to match LC or other national standard authority records against the local file.

_____*O = Operational   A = Available   D = Development   P = Planned   N = Not Available*

Explain:

3.4.4.2.   The ILS must support the ability for automatic matching to remote authority records.

_____*O = Operational   A = Available   D = Development   P = Planned   N = Not Available*

Explain:

3.4.4.3.   The ILS must generate SEE and SEE ALSO references from authority records to direct online catalog users to other headings as follows:

3.4.4.3.1.   See references (aeroplanes to airplanes)

_____*O = Operational   A = Available   D = Development   P = Planned   N = Not Available*

3.4.4.3.2.   Narrower terms (automobiles to sports cars)

_____*O = Operational   A = Available   D = Development   P = Planned   N = Not Available*

3.4.4.3.3.   Broader terms (automobiles to motor vehicles)

_____*O = Operational   A = Available   D = Development   P = Planned   N = Not Available*

3.4.4.3.4.   Related terms (airplanes to flying machines)

_____*O = Operational   A = Available   D = Development   P = Planned   N = Not Available*

Explain: (refer to item by number)

3.4.5.   Label Management

3.4.5.1.   The ILS must offer an easy to use, flexible label manager.

_____*O = Operational   A = Available   D = Development   P = Planned   N = Not Available*

Explain:

3.4.5.2.   The label manager must support the ability to produce spine labels individually on demand or batch run, on standard (non-proprietary) printers.

_____*O = Operational   A = Available   D = Development   P = Planned   N = Not Available*

Explain:

3.4.5.3.   The label manager must support printing of labels to single sheets or to continuous form feed stock.

_____*O = Operational   A = Available   D = Development   P = Planned   N = Not Available*

Explain:

3.4.5.4.   The label manager must support labels to be printed as they are generated or print all labels generated in a single operation.

_____*O = Operational   A = Available   D = Development   P = Planned   N = Not Available*

Explain:

3.4.5.5.   The label manager must support the ability to include volume or copy numbers as given on an item record where applicable, with no additional effort from staff.

_____*O = Operational   A = Available   D = Development   P = Planned   N = Not Available*

Explain:

3.4.6.   Highlight cataloging strengths:

3.5. Public Access Catalog Requirements

Public Access Catalog (PAC) refers to an integrated subsystem that allows patrons to search and browse the bibliographic database according to library-specified parameters.

3.5.1.   General

    3.5.1.1.   The PAC must be Web-accessible and support the following browsers, at a minimum. Versions listed below are minimal. It is assumed subsequent versions are supported unless vendor indicates otherwise.

        3.5.1.1.1.   Internet Explorer 6.x

      _____*O = Operational*   *A = Available*   *D = Development*   *P = Planned*   *N = Not Available*

        3.5.1.1.2.   Netscape Navigator 7.x

      _____*O = Operational*   *A = Available*   *D = Development*   *P = Planned*   *N = Not Available*

        3.5.1.1.3.   Mozilla Firefox

      _____*O = Operational*   *A = Available*   *D = Development*   *P = Planned*   *N = Not Available*

        3.5.1.1.4.   Opera 7.0

      _____*O = Operational*   *A = Available*   *D = Development*   *P = Planned*   *N = Not Available*

        3.5.1.1.5.   PWB 2.0

      _____*O = Operational*   *A = Available*   *D = Development*   *P = Planned*   *N = Not Available*

        3.5.1.1.6.   Safari 1.1

      _____*O = Operational*   *A = Available*   *D = Development*   *P = Planned*   *N = Not Available*

Explain: (refer to item by number)

    3.5.1.2.   The PAC must be fully compliant with MARC21 and Z39.50 standards.

      _____*O = Operational*   *A = Available*   *D = Development*   *P = Planned*   *N = Not Available*

Explain:

    3.5.1.3.   Pre-designed PAC screen themes must be readily available to easily reconfigure the look of PAC screens.

      _____*O = Operational*   *A = Available*   *D = Development*   *P = Planned*   *N = Not Available*

Explain:

    3.5.1.4.   The PAC must be governable by cascading style sheets so it can be easily made to seamlessly blend with the look of the library's website.

      _____*O = Operational*   *A = Available*   *D = Development*   *P = Planned*   *N = Not Available*

Explain:

    3.5.1.5.   The PAC must allow for item display in a bookshelf view, in which book jacket images are shown in shelf-list order.

      _____*O = Operational*   *A = Available*   *D = Development*   *P = Planned*   *N = Not Available*

Explain:

    3.5.1.6.   The PAC must allow easy access to bestseller lists, award winner lists, and other lists of the library's choosing with direct links from titles on the lists to those titles' entries in the catalog, or to a "request to order" form in cases when the library does not own the selected title.

      _____*O = Operational*   *A = Available*   *D = Development*   *P = Planned*   *N = Not Available*

Explain:

    3.5.1.7.   The PAC must include functionality that allows patrons to elect to be automatically placed on hold for any items by an author of their choosing that are added to the catalog or ordered. This service must include an automatic email alerting the patron that such a hold has been placed whenever a new item by that selected author triggers an automated hold. If the patron cannot be placed on hold automatically for an item because he or she already has reached the library-set limit of holds at any given time, an automatic notification must be generated and sent to the patron explaining that the hold could not be placed, with instructions for canceling an existing hold in order to create room for the new hold if the patron so desires.

_____*O = Operational*   *A = Available*   *D = Development*   *P = Planned*   *N = Not Available*

Explain:

3.5.1.8.   The PAC must offer the ability to toggle between regular sized view/font and large size view/font. This toggle must be easily identified and utilized by patrons who are unable to read standard-sized fonts.

_____*O = Operational*   *A = Available*   *D = Development*   *P = Planned*   *N = Not Available*

Explain:

3.5.1.9.   The ILS must support the ability for the library to produce custom lists and present them on specific pages of the PAC.

_____*O = Operational*   *A = Available*   *D = Development*   *P = Planned*   *N = Not Available*

Explain:

3.5.1.10.   The ILS must support integration of third-party tools that analyze web traffic, including but not limited to Google Analytics. It must be possible to track PAC usage including but not limited to unsuccessful search terms.

_____*O = Operational*   *A = Available*   *D = Development*   *P = Planned*   *N = Not Available*

Explain:

3.5.1.11.   The PAC must authenticate remote patrons who use the Web to access online resources, including eBooks and databases using EZproxy.

_____*O = Operational*   *A = Available*   *D = Development*   *P = Planned*   *N = Not Available*

Explain:

3.5.1.12.   The ILS must support Overdrive.

_____*O = Operational*   *A = Available*   *D = Development*   *P = Planned*   *N = Not Available*

Explain:

3.5.1.13.   The ILS must allow patrons to set up a user name online and change it online, if necessary. This user name can be used instead of a barcode when logging in to use PAC functions.

_____*O = Operational*   *A = Available*   *D = Development*   *P = Planned*   *N = Not Available*

Explain:

3.5.1.14.   The ILS must allow the library the option to require numeric passwords (PINs) that can be used to login to the PAC, self-check stations, or inbound phone notification system.

_____*O = Operational*   *A = Available*   *D = Development*   *P = Planned*   *N = Not Available*

Explain:

3.5.1.15.   The ILS must allow patrons to have forgotten PINs sent to their email addresses.

_____*O = Operational*   *A = Available*   *D = Development*   *P = Planned*   *N = Not Available*

Explain:

3.5.1.16.   The ILS must allow patrons to set up email and RSS alerts for new releases based on author preferences or other relevant criteria for print, eBooks, audio books, DVDs, music, electronic games (by title or format; Wii, PS3, etc.). These alerts must include a direct link to request the item.

_____O = *Operational*   A = *Available*   D = *Development*   P = *Planned*   N = *Not Available*

Explain:

3.5.1.17. The ILS must support the ability for the library to customize the PAC display of data, labels, and the order of data elements.

_____O = *Operational*   A = *Available*   D = *Development*   P = *Planned*   N = *Not Available*

Explain:

3.5.1.18. When renewing items via the PAC, patrons must be given a confirmation code that staff members can input into the staff client to view the details of that specific renewal transaction (including but not limited to the date and time of the renewal, which items were selected for renewal, and whether there were any alerts given, such as a message indicating that a particular item could not be renewed due to outstanding holds from other patrons) in the event of a dispute or other inquiry. It must also be possible to provide a confirmation code for staff client-based renewals done by phone.

_____O = *Operational*   A = *Available*   D = *Development*   P = *Planned*   N = *Not Available*

Explain:

3.5.2. Searching

3.5.2.1. The PAC must be able to search any Z39.50 compliant database or server, including digital collections and metadata. Detail any costs to develop/integrate particular targets, if applicable.

_____O = *Operational*   A = *Available*   D = *Development*   P = *Planned*   N = *Not Available*

Explain.

3.5.2.2. The ILS must support the ability for item-level detail availability to display in the PAC without leaving the results set.

_____O = *Operational*   A = *Available*   D = *Development*   P = *Planned*   N = *Not Available*

Explain:

3.5.2.3. The PAC must offer the patron the ability to send a text message containing an item call number to his or her mobile phone. If the patron is logged onto the PAC, his or her mobile phone number must be harvested automatically from his or her account with the option to input a different number for that specific text message if the patron so desires. If the patron chooses to enter a new phone number, a dialog box must appear that allows the patron to also overwrite that new phone number onto their account.

_____O = *Operational*   A = *Available*   D = *Development*   P = *Planned*   N = *Not Available*

Explain:

3.5.2.4. The PAC must offer an online automatic spell checker.

_____O = *Operational*   A = *Available*   D = *Development*   P = *Planned*   N = *Not Available*

Explain:

3.5.2.5. The PAC must offer a "did you mean" feature.

_____O = *Operational*   A = *Available*   D = *Development*   P = *Planned*   N = *Not Available*

Explain:

3.5.2.6. The PAC must have the ability to enable (or disable) automatic suggestions as patrons type quick, keyword, or phrase searches in the PAC.

_____O = *Operational*   A = *Available*   D = *Development*   P = *Planned*   N = *Not Available*

Explain:

3.5.2.7.   The ILS must support the ability for the library to specify its own alternate suggestions for specified search terms instead of the program's suggestions.

_____*O = Operational*   *A = Available*   *D = Development*   *P = Planned*   *N = Not Available*

Explain:

3.5.2.8.   The PAC must save previous searches done during a single session.

_____*O = Operational*   *A = Available*   *D = Development*   *P = Planned*   *N = Not Available*

Explain:

3.5.2.9.   The PAC must offer the ability to scope searches by collection.

_____*O = Operational*   *A = Available*   *D = Development*   *P = Planned*   *N = Not Available*

Explain:

3.5.2.10.   The PAC must provide search result relevancy ranking.

_____*O = Operational*   *A = Available*   *D = Development*   *P = Planned*   *N = Not Available*

Explain:

3.5.2.11.   The PAC must support the ability to print, export to email, and save to portable storage device a bibliography in several formats:

3.5.2.11.1. Brief bibliographic display

_____*O = Operational*   *A = Available*   *D = Development*   *P = Planned*   *N = Not Available*

3.5.2.11.2. Full bibliographic display

_____*O = Operational*   *A = Available*   *D = Development*   *P = Planned*   *N = Not Available*

3.5.2.11.3. American Psychological Association (APA)

_____*O = Operational*   *A = Available*   *D = Development*   *P = Planned*   *N = Not Available*

3.5.2.11.4. Chicago Manual of Style

_____*O = Operational*   *A = Available*   *D = Development*   *P = Planned*   *N = Not Available*

3.5.2.11.5. Modern Language Association (MLA)

_____*O = Operational*   *A = Available*   *D = Development*   *P = Planned*   *N = Not Available*

3.5.2.11.6. HTML

_____*O = Operational*   *A = Available*   *D = Development*   *P = Planned*   *N = Not Available*

3.5.2.11.7. MARC

_____*O = Operational*   *A = Available*   *D = Development*   *P = Planned*   *N = Not Available*

Explain: (refer to item by number)

3.5.2.12.   The ILS must support the ability for the library to determine PAC default search settings.

_____*O = Operational*   *A = Available*   *D = Development*   *P = Planned*   *N = Not Available*

Explain:

3.5.2.13.   Browse title search results must show a summary view with different physical formats (how many books, how many DVDs, etc. for a title).

_____*O = Operational*   *A = Available*   *D = Development*   *P = Planned*   *N = Not Available*

Explain:

3.5.2.14.   The PAC must offer the ability for libraries to allow patrons to share bookmarks to titles through sites such as Facebook™, Twitter™, and Digg™.

_____*O = Operational*   *A = Available*   *D = Development*   *P = Planned*   *N = Not Available*

Explain:

3.5.2.15. The patron must be able to link to a requested title directly from their patron account requests list.

_____*O = Operational*   *A = Available*   *D = Development*   *P = Planned*   *N = Not Available*

Explain:

3.5.2.16. The patron must be able to link to a title directly from their patron account items out list.

_____*O = Operational*   *A = Available*   *D = Development*   *P = Planned*   *N = Not Available*

Explain:

3.5.2.17. The PAC must support the ability for patrons to save searches.

_____*O = Operational*   *A = Available*   *D = Development*   *P = Planned*   *N = Not Available*

Explain:

3.5.2.18. Saved searches must:

3.5.2.18.1. Be able to be modified and reinitiated

_____*O = Operational*   *A = Available*   *D = Development*   *P = Planned*   *N = Not Available*

3.5.2.18.2. Be able to provide automated updates of what is new since the last search and provide alerts of these new materials to patrons via email and RSS feed

_____*O = Operational*   *A = Available*   *D = Development*   *P = Planned*   *N = Not Available*

Explain:

3.5.2.19. The PAC must support the ability for patrons to create and save a title list.

_____*O = Operational*   *A = Available*   *D = Development*   *P = Planned*   *N = Not Available*

Explain:

3.5.2.20. The patron must be able to add a title from the search results list directly to a saved title list or to a new title list.

_____*O = Operational*   *A = Available*   *D = Development*   *P = Planned*   *N = Not Available*

Explain:

3.5.2.21. The ILS must support integration of digital collections including but not limited to the Project Gutenberg collection on an item-level basis. These items must appear in PAC search results as with any other cataloged holdings, with a link given directly to the item itself.

_____*O = Operational*   *A = Available*   *D = Development*   *P = Planned*   *N = Not Available*

Explain:

3.5.2.22. The ILS must support integration of Overdrive and other eBook/digital audio book collections on an item-level basis. These items must appear in PAC search results lists as with any other cataloged holdings, with a link given directly to the item itself.

_____*O = Operational*   *A = Available*   *D = Development*   *P = Planned*   *N = Not Available*

Explain:

3.5.2.23. The ILS must enable a staff-mediated stop word list.

_____*O = Operational*   *A = Available*   *D = Development*   *P = Planned*   *N = Not Available*

Explain:

3.5.2.24. The ILS must support federated searching of library's databases from the PAC. If there is an additional charge for this service, include those costs below.

_____*O = Operational*   *A = Available*   *D = Development*   *P = Planned*   *N = Not Available*

Explain:

3.5.2.25. The ILS must support EZproxy for patron authentication with user's library card number.
_____O = *Operational*   A = *Available*   D = *Development*   P = *Planned*   N = *Not Available*

Explain:

3.5.3.   PAC Self-Service

3.5.3.1.   The PAC must allow patrons to register online for a library card.
_____O = *Operational*   A = *Available*   D = *Development*   P = *Planned*   N = *Not Available*

Explain:

3.5.3.2.   The PAC must allow authenticated patrons to:
3.5.3.2.1.   Change their password
_____O = *Operational*   A = *Available*   D = *Development*   P = *Planned*   N = *Not Available*

3.5.3.2.2.   Submit requested address changes for review and acceptance by staff
_____O = *Operational*   A = *Available*   D = *Development*   P = *Planned*   N = *Not Available*

3.5.3.2.3.   Review their items out, on-hold items, and outstanding fines/fees
_____O = *Operational*   A = *Available*   D = *Development*   P = *Planned*   N = *Not Available*

3.5.3.2.4.   Place and cancel holds
_____O = *Operational*   A = *Available*   D = *Development*   P = *Planned*   N = Not Availab le

Explain: (refer to item by number)

3.5.3.3.   The ILS must support the option of allowing patrons to renew items from the PAC, even if the patron registration would expire before the item's new due date.
_____O = *Operational*   A = *Available*   D = *Development*   P = *Planned*   N = *Not Available*

Explain:

3.5.3.4.   The ILS must alert patron when materials did not renew with an on-screen alert, and an optional text or email in addition, based on the patron preference.
_____O = *Operational*   A = *Available*   D = *Development*   P = *Planned*   N = *Not Available*

Explain:

3.5.3.5.   The ILS must support the ability for the library to offer an online credit card payment option for fines, fees, and donations. Note if convenience or processing fees will be imposed as well as the cost and payee responsibility.
_____O = *Operational*   A = *Available*   D = *Development*   P = *Planned*   N = *Not Available*

Explain:

3.5.3.6.   The PAC must include comment/suggestion functionality that allows users to submit messages to library staff. Describe the staff-side interface and its functionality for delegating or assigning messages to appropriate staff members or departments based on library policy, responding to messages, and otherwise processing messages.
_____O = *Operational*   A = *Available*   D = *Development*   P = *Planned*   N = *Not Available*

Explain:

3.5.4.   Highlight public access catalog strengths:

3.6. Acquisitions Requirements

3.6.1.   General

3.6.1.1.   The ILS must provide a fully functional, integrated acquisitions subsystem that automatically manages encumbrances, disencumbrances, and expenditures in multiple library-defined accounts based on acquisitions activities including but not limited to selecting, ordering, receiving, claiming, cancelling, invoicing, and reporting.

_____*O = Operational   A = Available   D = Development   P = Planned   N = Not Available*

Explain:

3.6.1.2.   The ILS must maintain a complete audit trail for fund allocations and adjustments by staff members.

_____*O = Operational   A = Available   D = Development   P = Planned   N = Not Available*

Explain:

3.6.1.3.   All accounting activities must take place in real time.

_____*O = Operational   A = Available   D = Development   P = Planned   N = Not Available*

Explain:

3.6.1.4.   The ILS must support the ability to move between acquisitions, serials, cataloging, and circulation subsystems without having to login to each subsystem.

_____*O = Operational   A = Available   D = Development   P = Planned   N = Not Available*

Explain:

3.6.1.5.   The ILS must provide support for different order types, including firm orders, subscriptions, continuations, donations, depository agreements, and gifts.

_____*O = Operational   A = Available   D = Development   P = Planned   N = Not Available*

Explain:

3.6.1.6.   Data stored and displayed in the acquisitions file must include but not be limited to:

3.6.1.6.1.   Bibliographic information

_____*O = Operational   A = Available   D = Development   P = Planned   N = Not Available*

3.6.1.6.2.   Acquisitions type (firm, gift, blanket, etc.)

_____*O = Operational   A = Available   D = Development   P = Planned   N = Not Available*

3.6.1.6.3.   Status information (on order, cancelled, received, etc.)

_____*O = Operational   A = Available   D = Development   P = Planned   N = Not Available*

3.6.1.6.4.   Library/copy/fund information

_____*O = Operational   A = Available   D = Development   P = Planned   N = Not Available*

3.6.1.6.5.   Invoice information

_____*O = Operational   A = Available   D = Development   P = Planned   N = Not Available*

3.6.1.6.6.   Vendor information

_____*O = Operational   A = Available   D = Development   P = Planned   N = Not Available*

3.6.1.6.7.   Vendor report information

_____*O = Operational   A = Available   D = Development   P = Planned   N = Not Available*

3.6.1.6.8.   Accounting information

_____*O = Operational   A = Available   D = Development   P = Planned   N = Not Available*

3.6.1.6.9.   Requestor information

_____*O = Operational   A = Available   D = Development   P = Planned   N = Not Available*

3.6.1.6.10. Instructions to vendor

_____*O = Operational   A = Available   D = Development   P = Planned   N = Not Available*

3.6.1.6.11. Internal processing instructions and notes

_____*O = Operational   A = Available   D = Development   P = Planned   N = Not Available*

3.6.1.6.12. Public notes

_____*O = Operational*   *A = Available*   *D = Development*   *P = Planned*   *N = Not Available*

Explain: (refer to item by number)

3.6.1.7.   Acquisitions records must be accessible online through at least the following access points:

3.6.1.7.1.   Purchase order number

_____*O = Operational*   *A = Available*   *D = Development*   *P = Planned*   *N = Not Available*

3.6.1.7.2.   Title

_____*O = Operational*   *A = Available*   *D = Development*   *P = Planned*   *N = Not Available*

3.6.1.7.3.   Author

_____*O = Operational*   *A = Available*   *D = Development*   *P = Planned*   *N = Not Available*

3.6.1.7.4.   Library of Congress card number

_____*O = Operational*   *A = Available*   *D = Development*   *P = Planned*   *N = Not Available*

3.6.1.7.5. ISSN/ISBN

_____*O = Operational*   *A = Available*   *D = Development*   *P = Planned*   *N = Not Available*

3.6.1.7.6. Bib number

_____*O = Operational*   *A = Available*   *D = Development*   *P = Planned*   *N = Not Available*

3.6.1.7.7. Vendor

_____*O = Operational*   *A = Available*   *D = Development*   *P = Planned*   *N = Not Available*

3.6.1.7.8. UPC code

_____*O = Operational*   *A = Available*   *D = Development*   *P = Planned*   *N = Not Available*

3.6.1.7.9. Notes field

_____*O = Operational*   *A = Available*   *D = Development*   *P = Planned*   *N = Not Available*

Explain: (refer to item by number)

3.6.2.   Fund Accounting

3.6.2.1.   The ILS must have the ability to support multiple overlapping fiscal periods in its fund accounting structure.

_____*O = Operational*   *A = Available*   *D = Development*   *P = Planned*   *N = Not Available*

Explain:

3.6.2.2.   The ILS must be capable of producing fund summary reports that include fund allocations, amount encumbered and expended, remaining available, and percentage encumbered and expended for a given fiscal year.

_____*O = Operational*   *A = Available*   *D = Development*   *P = Planned*   *N = Not Available*

Explain:

3.6.2.3.   The audit trail must track the date, time, and the user who made manual adjustments to the fund.

_____*O = Operational*   *A = Available*   *D = Development*   *P = Planned*   *N = Not Available*

Explain:

3.6.2.4.   The ILS must support the ability to transfer monies between funds.

_____*O = Operational*   *A = Available*   *D = Development*   *P = Planned*   *N = Not Available*

Explain:

3.6.2.5.   The ILS must support the ability to create, manipulate, and order/receive in multiple fiscal years.

_____*O = Operational*   *A = Available*   *D = Development*   *P = Planned*   N = Not Avail able

Explain:

 3.6.2.6. Fund file records must include amount budgeted, amount encumbered, amount expended, fund limits, uncommitted balance, and total fund balance.

_____*O = Operational* *A = Available* *D = Development* *P = Planned* *N = Not Available*

Explain:

3.6.3. Acquiring and Processing Materials

 3.6.3.1. The library must be able to pre-define URL links to web-based selection tools to support automatic launching from the acquisition client.

_____*O = Operational* *A = Available* *D = Development* *P = Planned* *N = Not Available*

Explain:

 3.6.3.2. The ILS must support electronic submission of orders to:
  3.6.3.2.1. AudioGo

_____*O = Operational* *A = Available* *D = Development* *P = Planned* *N = Not Available*

  3.6.3.2.2. Baker & Taylor

_____*O = Operational* *A = Available* *D = Development* *P = Planned* *N = Not Available*

  3.6.3.2.3. Book Wholesalers, Inc. (BWI)

_____*O = Operational* *A = Available* *D = Development* *P = Planned* *N = Not Available*

  3.6.3.2.4. Brodart

_____*O = Operational* *A = Available* *D = Development* *P = Planned* *N = Not Available*

  3.6.3.2.5. Ingram Books

_____*O = Operational* *A = Available* *D = Development* *P = Planned* *N = Not Available*

  3.6.3.2.6. Library Bound

_____*O = Operational* *A = Available* *D = Development* *P = Planned* *N = Not Available*

  3.6.3.2.7. Micro Marketing

_____*O = Operational* *A = Available* *D = Development* *P = Planned* *N = Not Available*

  3.6.3.2.8. Midwest Tape

_____*O = Operational* *A = Available* *D = Development* *P = Planned* *N = Not Available*

  3.6.3.2.9. Quality Books

_____*O = Operational* *A = Available* *D = Development* *P = Planned* *N = Not Available*

  3.6.3.2.10. Rainbow Books

_____*O = Operational* *A = Available* *D = Development* *P = Planned* *N = Not Available*

  3.6.3.2.11. Recorded Books

_____*O = Operational* *A = Available* *D = Development* *P = Planned* *N = Not Available*

  3.6.3.2.12. S&B Books

_____*O = Operational* *A = Available* *D = Development* *P = Planned* *N = Not Available*

  3.6.3.2.13. United Library Services

_____*O = Operational* *A = Available* *D = Development* *P = Planned* *N = Not Available*

  3.6.3.2.14. Whitehots, Inc.

_____*O = Operational* *A = Available* *D = Development* *P = Planned* *N = Not Available*

This list is not considered to be all-inclusive. List others if available:

 3.6.3.3. The ILS must support Electronic Data Interchange (EDI) X12 version 4010 or higher.

_____*O = Operational* *A = Available* *D = Development* *P = Planned* *N = Not Available*

Explain:

   3.6.3.4.   The ILS must support 9xx.

_____*O = Operational   A = Available   D = Development   P = Planned   N = Not Available*

Explain:

   3.6.3.5.   The ILS must permit the recording of holds against titles on order and in process.

_____*O = Operational   A = Available   D = Development   P = Planned   N = Not Available*

Explain:

   3.6.3.6.   The ILS must support the ability to determine the format (i.e., DVD, CD) when manually adding titles to an order for the purpose of ordering materials.

_____*O = Operational   A = Available   D = Development   P = Planned   N = Not Available*

Explain:

   3.6.3.7.   The ILS must automatically transfer holds placed on on-order items to full MARC records when they are cataloged.

_____*O = Operational   A = Available   D = Development   P = Planned   N = Not Available*

Explain:

   3.6.3.8.   The ILS must support receive and un-receive functions, and the ability to change the status of orders and individual items.

_____*O = Operational   A = Available   D = Development   P = Planned   N = Not Available*

Explain:

   3.6.3.9.   Full electronic invoicing, including automatic generation of vendor invoices in the ILS database, must be available.

_____*O = Operational   A = Available   D = Development   P = Planned   N = Not Available*

Explain:

   3.6.3.10.   The ILS must allow the operator to receive and invoice in one step.

_____*O = Operational   A = Available   D = Development   P = Planned   N = Not Available*

Explain:

   3.6.3.11.   The ILS must support the ability to place orders using over-encumbered funds.

Explain:

   3.6.3.12.   The ILS must support the ability to set up automatic patron notification when an on-order title is cancelled.

_____*O = Operational   A = Available   D = Development   P = Planned   N = Not Available*

Explain:

   3.6.3.13.   The ILS must show circulation use statistics, as an indication of how heavily a title is being circulated or requested, to aid in collection development.

_____*O = Operational   A = Available   D = Development   P = Planned   N = Not Available*

Explain:

   3.6.3.14.   The ILS must support the ability to split funds per order record.

_____*O = Operational   A = Available   D = Development   P = Planned   N = Not Availab le*

Explain:

   3.6.3.15.   The ILS must support the ability to receive entire cartons of shelf-ready items in one operation, simultaneously checking them in so they can circulate.

_____*O = Operational   A = Available   D = Development   P = Planned   N = Not Available*

Explain:

3.6.4.   Highlight acquisitions strengths:

3.7. Serials Control Requirements

3.7.1.   General

   3.7.1.1.   The ILS must include the following serials control capabilities:
   3.7.1.1.1.   Holdings and publication pattern maintenance
_____*O = Operational*   *A = Available*   *D = Development*   *P = Planned*   *N = Not Available*

   3.7.1.1.2.   Check-in
   3.7.1.1.3.   Claiming (including email and print claim notices)
_____*O = Operational*   *A = Available*   *D = Development*   *P = Planned*   *N = Not Available*

   3.7.1.1.4.   Routing
_____*O = Operational*   *A = Available*   *D = Development*   *P = Planned*   *N = Not Available*

   3.7.1.1.5.   Summary holdings, by copy
_____*O = Operational*   *A = Available*   *D = Development*   *P = Planned*   *N = Not Available*

   3.7.1.1.6.   Subscription maintenance (including payments)
_____*O = Operational*   *A = Available*   *D = Development*   *P = Planned*   *N = Not Available*

Explain: (refer to item by number)

   3.7.1.2.   The ILS must support the ability to accommodate all type of serials, including:
   3.7.1.2.1.   Periodicals
_____*O = Operational*   *A = Available*   *D = Development*   *P = Planned*   N = Not Av ailable

   3.7.1.2.2.   Continuations
_____*O = Operational*   *A = Available*   *D = Development*   *P = Planned*   *N = Not Available*

   3.7.1.2.3.   Law reports
_____*O = Operational*   *A = Available*   *D = Development*   *P = Planned*   N = Not Availabl e

   3.7.1.2.4.   Newspapers
_____*O = Operational*   *A = Available*   *D = Development*   *P = Planned*   *N = Not Available*

   3.7.1.2.5.   Annuals
_____*O = Operational*   *A = Available*   *D = Development*   *P = Planned*   *N = Not Available*

   3.7.1.2.6.   Governmentals
_____*O = Operational*   *A = Available*   *D = Development*   *P = Planned*   *N = Not Available*

   3.7.1.2.7.   Memoirs
_____*O = Operational*   *A = Available*   *D = Development*   *P = Planned*   *N = Not Available*

   3.7.1.2.8.   Proceedings
_____*O = Operational*   *A = Available*   *D = Development*   *P = Planned*   *N = Not Available*

   3.7.1.2.9.   Transactions
_____*O = Operational*   *A = Available*   *D = Development*   *P = Planned*   *N = Not Available*

   3.7.1.2.10.   Supplements
_____*O = Operational*   *A = Available*   *D = Development*   *P = Planned*   *N = Not Available*

   3.7.1.2.11.   Indexes
_____*O = Operational*   *A = Available*   *D = Development*   *P = Planned*   *N = Not Available*

3.7.1.2.12. Loose-leaf material
_____O = Operational   A = Available   D = Development   P = Planned   N = Not Available

Explain: (refer to item by number)

3.7.1.3.   For serials and continuations, the ILS must store data pertaining to:
3.7.1.3.1. Subscription dates (start, expiration)
_____O = Operational   A = Available   D = Development   P = Planned   N = Not Available

3.7.1.3.2. Source
_____O = Operational   A = Available   D = Development   P = Planned   N = Not Available

3.7.1.3.3. Frequency
_____O = Operational   A = Available   D = Development   P = Planned   N = Not Available

3.7.1.3.4. Subscription price
_____O = Operational   A = Available   D = Development   P = Planned   N = Not Available

3.7.1.3.5. Fund
_____O = Operational   A = Available   D = Development   P = Planned   N = Not Available

3.7.1.3.6. Location information
_____O = Operational   A = Available   D = Development   P = Planned   N = Not Available

3.7.1.3.7. Claiming information
_____O = Operational   A = Available   D = Development   P = Planned   N = Not Available

3.7.1.3.8. Prediction information
_____O = Operational   A = Available   D = Development   P = Planned   N = Not Available

3.7.1.3.9. Date of payment
_____O = Operational   A = Available   D = Development   P = Planned   N = Not Available

3.7.1.3.10. Holdings
_____O = Operational   A = Available   D = Development   P = Planned   N = Not Available

3.7.1.3.11. Routing information
_____O = Operational   A = Available   D = Development   P = Planned   N = Not Available

3.7.1.3.12. Note fields
_____O = Operational   A = Available   D = Development   P = Planned   N = Not Available

3.7.1.3.13. Active or non-active indicator
_____O = Operational   A = Available . D = Development   P = Planned   N = Not Available

Explain: (refer to item by number)

3.7.2.   Holdings and Publication Pattern Maintenance

3.7.2.1.   The ILS must support the ability to generate prediction patterns for determining when the next expected issue of a serial is scheduled to arrive.
_____O = Operational   A = Available   D = Development   P = Planned   N = Not Available

Explain:

3.7.2.2.   The ILS must support the ability to save patterns as templates for future use.
_____O = Operational   A = Available   D = Development   P = Planned   N = Not Available

Explain:

3.7.2.3.   The ILS must support regular, normalized irregular, and totally irregular prediction patterns.
_____O = Operational   A = Available   D = Development   P = Planned   N = Not Available

Explain:

3.7.2.4.   The ILS must support the ability to predict the issue chronology and enumeration based upon a pattern entered in the control record by the operator.

_____*O = Operational   A = Available   D = Development   P = Planned   N = Not Available*

Explain:

3.7.2.5.   The ILS must support the ability to review a pattern's expected issues prior to generating them in the system.

_____*O = Operational   A = Available   D = Development   P = Planned   N = Not Available*

Explain:

3.7.2.6.   The ILS must support the ability to delete issues or parts even if they are linked to an item record.

_____*O = Operational   A = Available   D = Development   P = Planned   N = Not Available*

Explain:

3.7.3.   Check-In

3.7.3.1.   With each check-in, the ILS must automatically record the issue enumeration and/or chronology, date received, notes, and claim any copies expected and not received.

_____*O = Operational   A = Available   D = Development   P = Planned   N = Not Available*

Explain:

3.7.3.2.   The ILS must support the ability for check-in to be performed by scanning the SICI.

_____*O = Operational   A = Available   D = Development   P = Planned   N = Not Available*

Explain:

3.7.3.3.   The ILS must support the ability to record the name/initials of the user when item is checked in.

_____*O = Operational   A = Available   D = Development   P = Planned   N = Not Available*

Explain:

3.7.3.4.   When checking in an issue, if the received issue is not the expected issue, but does conform to the predicting pattern, the ILS must allow the user to override the predicted number.

_____*O = Operational   A = Available   D = Development   P = Planned   N = Not Available*

Explain:

3.7.3.5.   The ILS must support the ability to combine issues that arrive unexpectedly as a combined issue.

_____*O = Operational   A = Available   D = Development   P = Planned   N = Not Available*

Explain:

3.7.3.6.   The ILS must support the ability to undo check-in of issues checked in by mistake.

_____*O = Operational   A = Available   D = Development   P = Planned   N = Not Available*

Explain:

3.7.3.7.   The ILS must support the option to print labels for each issue received as needed, individually and in batch.

_____*O = Operational   A = Available   D = Development   P = Planned   N = Not Available*

Explain:

    3.7.3.8.   The ILS must support the ability to print routing slips at serials check-in, individually and in batch.

_____*O = Operational*   *A = Available*   *D = Development*   *P = Planned*   *N = Not Available*

Explain:

    3.7.3.9.   The ILS must support the ability to suppress all issues linked to a particular holdings record from displaying in PAC.

_____*O = Operational*   *A = Available*   *D = Development*   *P = Planned*   *N = Not Available*

Explain:

    3.7.3.10. Retention information (i.e., last six issues retained) and a concise holdings statement must display in the PAC.

_____*O = Operational*   *A = Available*   *D = Development*   *P = Planned*   *N = Not Available*

Explain:

    3.7.3.11. The ILS must support the ability to automatically summarize individual issue holdings into a consolidated statement of holdings.

_____*O = Operational*   *A = Available*   *D = Development*   *P = Planned*   *N = Not Available*

Explain:

3.7.4.   Subscription Maintenance

    3.7.4.1.   The ILS must be able to manage subscriptions, including renewals and cancellations.

_____*O = Operational*   *A = Available*   *D = Development*   *P = Planned*   *N = Not Available*

Explain:

    3.7.4.2.   The ILS must support the ability to cancel a single serial subscription title where multiple copies are being received without disabling the ability to continue receipt of remaining subscriptions.

_____*O = Operational*   *A = Available*   *D = Development*   *P = Planned*   *N = Not Available*

Explain:

3.7.5.   Highlight serials control strengths:

3.8. Interlibrary Loan (ILL)

3.8.1.   The ILS must enable staff to place ILL requests electronically.

_____*O = Operational*   *A = Available*   *D = Development*   *P = Planned*   *N = Not Available*

Explain:

3.8.2.   The ILS must enable staff to send materials electronically.

_____*O = Operational*   *A = Available*   *D = Development*   *P = Planned*   *N = Not Available*

Explain:

3.8.3.   The ILS must enable staff to check out ILL materials to patrons.

_____*O = Operational*   *A = Available*   *D = Development*   *P = Planned*   *N = Not Available*

Explain:

3.8.4.   The ILL module must interact seamlessly with standard bibliographic utilities and third-party vendors.

_____*O = Operational*   *A = Available*   *D = Development*   *P = Planned*   *N = Not Available*

Explain:

3.8.5.   The PAC must allow patrons to request ILLs directly with or without staff review, based on the library's policies. If an additional cost is associated with this functionality, include the full details below.

_____O = *Operational*   A = *Available*   D = *Development*   P = *Planned*   N = *Not Available*

Explain:

3.8.6.   The ILS must enable staff to track ILL requests and patron usage.

_____O = *Operational*   A = *Available*   D = *Development*   P = *Planned*   N = *Not Available*

Explain:

3.8.7.   The ILS must support the ability to route a local hold request out to OCLC for ILL.

_____O = *Operational*   A = *Available*   D = *Development*   P = *Planned*   N = *Not Available*

Explain:

3.9. Web-Based Reporting Requirements

3.9.1.   The ILS must offer a separate reporting function that has a web-based graphical user interface.

_____O = *Operational*   A = *Available*   D = *Development*   P = *Planned*   N = *Not Available*

Explain:

3.9.2.   The web-based reporting function must not be based upon third-party software.

_____O = *Operational*   A = *Available*   D = *Development*   P = *Planned*   N = *Not Available*

Explain:

3.9.3.   Report output must be formatted in such a manner that the report results are neatly arranged and uniformly aligned throughout the results list to enable rapid staff review of the data. Provide a sample report output that demonstrates this.

_____O = *Operational*   A = *Available*   D = *Development*   P = *Planned*   N = *Not Available*

Explain:

3.9.4.   The web based reporting software must allow the user to create custom reports without any knowledge of SQL and with a basic knowledge of algebraic equations and Boolean logic, with little or no vendor assistance.

_____O = *Operational*   A = *Available*   D = *Development*   P = *Planned*   N = *Not Available*

Explain:

3.9.5.   The web-based reporting function must allow user to easily:

   3.9.5.1.   Create custom reports

_____O = *Operational*   A = *Available*   D = *Development*   P = *Planned*   N = *Not Available*

   3.9.5.2.   Generate report output files in a variety of file formats including Excel, PDF, HTML, and CSV

_____O = *Operational*   A = *Available*   D = *Development*   P = *Planned*   N = *Not Available*

   3.9.5.3.   Save custom report parameters

_____O = *Operational*   A = *Available*   D = *Development*   P = *Planned*   N = *Not Available*

   3.9.5.4.   Schedule saved reports

_____O = *Operational*   A = *Available*   D = *Development*   P = *Planned*   N = *Not Available*

   3.9.5.5.   Schedule saved reports in groups

_____O = *Operational*   A = *Available*   D = *Development*   P = *Planned*   N = *Not Available*

3.9.5.6. Execute saved reports
_____O = Operational   A = Available   D = Development   P = Planned   N = Not Available

3.9.5.7. Execute saved reports in groups
_____O = Operational   A = Available   D = Development   P = Planned   N = Not Available

3.9.5.8. Manage saved report parameters
_____O = Operational   A = Available   D = Development   P = Planned   N = Not Available

3.9.5.9. Administer user security and various configuration options
_____O = Operational   A = Available   D = Development   P = Planned   N = Not Available

3.9.5.10. Manage saved report output files
_____O = Operational   A = Available   D = Development   P = Planned   N = Not Available

3.9.5.11. Elect to save scheduled reports to a report list indefinitely or for a predetermined length of time (i.e., to save all the daily cash reports for one month only) at the library's option.
_____O = Operational   A = Available   D = Development   P = Planned   N = Not Available

3.9.5.12. Elect to have a report emailed automatically to one or more staff members immediately upon report processing and then to automatically save that report to the reports list if desired
_____O = Operational   A = Available   D = Development   P = Planned   N = Not Available

Explain: (refer to item by number)

3.9.6. Basic system cost includes canned reports for basic circulation, acquisitions, and cataloging functions. Give specific examples below and provide sample reports.
_____O = Operational   A = Available   D = Development   P = Planned   N = Not Available

Explain:

3.9.7. Library staff must have access to sample reports written by other customers and may modify these reports for their own purposes with no additional charges.
_____O = Operational   A = Available   D = Development   P = Planned   N = Not Available

Explain:

3.9.8. Customized reports must be available. If there is an additional cost for this service, provide base cost and any add-on charges per report. Define what constitutes customized reports.
_____O = Operational   A = Available   D = Development   P = Planned   N = Not Available

Explain:

3.9.9. Reports that automatically manage the complete interaction between the ILS and a collections agency such as Unique, Inc. must be provided in the basic system cost quoted in the cost proposal. Prompt technical support must be provided at any time and at no additional cost in order to resolve any and all issues that arise with the reporting of collections-related data via the ILS.
_____O = Operational   A = Available   D = Development   P = Planned   N = Not Available

Explain:

3.9.10. Highlight reporting strengths:

3.10. Inventory

3.10.1. The inventory module must support RFID and directly interface with EnvisionWare RFID Link. Provide specific details of this software interaction.
_____O = Operational   A = Available   D = Development   P = Planned   N = Not Available

Explain:

3.10.2. The inventory module must support item status API.
_____O = *Operational*   A = *Available*   D = *Development*   P = *Planned*   N = *Not Available*

Explain:

3.10.3. The inventory module must directly connect to the API.
_____O = *Operational*   A = *Available*   D = *Development*   P = *Planned*   N = *Not Available*

Explain:

3.10.4. The inventory module must be compatible with RFID wands from EnvisionWare, 3M, and other vendors. Specify all compatible wand vendors and models.
_____O = *Operational*   A = *Available*   D = *Development*   P = *Planned*   N = *Not Available*

Explain:

3.10.5. The ILS must provide an inventory utility that can be used on a notepad, Apple iPad, or similar device. Specify which devices are compatible.
_____O = *Operational*   A = *Available*   D = *Development*   P = *Planned*   N = Not Avail able

Explain:

3.10.6. The inventory utility must:

3.10.6.1. Download call number ranges of the library's collection for easy shelf comparison
_____O = *Operational*   A = *Available*   D = *Development*   P = *Planned*   N = *Not Available*

3.10.6.2. Scan barcodes on shelves or view list of items on shelves
_____O = *Operational*   A = *Available*   D = *Development*   P = *Planned*   N = *Not Available*

3.10.6.3. Work in offline mode when out of wireless range
_____O = *Operational*   A = *Available*   D = *Development*   P = *Planned*   N = *Not Available*

3.10.6.4. Be able to be used as a collection weeding tool
_____O = *Operational*   A = *Available*   D = *Development*   P = *Planned*   N = *Not Available*

3.10.6.5. Alert for items out of place or unaccounted for
_____O = *Operational*   A = *Available*   D = *Development*   P = *Planned*   N = *Not Available*

3.10.6.6. Run reports to identify exceptions or out of place items
_____O = *Operational*   A = *Available*   D = *Development*   P = *Planned*   N = *Not Available*

3.10.6.7. Use the Motion Tablet as a Windows 7 workstation for non-inventory times
_____O = *Operational*   A = *Available*   D = *Development*   P = *Planned*   N = *Not Available*

Explain: (refer to item by number)

3.10.7. The inventory module must fully support RFID-based inventory. If this is not operational or available, explain if this can be developed if necessary as a condition of contract award. Include all costs.
_____O = *Operational*   A = *Available*   D = *Development*   P = *Planned*   N = *Not Available*

Explain:

3.10.8. Highlight inventory manager strengths:

3.11. Mobile PAC Requirements

3.11.1. The ILS must provide a mobile PAC at no cost beyond those outlined in the cost proposal.
_____O = *Operational*   A = *Available*   D = *Development*   P = *Planned*   N = *Not Available*

Explain:

3.11.2. The mobile PAC must be a web-based, browser-based public access library catalog that has been optimized for mobile devices as follows:

  3.11.2.1. It must be device-independent
  _____*O = Operational*   *A = Available*   *D = Development*   *P = Planned*   *N = Not Available*

  3.11.2.2. It must not require an application to be downloaded and installed by the mobile device user
  _____*O = Operational*   *A = Available*   *D = Development*   *P = Planned*   *N = Not Available*

  3.11.2.3. It must be accessible by any device with a web browser, including desktop machines with standard web browsers and mobile devices with browsers optimized for mobile use
  _____*O = Operational*   *A = Available*   *D = Development*   *P = Planned*   *N = Not Available*

Explain (refer to item by number):

3.11.3. If a mobile device user enters the library's main web page address, the server must determine that the request is coming from a mobile device and automatically connect to the mobile PAC interface.
  _____*O = Operational*   *A = Available*   *D = Development*   *P = Planned*   *N = Not Available*

Explain:

3.11.4. The mobile PAC must allow patrons to perform real-time searches via keyword.
  _____*O = Operational*   *A = Available*   *D = Development*   *P = Planned*   *N = Not Available*

Explain:

3.11.5. The mobile PAC must include at minimum a link to the full library website/PAC, library hours, and library contact information. The layout and content of this menu and data elements, as well as the option to add other elements, must be under the library's control via a graphical user interface.
  _____*O = Operational*   *A = Available*   *D = Development*   *P = Planned*   *N = Not Available*

Explain:

3.11.6. Highlight mobile PAC strengths:

3.12. Other

3.12.1. A smart phone app must be available for the PAC. The app must be a free download for patrons and must be offered to the library at no cost beyond the basic system costs quoted in the cost proposal. Specify for which devices/platforms an app is available (i.e., iPhone, Android, etc.)
  _____*O = Operational*   *A = Available*   *D = Development*   *P = Planned*   *N = Not Available*

Explain:

3.12.2. The ILS supports workstations using Windows 7 (32 bit).
  _____*O = Operational*   *A = Available*   *D = Development*   *P = Planned*   *N = Not Available*

Explain:

3.12.3. The ILS supports workstations using Windows 7 (64 bit).
  _____*O = Operational*   *A = Available*   *D = Development*   *P = Planned*   *N = Not Available*

Explain:

3.12.4. The ILS supports text messaging.
  _____*O = Operational*   *A = Available*   *D = Development*   *P = Planned*   *N = Not Available*

Explain:

3.12.5. The ILS supports Facebook™.
_____O = Operational   A = Available   D = Development   P = Planned   N = Not Available

Explain:

3.12.6. The ILS supports Twitter™.
_____O = Operational   A = Available   D = Development   P = Planned   N = Not Available

Explain:

3.12.7. The ILS supports other e-resources such as QR codes. List all applicable supported e-resources.
_____O = Operational   A = Available   D = Development   P = Planned   N = Not Available

Explain:

3.13. Customer Support

3.13.1. State the customer support hours of operation (with corresponding days of the week) and holiday closing schedule. Describe emergency procedures that will be followed if the library system goes down after the standard hours of support.

3.13.2. Explain whether support is unlimited and provided at no additional cost beyond basic annual maintenance as quoted in the cost proposal. If not, explain all service tier options with a full cost breakdown.

3.13.3. The vendor must perform preventative maintenance with daily scans of the library's servers as part of maintenance. Please describe and indicate if this is included in the basic maintenance or at an additional cost.

3.13.4. The vendor must track all bug or hotline incidents reported by the library. The library must be able to view all incidents (including open and closed) via the vendor's extranet. Describe how help requests are handled (phone calls, email, chat, etc.). Explain whether help requests are placed in a queue, and if a triage format is applied if assistance cannot be provided immediately. Explain whether the library would have input on when a request ticket is closed.

3.13.5. 100% of the database schema must be available online to library customers for purposes of developing custom reports, SQL scripts, and/or tabled reports. If not 100%, describe extent.

3.13.6. The library staff must be able to search the vendor's knowledge base as a self-service. Describe the knowledge base contents and frequency of updates.

3.13.7. The full ILS documentation must be available online and must be fully searchable by keyword. Describe the available documentation.

3.13.8. The extranet must allow the library to download customer-developed custom reports and to upload its own custom reports to share with other vendor customers.

3.13.9. If the vendor subcontracts with another company for support, the vendor must list below which subcontractors are used and which support services they will supply.

3.13.10. Highlight customer support strengths:

3.14. Data Migration

3.14.1. Describe data conversion and implementation services, including vendor and library roles and responsibilities in the data conversion process. Include information on whether one person or a team would be assigned to the project, and the nature of the access the library would have to that person or team (including available contact methods and the length of time the library would have access to that person or team).

3.14.2. The library requires that a representative from the ILS vendor is on-site for the soft launch and full launch days in full, at a minimum. Explain the services the library can expect to receive from the representative and whether additional on-site days are included in the cost proposal.

3.14.3. Provide a migration and implementation plan including timetables and whether parallel operation of the old and new system is required.

3.14.4. Describe system tests prior to complete conversion of all modules. Include a description of the method used to ensure that the mapping of fields is successful, and corrective action taken in the event a discrepancy is detected.

3.14.5. Detail data conversion costs and authority file cleanup costs. Specify all other additional migration-related anticipated expenses not included in the cost proposal.

3.14.6. Provide a detailed timeline of the migration process. Describe handling of gap files and downtimes. If patron service will be interrupted for any length of time during open library hours, or after hours in connection to the OPAC, provide detailed information on this service interruption. Vendors are advised that the library will not permit any alteration of normal library operating hours for any phase of this project, including but not limited to migration of data. The library operates seven days per week and will not close for any partial or full day, or reduce services, as a part of this implementation.

3.14.7. Describe policy file transfers, loan rules, and code migration. Does the vendor provide training in developing policy files?

3.14.8. Describe the capabilities of patron, bibliographic, and serial record transfers.

3.14.9. Outline and describe data conversion, testing, and implementation.

3.14.10. Describe exactly what types of data the library will have access to at key points in the migration timeline.

3.14.11. The library requires that the loading profile not perform an OCLC prefix-removal operation on the 001 field. Explain how this requirement will be met.

3.14.12. Describe whether the following post-implementation acceptance tests, or alternate tests, would be performed as a part of pre-finalization procedures:

   3.14.12.1. A review to determine that all specified features are present
   3.14.12.2. A measurement of response times
   3.14.12.3. A measurement of reliability over a period of 30 consecutive days following the library's written acceptance of the system as fully installed and operational
   3.14.12.4. An inspection to determine if all features are available and performing at full capacity while the maximum number of concurrent users for which the system is licensed are active
   3.14.12.5. An inspection to ensure that the system meets the requirement of 99.9% uptime during library hours during the first 30 days

3.14.13. Highlight data migration strengths:

3.15. Training Requirements

Provide details of what the vendor will provide for each of the following areas.

3.15.1. The vendor must provide basic on-site training in all functioning subsystems for the independent operation of the system, including regular maintenance and troubleshooting. Trainers must be experienced in all functions or the vendor may provide trainers specializing in areas of expertise, so long as all training is conducted by an individual who has extensive and direct experience with the content of the training.

3.15.2. The vendor must provide specialized training for personnel who will manage the system. Library staff and/or City of Brentwood IT staff must be trained to manage and operate the system on a daily basis. As above, trainers must have extensive and direct experience with the content of the training.

3.15.3. Training must be planned in accordance with a mutually agreeable schedule between the library and the vendor. Multiple training sessions will be necessary to accommodate staff schedules and to ensure proper coverage of service areas.

3.15.4. Training must include the following, performed in each case by trainers who have extensive and direct experience with the area in which they are to be training:

    3.15.4.1. Project implementation visit to cover the implementation process, policy files creation, data migration issues, project planning, and staff client system administration

    3.15.4.2. Application training to cover the PAC, patron services, cataloging, acquisitions, serials control, and workflow

    3.15.4.3. System administration training to cover the system administration interface, ILS database structure and reports, database maintenance, user management, client installation, and basic report writing using vendor customer resources, ILS system canned reports, and/or ILS interfaces

    3.15.4.4. Four months after the full launch, the vendor must provide a post-implementation training follow-up with library principles covering topics designated by Brentwood Library staff. Training is to be no less than three days or more than five days. If training less than five days, other training follow-ups may be negotiated.

3.15.5. The vendor must describe other post-implementation training opportunities including the following but not to the exclusion of other resources to be described by the vendor. Detail costs below with full itemized description of these resources, and designate whether these costs are inclusive of the cost proposal or incur additional costs.

    3.15.5.1. Webinars

    3.15.5.2. Tutorials

    3.15.5.3. User groups

    3.15.5.4. Off-site training

    3.15.5.5. System documentation

        3.15.5.5.1. Online training materials
        3.15.5.5.2. Print-based training materials

    3.15.5.6. Training videos, including screencasts

    3.15.5.7. Test server available for staff for post-implementation training

    3.15.5.8. Other

3.15.6. The vendor must provide training to key personnel for upgrades and implementation of upgrades via documentation, telephone, webinar, and or other appropriate communication. Describe how this training will be administered, and list any additional costs.

3.15.7. Describe how much time is devoted for library staff training. Provide detailed costs (inclusive of travel, per diem, and any other associated costs) for initial training and post-implementation training to occur approximately four months after the full launch date.

3.15.8. Within four months of the full launch, a workflow analysis consisting of four full on-site workdays of workflow observation and assessment must be performed, and a full report with details of recommended workflow improvements delivered within two weeks of the analysis. This must be included in the basic quoted costs in the cost proposal. Describe the specific tasks that will be completed during the analysis to ensure that the library is making the most effective possible use of the ILS.

3.15.9. Highlight training strengths:

4. COST PROPOSAL

4.1.   Show below or attach initial costs and five years of ongoing costs for all required software, hardware, and related services including installation, implementation, maintenance, and training. Provide a breakdown of the amount and timing of payments for the initial costs. Optional software, hardware, and related services should be quoted separately and fully. Software and other additional functionality developed by the vendor's other clients must be fully available to the Brentwood Library at no cost above the basic annual maintenance fees given in the cost proposal; include a statement in the cost proposal that provides written agreement to this requirement. Service contracts must be quoted with a locked price for five years or longer. A fixed price must be given for all third-party interfaces, including any APIs, SIP licenses, NCIP, or other protocols.

4.2.   Fully explain all deviations from specifications, including added costs and items or services that are requested in the above specifications but are not included in the cost proposal despite availability.

4.3.   The library must be able to cancel, at any time and for any reason that the library deems to be in its best interests, any contract signed in connection to a proposal received in response to this RFP with no penalty, for a prorated refund. Explain all instances in which this requirement would not be honored.

5. CONTRACT AND STATEMENT OF NON-DISCRIMINATION

5.1.   Provide an unsigned copy of your proposed service agreement for our review and any other stipulations of which we should be aware. Any proposed contract form submitted by a proposer for the City's approval must be compatible with the terms and conditions included in this RFP, unless any incompatible language is specifically identified by the proposer and accepted by the City. The indemnification agreement included with this RFP must be attached to the proposed contract, or similar indemnification language must be included within the contract form.

5.2.   Show below or attach your organization's statement of non-discrimination.

6. DISASTER RECOVERY PLAN

6.1.   Describe disaster recovery procedures in detail, including locations and backup schedules.

7. CUSTOMER REFERENCES

7.1.   Provide three references that are similar in size to the Brentwood Library, and ideally have migrated from the same system we currently use. These installations must have been completed in the past three years.

Reference 1:

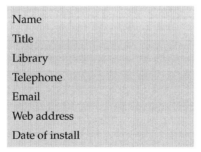

Name

Title

Library

Telephone

Email

Web address

Date of install

Reference 2:

Name

Title

Library

Telephone

Email

Web address

Date of install

Reference 3:

Name

Title

Library

Telephone

Email

Web address

Date of install

8. SERVER AND IT SUPPORT REQUIREMENTS

8.1. Describe the level of support needed from library staff and City of Brentwood IT staff, and the level of support provided by vendor during the pre-implementation and implementation phases (from the time a contract is signed until a final acceptance document is signed).

8.2. Describe level of support needed from library staff and City of Brentwood IT staff, and the level of support provided by vendor after the implementation is complete.

8.3. Upgrades must be completed without any interruption to library service, either in-house service or service delivered via the OPAC. If service would potentially be interrupted for an upgrade, then the upgrade must be completed between 11:00 p.m. CST and 6:00 a.m. CST only, at no additional cost to the library. Explain specifically how this requirement will be met.

8.4. Both daily backups and additional backups as requested by the library must be included in the service provided in the basic quoted maintenance costs given in the cost proposal. Explain policies related to backups.

8.5. Library staff must have access to schedule jobs on the system. Explain any limitations to this access.

9. WORKSTATION AND SERVER REQUIREMENTS

9.1. Describe the minimum and recommended PC configuration for staff and public clients.

9.2. Describe the minimum hardware specifications for the servers and the number of servers needed.

10. GENERAL TERMS AND CONDITIONS

10.1. By submitting a proposal, each proposer will be deemed to have agreed to the general terms and conditions set forth below, unless the proposal specifically takes exception to any of the general terms and conditions. Each proposal must include a statement attesting that the general terms and conditions are accepted, except for those exceptions which are specifically identified by the proposer.

a. Cost proposal: The cost proposal submitted with the proposal shall include the cost of all equipment, labor, insurance coverages, materials and delivery and/or freight charges, and any required trade and/or license fees, business license fees and permit(s), necessary to render the specified services.

b. Payments: Unless otherwise agreed to in writing between the successful proposer and the City of Brentwood, payments by the City will be made within 20 days after receipt of an accurate, complete and itemized invoice for the work specified herein, or within 20 days after such work has been accepted by the City, whichever occurs later.

c. Licenses and permits. The successful proposer shall obtain all required licenses and permits, in accordance with applicable state and local regulations, necessary to render the specified services.

d. Applicable laws and regulations: All applicable federal and state laws, city ordinances, orders, rules and regulations of all authorities having jurisdiction over the specified work shall apply to the successful proposer, and they will be deemed to be included in these specifications the same as though they are written out in full herein.

e. Safe work area: The successful proposer will be expected to utilize best practices to minimize the risk of personal injury to the public, City personnel and employees of the proposer and/or the proposer's subcontractors and agents, if any.

f. Inspection of work. The City's representatives shall have the authority to inspect all work, and to reject any materials or work which do not conform to these RFP documents or the proposal; to direct application of forces to any portion of the work which requires it, in the judgment of the City's representatives; and to decide questions which arise between the parties relative to the execution of the work.

g. Damages: The successful proposer will be responsible for any damages it causes in the course of performing the specified services, and shall repair or replace any damaged property to the satisfaction of the City of Brentwood at the proposer's own expense.

h. Other documents to be required of the successful proposer: Prior to commencement of work, the successful proposer must provide the following documents:

   1. Two signed copies of the proposed contract, as approved by the City Attorney.
   2. Indemnification agreement, as included with this RFP, executed in full by a duly authorized representative of the successful proposer; provided that similar indemnification language, acceptable to the City Attorney may be incorporated into the proposed contract form in lieu of a separate indemnification agreement.
   3. Certificate of Insurance that meets or exceeds the City's insurance requirements (see below.)
   4. IRS Form W-9 (forms available upon request from the City's Finance Department.)

i. Insurance: The successful proposer shall maintain insurance satisfactory to the City to protect both itself and the City from claims under workers compensation acts and from any other demands for personal injury, deaths or property damage which may arise from operations under the work performed by the proposer for the City, whether such operations be by the proposer or any subcontractor or anyone directly or indirectly employed by either of them. Certificates of such insurance, naming the City as an additional insured, shall be filed with the City Attorney and shall be subject to his approval for adequacy of protection. At a minimum, the successful proposer must maintain comprehensive general liability insurance in amounts no less than $1,000,000, each occurrence, for bodily injury, and $1,000,000, each occurrence, for property damage. The insurance coverage required hereunder shall be maintained with a company or companies having a current "A-" or better rating from the A.M. Best Company. The successful proposer may purchase at its own expense such additional or other insurance protection as it may deem necessary. Maintenance of the required minimum insurance protection does not relieve the successful proposer of responsibility for any losses not covered by its insurance. The proposer acknowledges that the City is not liable for the safety, security or condition of the equipment or materials to remain under the ownership of the proposer.

j. Termination: If, though any cause, the successful proposer shall fail to fulfill in a timely and proper manner the obligations imposed by this RFP, or if the successful proposer shall violate any of the agreed upon terms or conditions, the City, through its Library Director or City Manager, shall thereupon have the right to terminate the work by giving written notice to the successful proposer of such termination and specify the effective date thereof. In such event, all materials and supplies delivered to the City for the work to be performed for the City shall, at the option of the City, become the City's property and the proposer shall be entitled to receive just and equitable compensation for any work satisfactorily completed to the point of termination.

k. Errors and omissions in proposals: Uncorrected errors included in proposal or elsewhere in the materials submitted by the proposer shall be considered on a case-by-case basis by the City. Uncorrected errors made by the proposer may be deemed by the City to be so severe as to make the proposal non-responsive. At the discretion of the City, proposers may be permitted to clarify a submitted proposer. In the case of a discrepancy between the proposer's unit price for a particular line item as quoted in the proposal and the unit price calculated by dividing the proposer's extension price for that same line item by the quantity indicated for that same line item, then the proposer's unit price for that line item as quoted in the proposal shall prevail. Omissions from a proposer's submittal shall be considered on a case-by-case basis by the City. Omissions may be deemed by the City to be so severe as to make the proposal non-responsive. At the discretion of the City, proposers may be permitted to clarify or supplement materials accompanying a submitted proposal.

l. Confidential and/or proprietary information; trade secrets: All contents of all submittals are subject to public disclosure and shall be deemed not to contain any confidential information. Further, by submitting its proposal, the proposal indemnifies and holds the City of Brentwood harmless against any loss or damage, including reasonable attorney fees, it may incur as a result of the City's reliance upon the proposer's representation that materials supplied by the proposer do not contain trade secrets or proprietary information which is not subject to public disclosure.

m. Antidiscrimination: The successful proposer, in performing the work covered by these documents, shall not discriminate against any person seeking employment with or by the proposer because of race, color, sex, creed, religion, ancestry, disability, familial status, or national origin.

n. Agreement to procurement terms and conditions: By submitting a proposal, each proposal certifies that it has read and accepts all terms, conditions and requirements of this solicitation. All procurements by the City of Brentwood are also subject to Section 2–209 (Purchasing) of the Brentwood Municipal Code, a copy of which may be reviewed at the office of the City Recorder, or online at www.brentwood-tn.org.

o. Governing law: Any dispute or default arising from the work described in this RFP shall be governed by the laws of the State of Tennessee. Proposers agree to submit to the jurisdiction and venue of the courts of Williamson County, Tennessee, or the federal district court of the Middle District of Tennessee.

p. Proposal expiration: Prior to award, all proposals and associated pricing as submitted shall be considered valid and may be accepted by the City for as long as the proposer is willing to do so but for at least 90 days after the date proposals are due.

INDEMNIFICATION AGREEMENT

_____ ("Vendor") does hereby release, hold harmless and indemnify the City of Brentwood, Tennessee and each of its employees, officers and agents from any liability or claims (including court costs and reasonable attorneys' fees) which may be asserted in regard to personal injuries or property damage, real or alleged, arising out of work conducted by or on behalf of the Vendor pursuant to Vendor's proposal for an integrated library system for the Brentwood Library, dated _____, 2011, excepting only such losses as shall be occasioned solely by the negligence of the City of Brentwood.

VENDOR:

By: _____

Authorized official

Print Name: _____

Glossary of Terms

AACR2R: Anglo-American Cataloging Rules, Second Revised Edition (1988). A bibliographic standard based on a set of rules used to describe various types of library materials.

Application Programming Interface (API): A set of codes and specifications for software programs to follow in order to communicate with one another. It acts as an "intermediary" or interface between the software programs. In a library setting, staff may use the integrated library system (ILS) software program to communicate with the respective automation company's ILS software program through API in order to modify certain features and use process data.

Barcode: a set of numbers represented by a pattern of bars that once scanned can be recognized by automation software. There are two main types of barcodes: traditional (smart and dumb) and RFID.

Baseline Project Plan (BPP): planning document that summarizes the results of the feasibility assessment studies and provides a project's scope, justification for the project, project requirements, cost estimate, resource requirements, and recommendations.

BIBFRAME: The Library of Congress Bibliographic Framework Initiative–proposed linked data model that will replace the MARC 21 format and establish the foundation for the future of bibliographic description of data in the web environment.

Boolean Operators: AND to narrow search results, OR to expand search results, and NOT to narrow search results by eliminating unwanted terms.

Broadband: Internet access that provides users with speeds significantly higher than those available through dial-up: DSL, coaxial cable, fiber optic cable, and wireless.

Cloud Computing: "A model for enabling ubiquitous, convenient, on-demand network access to a shared pool of configurable computing resources (e.g., networks, servers, storage, applications, and services) that can be rapidly provisioned and released with minimal management effort or service provider interaction."

Cloud Hosting: a hosting model in which the provider stores or installs the software on a computer platform run by the hosting company instead of on traditional in-house servers.

Coaxial Cable: provides high-speed Internet connections through use of the cable television company's infrastructure.

Digital Subscriber Line (DSL): a high-speed Internet connection that receives data ranging from 1.54 Mbps to 8.45 Mbps (downstream) and sends data ranging from 128 kbps to 640 kbps (upstream).

Discovery Interface: the next-generation online catalog—software that works with an existing ILS to retrieve multiple library resources, including print and digital works; it includes spell-check, relevance ranking, recommender services, and faceted searching.

Discovery Service: cloud-based next-generation discovery interface that integrates with all of a library's collections in a single interface; one search box retrieves materials in all formats.

Dumb Barcode: Generic barcode that is not linked to an item during retrospective conversion. A dumb barcode may contain only the name of the library. See also smart barcode.

eXtensible Markup Language (XML): a coding language for the web that describes the content of a webpage in terms of what data are being described rather than in terms of how they are displayed. This language is ideal for coding MARC records for the web due to its flexibility.

Fiber Optic Cable: a type of cable that delivers high-speed Internet access; a thin, flexible medium that conducts pulses of light, with each light representing a bit.

Folksonomy: subject categories or headings organized on the basis of tagged content created by patrons.

FRBR (Functional Requirements for Bibliographic Data): a conceptual model that defines four different entities, attempting to make catalog records more accessible to users.

Graphical User Interface (GUI): a computer program that enables a person to communicate with a computer through the use of symbols, visual metaphors, and pointing devices.

Infrastructure-as-a-Service (IaaS): the provision model in which an organization outsources the equipment used to support operations, including storage, hardware, servers, and networking components.

Integrated Library System (ILS): a computer-based information system consisting of a set of interrelated components and subcomponents, designed to perform specific tasks.

Library Automation Life Cycle (LALC): a conceptual model of five iterative phases and a set of tasks and procedures used for carrying out a library automation project.

Library Services Platforms (LSPs): Next-generation integrated library systems (LSPs) that are designed to be deployed through software as a service. LSPs provide one search box for searching and retrieving relevant materials in all formats, including journal articles from subscription databases. LSPs integrate and streamline the management of print, digital, and electronic materials.

LibraryThing: a social networking site where users build and share their own collections of books and other materials.

MARC 21: machine-readable cataloging of the 21st century. It is a bibliographic standard that was developed by the Library of Congress.

MARCXML: a framework for working with MARC data in an XML environment, including schemas, style sheets, and software tools.

Migration: the process of moving ILS applications from one ILS to another that better meets the library's needs.

Module: a component of a software program that represents a function and performs tasks associated with it.

Multitenant Model: software hosting model in which a single instance of the ILS or application is shared by multiple tenants. It is one of the main characteristics of true cloud computing.

Network Architecture: a set of specifications that defines every aspect of a network's communication system, including but not limited to the types of user interfaces employed, the networking protocols, standards, and types of network cabling used.

Network Topology: the physical layout of computers and devices connected in a network.

Online Catalog: software for managing various library operations including circulation, cataloging, serials, acquisitions, digital asset, and electronic resources. The software has an interface for public access that is traditionally known as OPAC.

Online Computer Library Center (OCLC): a nationwide bibliographic utility that enables resource sharing among libraries and other member institutions.

Online Public Access Catalog (OPAC): the traditional name of an online catalog interface that patrons use to access and retrieve information. See also discovery interface and discovery service.

OPAC: see Online Public Access Catalog

Open-Source Initiative (OSI): a nonprofit corporation with the purpose of educating about and advocating for the benefits of open-source software. It is a community-recognized body for reviewing and approving licenses as open-source conformant.

Open-Source Software: software that allows the user access to the program source code for modification and free distribution based on 10 specific criteria regulated by the Open-Source Initiative.

Platform-as-a-Service (PaaS): a hardware hosting model for renting hardware, operating systems, storage and network capacity through a cloud service provider.

Program Evaluation Review Technique (PERT): a strategy for creating optimistic, pessimistic, and realistic time estimates to complete a task (based on the equation $ET = O + 4r + p/6$).

Proprietary Software: software supplied by a commercial vendor, who is responsible for maintaining, updating, providing technical support, and training (also known as *turnkey* or *off-the-shelf*).

Protocol: a set of rules that describes how to transmit data across a network.

QR Codes: 2D-rich matrix that encodes information and requires a generator or a barcode reader (used to provide access to digital content from a user's smart phone or other mobile devices).

RDA (Resource Description and Access): the new standard for resource description and access: based on the conceptual models of FRBR.

Remote Hosting Model: a service model in which the ILS provider hosts the ILS software on behalf of the library and runs the hosted application remotely on existing hardware; the provider does not maintain the software, so it is not a "true" cloud computing service model.

Request for Information (RFI): a request initiated by the library to obtain information about software, hardware, and other services a library automation company or firm provides. It is not the same as a Request for Proposal.

Request for Proposal (RFP): a document that describes a library's specifications for essential, desirable, and other features in an ILS. It also contains the library's terms and conditions, how to respond to use and respond to the RFP.

Retrospective Conversion (Recon): the process of converting a library's shelflist cards or an item's bibliographic information into a MARC format.

RFID System: Radio Frequency Identification system. A technology that uses electronic tags placed on books and other materials to relay identifying information to an electronic reader (RFID reader) by means of radio waves.

SDLC: see System Development Life Cycle

Shelflist: a section of a card catalog that contains a master copy of each cataloged item in a library's collection. Shelflist cards are usually filed by call number (e.g. Dewey Decimal, Library of Congress).

Single-Tenant Model: software hosting model in which a tenant's software application is hosted individually rather than shared with others.

Smart Barcode: a barcode linked to its respective item during retrospective conversion that identifies the essential information of the item (e.g., title, author, and name of the holding library).

Social OPAC: see SOPAC

SOPAC: open-source social discovery platform for sharing library bibliographic data.

Software Architecture: software deployment models available for hosting the library's ILS.

Software-as-a-Service (SaaS): a "true" cloud computing model in which a designated service provider provides the capability to run multiple ILSs and other applications on a cloud infrastructure that is shared among libraries using this deployment model.

System Development Life Cycle (SDLC): a conceptual model used to describe the phases and procedures for carrying out a system development project.

Usability: a method for assessing the effectiveness of an interface in relation to the user's experience and goals rather than to the system's specifications. Usability emerges from the Human–Computer Interaction (HCI) field.

Usability Heuristics: a set of predefined rules of thumb that describe the common properties of usable interfaces.

Web 2.0: a set of technologies and trends that characterize the second generation of the web. It supports dynamic user–generated content, collaboration, and social media across varied platforms.

Wireless Broadband: a technology which uses a radio link between a user's location and the wireless service provider's facility.

Index

About the Author

DANIA BILAL is professor of information sciences at the School of Information Sciences, College of Communication and Information at the University of Tennessee, Knoxville, TN. Experienced in academic, school, and special libraries, she teaches courses in information systems design and implementation, human–computer interaction, research methods, and mining the web. Her published works include two editions of Libraries Unlimited's *Automating Media Centers and Small Libraries: A Microcomputer-Based Approach*; *Information and Emotion: The Emergent Affective Paradigm in Information Behavior Research and Theory* (coedited with Diane Nahl); and numerous articles in scholarly journals. Her research focuses on user information behavior; interaction with information systems such as web search engines, digital libraries, and online catalogs; evaluation of these systems through usability assessment; and the design of interfaces from the users' perspectives. Bilal holds a master's degree and doctorate in library and information studies from Florida State University.

Printed in Great Britain
by Amazon